Beverage Management

Beverage Management
Product Knowledge and Cost Control

Michael M. Coltman

Van Nostrand Reinhold
New York

Library of Congress Catalog Card Number 88-34330
ISBN 0-442-20659-3

Printed in the United States of America
Designed by East End Graphic Arts
Cover photo © by Michael Melford/The Image Bank

Van Nostrand Reinhold
115 Fifth Avenue
New York, New York 10003

Van Nostrand Reinhold International Company Limited
11 New Fetter Lane
London EC4P 4EE, England

Van Nostrand Reinhold
480 La Trobe Street
Melbourne, Victoria 3000, Australia

Macmillan of Canada
Division of Canada Publishing Corporation
164 Commander Boulevard
Agincourt, Ontario M1S 3C7, Canada

16 15 14 13 12 11 10 9 8 7 6 5 4 3 2 1

Library of Congress Cataloging-in-Publication Data

Coltman, Michael M., 1930–
  Beverage management : product knowledge and cost control / Michael
M. Coltman.
    p. cm.
  Bibliography: p.
  ISBN 0-442-20659-3
  1. Bartending. 2. Alcoholic beverages. I. Title.
TX950.7.C65 1989
647'.95—dc19   88-34330
                                                                  CIP

Contents

1

Introduction

All alcoholic beverages are made from a fermented product. Fermentation is a completely natural process. For example, if a bunch of ripened grapes are put in a bowl, the weight of the upper grapes will cause the skins of those underneath to break. Natural yeast on the outer skins of those underneath grapes will then act on the sugar in their juice, turning it into alcohol and carbon dioxide. The carbon dioxide then escapes and the alcohol is left.

Even though this uncontrolled fermentation process creates alcohol (in the form of wine), it will also turn that wine into vinegar in time if the wine is left exposed to air. Thus in commercial wine making, the process of creating alcohol is much more carefully controlled.

Beer and distilled spirits also require fermentation as a first step. In the case of beer, the product fermented is not grapes but grain—usually malted barley and/or other starch cereals such as rice or corn. In the case of distilled products, the starting product can be virtually anything that contains starch or sugar. Distillation simply takes the process of fermentation one step further to produce a product with a far higher alcohol content.

HISTORY OF ALCOHOL

Wine is probably the earliest of the alcoholic beverages, simply because it could be made without the maker's having to understand the chemical changes that turned the sugar in grapes, other fruits, and other products into alcohol. Some of these earlier wines were made from honey and were known as mead. Indeed, wine may have been made as long as ten thousand years ago.

Wine is mentioned in documents three thousand years old, as well as in the Bible and in the literature of the Greeks and Romans. Beer has been known for almost as long as wine has: It is known to have been brewed in Mesopotamia as long as six thousand years ago. In fact, grain was turned into beer long before it was used to make bread, and beer was used for its carbohydrate content as a food.

It was the Greeks who discovered that wine could be stored—and would often improve with age—if it were kept out of contact with air. They stored their wine in large vessels known as *amphorae,* which were airtight and could be filled with wine and then stoppered, to allow the wine to age. When the Greeks passed on to the Romans their skills in wine making, they also taught them about using amphorae. And so for thousands of years, wine was made, and the process for aging and improving it was passed on from generation to generation. But when the Roman Empire collapsed in about A.D. 500, so did a great deal of the knowledge about aging wine, the use of the amphorae, and the art of pottery making.

For about one thousand years, wooden casks took the place of the amphorae for storing wine, but the casks were porous, thereby allowing the wine to turn into vinegar. Good wine was still being made, but it had to be consumed relatively quickly; that is, those wines that would improve with age were not allowed to, for without a replacement for the ancient amphorae, there were no suitable containers. As a result, for hundreds of years, wine had to be consumed within a year, in the same way that only enough bread and beer was made from one season's grain to last until the next season.

Wine was made and consumed in those countries that could grow grapes, whereas beer was made and drunk in countries, such as England, where grapes could not grow or, if they could, would not produce quality wines.

Through the Middle Ages, beer and wine were the drink of all classes in Europe. The available water was generally not fit to drink, and so people drank beer or ale at breakfast or lunch and wine at dinner. These drinks were commonly available and cheap. Wine consumed in countries such as England was shipped over in casks from France and was expected to be drunk young. Although glass was known, and wineglasses were used for drinking wine, glass wine bottles did not begin to be used until about three hundred years ago. Earlier wine containers (apart from wooden casks) were simply carafes or decanters that were filled from the casks and used to bring the wine to the table.

Wine Bottles

Once a cask of wine was opened, the wine was soon consumed, as it was used to quench thirst rather than to be sipped for enjoyment, and casks had to be emptied quickly to avoid the wine's spoiling. The early "bottles" were made of leather, pewter, pottery, or even wood and were used by people traveling long distances on both foot and horseback on business, pleasure, or pilgrimage. The most useful "bottle" was a flat, almost pear-shaped leather container with a pouring spout and a couple of rings at the top through which a rope could be passed so that it could be flung over the shoulder for traveling. It held about a quart of wine and was known as a *costrel*. Its design still exists today in the form of the *Bocksbeutel*, a glass bottle used for the white wines of West Germany's Franconia district.

Even when glass bottles were invented, they could not be used for shipping wine, as there was no known way of firmly stoppering them; corks were first used only in the early 1600s. Of course, with the advent of corks (and corkscrews to remove the corks), wine could be shipped in bottles, and its trade increased accordingly.

Distilled Spirits

Although both wine and beer have a long history, it was not until much later that fermented beverages were distilled. The process of distillation was known in the ancient world, and even Aristotle wrote that seawater could be made potable by distilling it. But it did not occur to the ancients to distill wine or beer, as they were happy drinking them as they were.

Distillation is a fairly simple process. Water boils at 212° F (100° C) and alcohol at 176° F (80° C). Therefore, by heating a fermented product containing alcohol to a temperature higher than 176° F (80° C) but below 212° F (100° C), the alcohol will evaporate and water will be left behind. If this alcohol vapor is then collected and cooled, it will recondense into a liquid with a considerably higher alcohol content.

Distilled spirits were first produced in the Western world three hundred to four hundred years ago. The process was first used to produce a product that would cure diseases when consumed, and the resulting distilled alcohol was given the name *aqua vitae,* or "water of life." As we know today, distilled alcohol—or distilled spirits—does not cure disease, but distilled spirits have persevered as a popular drink and, along with wine and beer, have become a third major category of alcoholic beverage.

We shall turn now to each of these three categories (wine, beer, and spirits) and explore each of them in more detail. We shall conclude with discussions of beverage purchasing, receiving, storing, control, and sales.

The reader should note that this book is not intended to provide an encyclopedic knowledge of alcoholic beverages, and of wine in particular. It is meant only as an introduction to the fascinating study of alcoholic beverages. The interested reader wishing to pursue this study further is referred to the bibliography, which lists books providing far more detailed information.

2

Wine Types, Manufacture, and Vintages

CHAPTER OBJECTIVES

After studying this chapter the reader should be able to

- Discuss factors such as soil and climate that affect wine quality.
- State the name of the vine that produces the world's best wine and list the major countries where this vine flourishes.
- List the names of five well-known white and five well-known red grape varieties.
- State the alcohol content range of still wines and define descriptive wine terms such as *dry.*
- Differentiate still wines from sparkling and fortified wines.
- Discuss the various steps in the manufacture of wine and define wine-making terms such as *must, chaptalization, carbonic maceration,* and *racking.*
- Explain the role of corks in the bottling of certain wines.
- Discuss the term *vintage* and the legal requirements that certain countries have with reference to vintage-dated wines.
- Define the common terms used to describe wines.

One of the reasons that early humans traveled was to seek land on which to grow vines for making wine and to grow grain for making beer. Wine, as we now know, has been fermented from grapes (as well as other fruits) for some ten thousand years. These early wines were considered God's gift and were closely related to religious rites and also used on joyous occasions such as battle victories or weddings. Alcohol was also mixed with various herbs and used as a medical cure.

Early knowledge of wine making was passed on from the Greeks to the Egyptians and then to the Romans. As the Romans expanded their empire, they spread their wine-making skills into other European countries. The medieval monks further developed this art, making wine both to drink themselves and to sell to raise cash for their monasteries. Eventually the early colonists brought the art of wine making to North America and to other areas around the world.

GRAPES AND FERMENTATION

Any liquid that contains sugar can be fermented with the addition of yeast, but grape wine makes itself, as the grapes' outer skins contain yeast molds. The sugar in the grape juice is turned into alcohol, and so the higher the grapes' sugar content is, the higher will be the wine's alcohol content.

Chemical Control

In commercial wine making the production of wine is a carefully controlled process in which the chemistry of fermentation can be regulated according to the type of grapes and their origin. Despite this regimentation, however, wines often cannot be duplicated elsewhere either chemically or naturally. Indeed, a vine that produces a particular type of grape and wine in a certain location, if grown elsewhere, will produce grapes that generate a different type of wine. For that same reason, grapes from a lower part of a hill may produce a far different wine than will the same grapes grown higher on the same hill. This is the charm of wine. Although some wine-tasting experts claim to know whether a wine comes from a particular vineyard, or even the lower slope or the higher slope of a particular hill, others scoff that such precise geographic wine origins cannot be determined from taste alone. However, it is still true that the specific location of a vineyard will have a recognizable effect year after year on the quality of its wine. The slope of the hill, exposure to sun, drainage, subsoil nutritives that the roots feed on, and many other factors all have a bearing on a wine's quality and will distinguish it from wine produced in an adjoining area.

Factors Affecting Wine Quality

A number of factors affect wine quality, the most important being the type of grape used: The best grapevine is the *vitis vinifera,* which has many different varieties. The grape yield per acre is also a factor. The higher the yield is, the lower the wine quality will generally be. Conversely, the lower the yield is, the more concentrated the grape flavor, and the better the wine quality, will be. The better vineyards produce from two to four tons of grapes per acre. Normally, a ton of crushed grapes yields an average of 170 gallons of table wine.

Soil is also a factor, the best being one that offers good drainage, which is why gravel and sand are better than clay. Good drainage forces the vines' roots to seek deeper moisture, which causes their roots to become longer. These longer roots are able to reach deep mineral deposits, and these minerals, in turn, add flavor to grapes and thus to the wines.

Another factor is climate. Grapevines like cool nights and sunny, warm days, as these help them maintain the right balance between acid and sugar in the grapes. However, too hot weather when the grapes are maturing, near harvest time, will decrease the acid and increase the sugar and will produce a wine that may not age well. On the other hand, too little sunshine will reduce the amount of grape sugar and produce a wine low in alcohol, and as a result, sugar may have to be added before fermentation to raise that alcohol level. Also, rain at harvest time can dilute the grapes' sugar and encourage rotting, thereby lowering the quality of the wine. Mechanical grape-picking equipment can give grape growers more control over the grapes' quality than hand picking can, as all the grapes can be picked quickly when they are at their peak of ripeness. But if rain has spoiled some of the grape bunches, hand picking will allow those to be bypassed.

Finally, the skill of the winemaker is extremely important, as it can affect the personality and quality of the wine produced. The vintner's skills can also vary, because of local tradition, and will dictate the type of wine made. The market for whom the wine is to be manufactured also calls upon different wine-making skills. For example, is the wine to be made in a smaller quantity with a high quality, or in a larger quantity, with a lesser quality, for a broader market?

Vitis Vinifera

The best wines are made from a type of vine known as *vitis vinifera,* some of which are known to be three hundred years old. This vine grows best in two broad belts, one north and the other south of the equator. Grapes can be grown outside these belts and be turned into wine, but its quality is not considered as high as that from vines grown within these belts. The northern belt includes acknowledged wine-making countries such as France, Italy, Germany, and the United States. The southern belt embraces Chile, Argentina, Australia, New Zealand, and South Africa. Sometimes two or more vines are crossbred to produce a different type of grape with special characteristics such as climatic adaptability, disease resistance, or yield. These crossed vines are known as *hybrids*.

Strangely, the type of soil in which the *vitis vinifera* flourishes does not have to be rich and fertile. Rather, the most hospitable soil is composed mostly of chalk, sand, clay, gravel, and even slate. Most grapes grow best on slopes that can catch a maximum of sun and warmth both directly and reflected from the soil. Some rain is necessary during the approximately one hundred days of the growing season from blossoming to harvesting, but good drainage is normally essential. Vines will yield more grapes when planted in fertile soil on flat land, but the wine made from such grapes will seldom be comparable in quality to wine made from grapes grown on sunny slopes in soil that may not be fertile but is rich in the minerals that create a special characteristic, known as *bouquet*, that is present in all quality wines.

As the grapes mature, their sugar content increases and their acid content decreases. Grape growers thus must know when the balance between sugar and acid is just right to produce the best wine.

Common *Vitis Vinifera*

The following are some of the best-known types of *vitis vinifera* grapes:

White	Red
Chardonnay	Cabernet Sauvignon
Chenin Blanc	Gamay
Gewürztraminer	Merlot
Müller-Thurgau	Nebbiolo
Muscat	Pinot Noir
Pinot Blanc	Syrah
Riesling	Zinfandel
Sauvignon Blanc	
Trebbiano	

TYPES OF WINE

There are three basic types of wine: still, sparkling, and fortified. All three will be covered in more detail in later chapters.

Still Wine

Most wine is *still wine*, which is also known as *dinner* or *table wine*. It can be produced in various shades of red, rosé, and white and has an alcohol content generally ranging from 9 to 14 percent by volume.

Red wine is often more full bodied than rosé or white and is often heartier, tarter, and drier. (The word *dry* when used in regard to wine refers to an absence of sweetness.) Red wine is best served at room temperature, although some young red wines can be served chilled.

The color of rosé wine varies from pale pink to red. It may be slightly sweet and often has a fruity flavor. Rosé wines tend to be more like white wines than like red ones. Rosé wines are best served chilled.

White wines vary from a pale straw color to a deep gold. Whites are lighter bodied and more delicate than reds and have a much less pronounced flavor. They range from extremely dry to extremely sweet and are served chilled.

Much still wine is referred to by the French term *vin ordinaire* (ordinary wine) to differentiate it from more expensive quality wines. In France, the term *vin ordinaire* is used to describe an inexpensive wine of agreeable quality produced in great quantities for everyday consumption by the inhabitants of France and other European countries. Very little of this type of wine is exported to North America, and any that is will compete primarily with the so-called jug wines produced in North America. *Vin ordinaire* is nevertheless classified as a still wine, even if it costs only $5 a bottle. And a high-quality, well-aged, expensive bottle of wine is also a still wine, even though its quality is vastly superior to a budget bottle of still wine. In other words, the term *still wine* should be used to differentiate it from the other two types of wine, sparkling and fortified, and not as a determinant of quality.

Sparkling Wine

Sparkling wines contain carbon dioxide bubbles, which provide their effervescence. The carbon dioxide is produced either through a natural process of fermentation that does not allow the carbon dioxide to escape during the conversion of the grape sugar into alcohol and carbon dioxide, or it is added to still wine after the fermentation is complete.

Red, rosé, and white wines all can be made into sparkling wines. Whatever the color, sparkling wine is best served chilled. Like still wines, sparkling wines range from 9 to 14 percent alcohol by volume.

The best-known naturally produced sparkling wine is champagne. Although only the sparkling wine produced in the Champagne region of

France is true Champagne (with a capital C), the champagne *method* can be applied to any wine to make it sparkling. In Germany, sparkling wine is given the name *Schaumwein,* and in Italy, it is *spumante.* (Champagne and other sparkling wines will be covered in more detail in Chapter 9.)

Fortified Wine

Fortified wines are still wines to which has been added a distilled grape spirit such as brandy. This fortification considerably increases the wines' alcohol content, which ranges from 15 percent to as high as 24 percent by volume. Fortified wines vary from very dry to very sweet and are usually served before or at the conclusion of a meal. The best-known fortified wines are port, sherry, vermouth, Madeira, and Marsala. (Fortified wines will be discussed in more depth in Chapter 8.)

MANUFACTURING STILL WINE

There are six steps in the manufacture of still wine: crushing, fermenting, racking, maturing, filtering, and bottling, as illustrated in Figure 2-1.

Crushing

Crushing is the process in which whole grapes are pressed or lightly crushed to produce *must.* For some types of wine, the stems are removed during the crushing process. In other cases, they are left in the must. This must is then transferred to fermenting tanks made of wood (the traditional material) or, more likely today, plastic-lined, fiberglass, or stainless steel tanks, which are easier to clean and maintain. Stainless steel, in particular, allows the temperature of the fermenting must to be more precisely controlled.

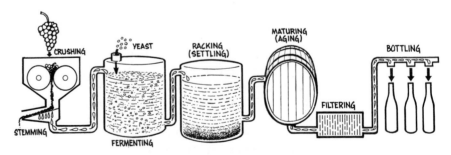

Figure 2-1   Steps in the manufacture of still wine.

Fermenting

Wines will ferment as a result of yeast mold naturally found on the grapes' outer skin, but commercial wine makers use commercial yeasts, rather than natural ones. These commercial yeasts allow the fermentation process to be better controlled to produce the desired quality of wine. If the new must were left to ferment naturally, it might extract too much acidity and tannin from the pips and stems (if they have not been removed), and too much color from the skins of dark grapes, which could be objectionable later on.

Therefore, even though grape-growing weather conditions are beyond human control, the fermenting of the grape must, the most important stage in wine production, can be regulated. Different fermentation processes are used to vary the chemical composition of the must, so as to produce a particular end product. White wines are usually fermented in a closed container to prevent oxidation resulting from contact with air. But red wines are usually fermented in open containers, as they can be fermented at a higher temperature, thereby producing a more violent fermentation that prevents oxidation.

Temperature is also important. If the must gets too cold or too hot, the fermentation will stop and is very difficult to start again. In particular, white wines should ferment slowly at relatively low temperatures so as to retain the freshness and fruity flavor that are their main features. Whites are fermented between 45° and 65° F (7° to 18° C), and reds between 70° and 90° F (21° to 32° C). Some wines are produced by what is known as *cold fermentation,* which slows the fermentation process. Cold fermentation takes place at temperatures from 54° to 59° F (12° to 15° C) for whites and from 65° to 70° F (18° to 21° C) for reds. This adds a fresh, fruity flavor to the wine.

The juice of all grapes is white, and in the manufacture of white wines, the skins are removed from the must before fermentation begins. That is, only the juice is allowed to ferment. White wine can be made from the juice of either white or red grapes.

The color of rosé and red wines comes from the skins of red grapes, and in the manufacture of those wines the skins are not removed before fermentation. That is, rosé and red wines can be made only from red grapes. For rosé wines the skins are removed after a day or so of fermenting, after some color has been extracted. For red wines, the skins may remain in the fermenting must until the end of fermentation, which can take up to two or three weeks. At that point the skins are pressed out and removed. For both rosé and red wines, the coloring matter and tannin are extracted from the skins, in a process known as *vatting (cuvaison* in French). Short vatting is used for wines whose main feature is fruitiness, and longer vatting is used for wines in which depth of flavor and longevity are desired. The tannin extracted during the vatting of red wines gives young wines an astringent taste, and it is this feature, absent in white wines, that is the main difference between the taste of red and white wines.

Fermentation turns the sugar in the grape juice into alcohol and carbon dioxide. To make still wines, the carbon dioxide gas is allowed to escape. Fermentation can take up to two weeks, or until the alcohol content is high enough (usually 14 percent by volume) to kill any remaining yeast that would stop the fermentation. In other words, a natural still wine can rarely exceed 14 percent alcohol by volume. The rate of fermentation is controlled in part by the amount of sugar present in the grape juice. If a sweeter wine is wanted, the fermentation process can be stopped. But if all the sugar present is converted to alcohol, the wine will be dry.

With rare exceptions, red table wines are fermented until they are completely dry, and the only thing that makes one red wine taste drier than another is the amount of tannin or acid that it contains. However, some red wines from Italy and Spain do taste slightly sweet, and some North American red wines are artificially sweetened by the addition of a small amount of sugar during the bottling process.

Most still wines contain between 11 and 14 percent alcohol by volume, although some wines (mainly the white wines of Germany) contain only 8 or 9 percent. In the case of some white wines, a poor grape-growing season may have produced grapes that have not ripened properly and contain too little natural sugar. In such cases sugar may be added to the must during fermentation, in a process known as *chaptalization*. Without chaptalization the wine would have too low an alcohol content and may even become unstable. Thus chaptalization increases the wine's alcohol content to a normal level.

In contrast, some white wines made from grapes with a high sugar content are produced before the fermentation process is completed. Such a wine will contain some residual sugar and will have a naturally sweet flavor. The white wines of Sauternes, in France's Bordeaux region, are noted for this, as are some of the wines from Germany and California.

Some wines are fermented using a process known as *carbonic maceration*. This removes a large proportion of acids and produces a lighter, more fruity wine than if it were fermented normally. With carbonic maceration the uncrushed grapes are initially placed in an airtight fermenting container that produces a blanket of carbon dioxide while the grapes ferment in their skins. This process is used primarily for fresh red wines such as Beaujolais Nouveau.

Racking

After the fermentation is complete, the wine is placed in casks, barrels, or tanks. As the wine rests in these containers, the residue of dead yeast cells and skin particles (known as *lees*) settles. From time to time the wine is *racked,* or transferred to new casks or tanks, leaving the lees behind, so that the racked wine can settle further. A wine may be racked several times until it is clear, and to help remove the lees, some wines may be filtered during racking.

Maturing

After racking, most wines are allowed to mature further. Rosé and white wines are matured in large stainless steel or glass-lined containers. Some white wines are matured for only a few months so that they will retain their youthful characteristics. That is, they are bottled relatively quickly. Most reds are matured in casks, often made of oak. The porous oak wood allows the air to interact with the maturing wine to produce a more mellow product and help develop the wine's particular character. This maturing can last for a few months, or even for as long as several years. The better red wines may remain two or three years in maturing containers.

Most wines are matured, or aged, in large stainless steel, concrete, or wood containers. The length of time a wine is aged affects its color, aroma, and flavor. For example, if a wine is aged for a long time in an oak vat, its color will deepen, it will have a stronger flavor of wood, and it will have a higher tannin content.

Filtering

After maturing, the wine is *filtered,* to help stabilize it. This process is sometimes referred to as *fining* or *clarifying.* Fining removes any solid particles still in the wine. The wine is then clarified by adding substances such as albumen (egg whites), gelatin, or bentonite (a fine clay) which sink to the bottom of the vat, taking any particles in the wine down with them. Some wine makers stabilize their wine by means of pasteurization, or heating the wine to about 140° F (60° C) and then rapidly cooling it. However, this process kills ingredients in the wine that give it its flavor and character and, by sterilizing it, prevents any further improvements to it. Many North American wine producers filter their wines very finely to make the wine as absolutely clear as possible, but this process can also reduce the wine's body and depth of flavor. Other wine producers do not filter their wines at all, because they believe that not filtering results in a more natural product. In this case the bottle's wine label may state that the wine is unfiltered or unfined. Some wine makers use cold filtration or stabilization, which requires chilling the wine to several degrees below freezing. This precipitates harmless wine crystals known as *tartrates* which can then be removed. After the final filtering the wine is ready for bottling.

Bottling

The final step in wine manufacturing is bottling. Bottles are a more permanent and convenient method for storing wine than are barrels or casks. Most wines continue to improve, or age, in the bottle. This continued aging is shorter for whites than for reds. Some notable reds need years of aging, and some outstanding wines continue to improve in the bottle for decades. This aging in the bottle is caused by the various elements present in the wine (such as acids, pigments, and tannins) interacting and combining with one another to create the wine's specific character.

But the length of time a wine stays in the bottle does not determine its quality, as only the very best wines are hardy enough to continue to improve over many years. Some wines, and particularly some white wines, are at their best if they are consumed within a few months of bottling. Most other white, rosé, and light red wines are best if left in the bottle no more than two or three years. However, some dry white wines, as well as most of the best naturally sweet white wines are best left longer in the bottle. The best reds continue to improve for up to four or five years, and in some cases much longer, in the bottle. It is only after this time that they show their real character, complexity, and richness of body.

Most bottled wines are blends of several wines. Only the very best wines are not blended. One of the reasons for blending is to ensure the product's consistency from year to year. Wine is not a standard product, and its quality can differ from year to year even when made from grapes from the same vineyard. Thus blending can often produce a finer wine, and it ensures a wine that will satisfy its consumers' taste. Blending is also sometimes necessary when the grapes from the bad harvest of a particular vineyard are used. Or different grapes are mixed when they are crushed. In other cases the product is blended after fermentation and before bottling.

Many cheap wines are pasteurized after being bottled to prevent bacteria from multiplying and spoiling the wine. This pasteurization can also prevent a wine from fermenting further in the bottle, but it can add an undesirable flavor because of exposure to the high heat used during the pasteurization process. Extremely fine filtering, discussed earlier, can often accomplish the same result without the side effects of pasteurization.

Quality wines develop more slowly and sometimes more completely in larger containers, and even though it sometimes pays to buy half-bottles (for example, when testing a new wine), the wine may not be as good (as it will have aged more quickly) as the same wine in a larger bottle such as a *magnum* (two full bottles).

When the wine is shipped, the maintenance of a constant temperature is important for preserving the wine's quality, particularly if the wine is shipped overseas. Extremes of temperature can prematurely age a wine and/or cause it to oxidize. And if the wine is continually agitated during shipping, that can also cause premature aging.

Bottle Corks

Most quality wine bottles are stoppered with porous cork, as the continued air contact is important. Only minute quantities of air do get through the cork, but it is enough to make a difference. In many cases the cork is covered with a plastic or tinfoil cap to protect it. Unfortunately, cork has become scarce and costly in recent years.

Cork is made from the bark of a type of oak tree that only grows in certain European countries such as Portugal. Only so much cork can be produced each year, as the trees are protected by government decree. As a result, fiberboard has replaced cork in some wine bottles, and there is an increasing trend toward using screw-top bottles rather than cork. But for wines that do not age in the bottle (which is the case with many cheaper wines), the lack of a cork makes no great difference.

For wine bottles that have been corked, it is important that they be stored and aged on their sides. In this way the wine is kept in contact with the cork and keeps it moist. If these wines are stored upright, the corks will dry out; there will be too much air contact; and the wine may spoil.

The wine bottles' corks are usually branded with the name of the winery, shipper, and year of bottling—a practice used to discourage fraud. For example, restaurants have been known to transfer cheap wine to empty quality-wine bottles and then to recork them with new unbranded corks (because the original, removed cork cannot be used again). An unbranded cork used with a bottle labeled as a quality wine will likely indicate this.

VINTAGE WINE

Many people, particularly those new to wine, want to know whether the date on a wine bottle's label represents a "good" year. They refer to these good years as *vintage years*. But every year for wine production is a vintage year, as the word *vintage* means a grape harvesting and, strictly speaking, has no particular meaning other than that.

There are many different variables that make one vintage better than another. For example, as grapes ripen, their sugar content increases and their acidity decreases—and a good wine is produced when the sugar and acid levels are at their best balance. The correct amount of sugar ensures that the wine will contain enough alcohol and be a more stable product, and have enough acidity to enhance its flavor. In poorer years the wines will have less alcohol and more acid (that is, be more tart). Generally, because white grapes do not normally require as long a growing season as red ones do, and can produce quality wines with lower sugar levels, there tend to be more good vintages for wines made from white rather than red grapes.

Sometimes a good vintage is declared before the grapes are picked, but a good vintage can be surely determined only once the fermentation has been finished. Some wine sophisticates say that it is still best to wait until the following year to declare the quality of the vintage.

Vintage Laws

We now come to the reliability of a vintage date on a bottle. First, any date on the bottle is supposed to represent the year in which the grapes from a particular area were picked. Some countries have laws regarding this. In France, 100 percent of the grapes must come from the year shown on the label date, and in West Germany, the figure is 85 percent (the rest of the wine may be blended from other years' grapes). In the United States, 95 percent of the grapes of wines with a vintage date must have been picked in the year shown on the label. If a wine from any of these three countries does not have a date on the label, then it does not conform to these standards and is likely a fully blended wine. But this does not mean that it is not a good wine, as more than a vintage date is needed to produce a quality wine.

However, a general rule is that the more expensive a bottle of wine is, the more likely it is to be a quality wine, and thus the more important the vintage date on the bottle is. But how does one know whether the date is significant? This question can be answered only with serious study.

It is a fact that a good year in France for grapes may not be a good year in Italy and a bad year in Germany may be a good year in the United States. But even within a country, a good year for French Bordeaux may be a bad year for French Burgundy, and even within the Bordeaux region one wine village may have a good year while the village next door does not. Indeed, a specific vine in a particular vineyard may produce a good vintage year while its next door neighbor's wine from a different type of grape will compare poorly. And even red and white wines produced from the same vineyard may not both be good vintages. In other words, without special study it is impossible for anyone to know all the information about good and bad vintage years.

Vintage Charts

Vintage charts, which show a numerical scale of quality, are often produced by shippers and importers, but these can be only a rough guide, as they cannot discuss each vineyard and are often produced to serve the needs of the shipper and/or importer. Therefore they should be used with caution by the general purchaser or consumer and should not be used as the only determinant of a quality wine.

Remember also that a quality wine listed on a vintage chart cannot be assumed to be a quality wine forever. Like any product, wines have life cycles. Some quality wines mature in a couple of years and then decline in quality, whereas others need several years to reach their peak and then hold that high quality for many more years before starting to decline. Unfortunately, some people buy these quality wines because of their date and then consume them too soon before they reach maturity. In other words, a date on the bottle is not a guarantee of quality at the time the wine is consumed. It is complete knowledge about the wine that counts.

Finally, note that most of the world's wines are blended and are meant to be consumed within a year of grape harvesting. Freshness and youth are the important attributes of these wines, rather than quality based on a good vintage year.

DISCUSSION QUESTIONS

1. What is the name of the vine from which the best wine is made?
2. What factors affect the quality of a wine?
3. What is a hybrid vine?
4. List three important wine-making countries in the northern, and three in the southern, wine-making belts.
5. List five well-known types of red wine grapes and five well-known types of white wine grapes.
6. In what range is the alcohol content, by volume, of most still wine?
7. What does dry mean in reference to wine?
8. What gives sparkling wines their effervescence?
9. How are wines fortified?
10. In wine manufacture, what is must?
11. Why is it important to control the temperature when fermenting wine? What is cold fermentation?
12. Define the terms *chaptalization* and *carbonic maceration* as used in the fermenting process.
13. How does red wine obtain its color?
14. In wine manufacturing, what is racking, and what purpose does it serve?
15. Give two reasons that many wines are blended.
16. Why should corked wine bottles be stored on their sides rather than upright?
17. What does the word *vintage* mean?
18. State the legal requirement in France, Germany, and Italy for grapes that are used in a vintage-dated wine.

3

Wines of France

CHAPTER OBJECTIVES

After studying this chapter the reader should be able to

- Describe the disease that nearly wiped out the European wine industry in the nineteenth century.
- Explain the acronyms AOC and VDQS with reference to French wines and list the two other categories of French wine.
- List the seven requirements for labeling a bottle of French wine and explain the meaning of French terms that may appear on a label, such as *château, négociant,* and *mise en bouteille à la propriété.*
- List the major wine-producing regions of France.
- Define claret, and list the five districts in the Bordeaux region that are noted for their quality wines.
- Explain the term *cru classé* and its use with reference to Bordeaux wines and identify the five wines in the Bordeaux region that are entitled to the top-quality *premier cru* designation.
- Discuss the term *pourriture noble* and its effect on grapes and wines.
- State the predominant grape varieties used in Burgundy, discuss the difficulties in identifying Burgundy wines based on their labels, and define French terms such as *mis en bouteilles dans nos caves* used on Burgundy wine labels.
- List the Côte d'Or's two subdistricts as well as the other four Burgundy wine districts and identify in which district specific wines such as Pouilly-Fuissé are produced.
- Discuss the wines of Beaujolais, including Beaujolais Nouveau, and list five of the nine Beaujolais *grand cru* wines.
- Discuss the wines of the Côtes-du-Rhone and the Loire Valley and identify some of them.
- Discuss the wines of Alsace and identify the major grape varieties used to produce them.

INTRODUCTION

Grapevines grew wild in many parts of what is now France long before there were people to eat the grapes or to make wine from them.

When the Romans moved north and west into the rest of Europe, it was to seek out flatlands for growing grain. They already had sufficient wine for their own needs in Italy and were even able to export their surplus to conquered lands such as France. Eventually, the local people of France were encouraged to plant their own wine grapevines along the riverbanks. Today those same riverbanks are the home of France's great vineyards.

By the middle of the nineteenth century the wine-making industry was well established in France. Indeed, there was probably more wine made each year in France than in all the other countries of the world together. There was so much wine, and it was of such good quality, that the French learned that many of the stored surplus wines improved even further with aging.

But then disaster struck the French wine industry. Hardy as the vines are, most of them were killed over a twenty-year period. By the 1870s the great vineyards of Bordeaux had been wiped out, and within the next ten years those of Burgundy and Champagne were dead or dying. The vines were attacked by a disease known as *phylloxera* which had inadvertently been brought to Europe from North America.

However, the salvation came from the same source as the disease. North American vines, particularly those from the Northeast, were virtually immune to phylloxera. European vines were grafted onto American rootstock (and have been ever since). Millions of vines were replanted at mammoth cost, and today those vineyards of France, and of other European countries, continue producing great wines from the same North American rootstock.

THE WINE LAWS OF FRANCE

The first wine laws of France were passed by the government in the early 1900s and were refined over time and then codified in the 1930s. They are known as *appellation contrôlée* (controlled name) laws and were originally designed to control the authenticity of quality French wines after the vineyards were replanted following the phylloxera destruction. Laws were also introduced to prevent fraud, such as adulterating good wines with lesser ones (or with water or prohibited chemical products), to prevent the use of misleading labels or the falsification of documents describing the wine, and to try to encourage each district to produce better wine. Each wine district is strictly delineated, and for each, the kinds of grapes that may be grown and the amount of wine that can be produced per hectare are defined. Finally, the laws state how the vines are to be pruned and what the minimum alcohol content of the wine must be, and sometimes how it is to be aged. Wines must also pass a taste test.

AOC Wines

The highest-quality French wines are known as *appellation d'origine contrôlée* (controlled origin name), often abbreviated to AOC. The AOC designation is used for outstanding quality wines, with the government's guarantee that the place name on the label is in fact where the wine comes from. Origin is important, because what differentiates these wines from lesser ones is the superior quality of the soil in which the vines are grown. Any wines in this category thus must have the words *appellation contrôlée* (spelled out in full) on the label. Some AOC labels insert the name of the actual region between the words *appellation* and *contrôlée*. For example, a controlled-area wine from Bordeaux might be labeled *appellation Bordeaux contrôlée*. In other cases, the origin will appear above the AOC designation. The origin may be a region (for example, Bordeaux), a district within a region (for example, Médoc, a district within the Bordeaux region), a village within a district (for example, St. Julien, a village within the Médoc district), or even an individual vineyard, which is often the common practice in the Bordeaux region (for example, Château Lagrange vineyard in St. Julien village). AOC wines presently comprise about 25 percent of France's total production.

VDQS Wines

One notch down from outstanding quality wines are the *vins délimités de qualité supérieur* (superior quality wines), and those words, or the abbreviation VDQS, must appear on the label. The quality of these wines is not quite as high, or as consistent, as that of the AOC wines. The total production of VDQS wines is about 5 percent of France's total.

Other Wines

Two other qualities of wine are also available but are not seen as often outside France, even though they comprise about 70 percent of the total wine production in that country. These are *vins de pays* (country or regional wines) and *vins de table* (table wine).

Vins de pays must come from a specific zone of production, mentioned on the label, and from a particular grape variety. Note that there is also a distinction between *vin de pays*—a government-controlled term—and *vin du pays* (regional wine), a term conversationally given to whatever wine is produced locally without any government-controlled labeling.

Vins de table often have no geographical indication of their origin on the label and are generally known to customers under a commercial brand name, with their prices, alcohol content, and quality being highly variable. To control some of these variables, vintners will frequently blend wines of different origins, with one type contributing, for example, a certain acidity; a second, strength; and a third, quality.

Illustrations may, and frequently do, appear on French wine labels. However, certain designated words such as *château* (strictly meaning a castle, but commonly meaning a wine estate or vineyard, and a word commonly used on the labels of the very best Bordeaux wines) may be used only for products having the right to an *appellation contrôlée* designation and coming from wine estates that do actually exist.

Over time, wines can be moved up or down in each of the four categories. That is, a *vin de pays* can move up to the VDQS category, and in the same way, a VDQS wine can move up to the AOC category.

There is, of course, no guarantee that such strict wine laws will protect consumers from fraud. Indeed, in the mid-1970s some of the best-known shippers in the premier wine-making region of Bordeaux were caught putting ordinary wine into AOC-labeled bottles and altering the accompanying legal documents authenticating the wines as quality ones.

Also, despite the French government's attempts to control labeling, confusion can still exist. For example, a label might read "M. Charpentier, Négociant à Bordeaux" (*négociant* meaning "bottler" or "shipper"). But this does not necessarily mean that the wine is from Bordeaux; it may be an ordinary table wine from some other region that just happens to have been bottled in Bordeaux because the shipper's premises are there. Again, origin can be determined only if the words *appellation d'origine contrôlée* or *appellation contrôlée* appear on the label.

Indeed, consumers in North America can easily be confused, as today many French wines are marketed by well-known French AOC shipping firms when, in fact, those wines are only ordinary table wines (often blended) designed to compete with the jug wines produced in North America. If purchasers buy by the vintner's or bottler's name, they may end up believing that the wine is of a higher quality than it actually is and be paying more than the wine is really worth. The best protection for purchasers in regard to quality is thus to seek out the labels that indicate whether the wine is an AOC or a VDQS.

Wine Bottle Labels

For French wines imported into North America, seven categories of information are required in addition to the wine's name:

1. A statement that the wine is a product of France.
2. The region where the wine was produced.

3. The appellation of the wine (AOC, VDQS, *vin de pays*, or *vin de table*).
4. The name and address of the shipper.
5. The name and address of the importer.
6. The percentage of alcohol by volume.
7. The net content of the bottle.

A label might look like the one in Figure 3-1, and sometimes the following words appear on French wine bottle labels:

Cave—Cellar.
Chais—Above-ground wine storage area.
Château—An estate usually owned by a single vintner or wine producer.
Clos—A vineyard.
Côte—A riverbank or slope.
Cru—A growth or place of origin.
Cuvaison—Vatting.
Cuve—Vat.
Cuvée—A blend of several grape varieties.
Domaine—An estate usually owned by a single vintner or wine producer.
Mis(e) en bouteille(s) au château or *mis(e) en bouteille(s) à la propriété*—Estate bottled, meaning that 100 percent of the grapes come from that vineyard. These terms may appear on any label.
Mis(e) au château or *mis(e) au domaine*—Also meaning estate bottled. However, these two terms may be used only for wines entitled to an *appellation contrôlée*.
Mis(e) en bouteille(s) dans la région de production—Bottled where produced. This term may be used only with *appellation contrôlée* wines.
Propriétaire—Owner or proprietor.

DOMAINE DE LA SALLE

Chusclan

Côtes-du-Rhône

APPELLATION CÔTES DU RHÔNE VILLAGES CONTRÔLÉE

SHIPPED BY:
M. Roussilie Viticulteur à
Chusclan (Gard) embouteillé
et distribué par S.A. Sofip,
3, rue du Chais, Paris 6ᵉ

IMPORTED BY:
Novum Wholesale Wines
New York, NY

750 ml   Product of France   12.5% alc./vol.

Figure 3-1   Label information on imported French wine bottles.

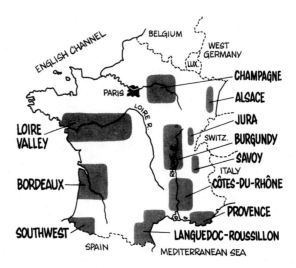

Figure 3-2   Map of French wine-producing regions.

Vigneron—Vintner.
Viticulteur—Wine maker.

French Wine Regions

There are six major French wine-producing regions, each containing many different districts. These regions are Bordeaux, Burgundy, Côtes-du-Rhône, Loire Valley, Alsace and Champagne. Less important regions are Jura, Provence, Languedoc-Roussillon, Savoy, and the Southwest. The general location of these French regions is illustrated in Figure 3-2. Wines from the various French regions can often be identified just from the shape of the bottle, with each region generally using a distinctive shape. These shapes are shown in Figure 3-3.

Figure 3-3   Typical French regional wine bottle shapes.

BORDEAUX

Bordeaux has been famous as a wine-producing area since Roman times. The Bordeaux wine region is often said to produce the queen of French red wines (Burgundy, by contrast, produces the king of French red wines). But both Bordeaux and Burgundy are also well known for their white wines. Although Bordeaux produces only about 5 percent of France's wines, this 5 percent accounts for about 25 percent of those entitled to the category of *appellation contrôlée.*

The Bordeaux region takes its name from its principal city, Bordeaux. Vines in Bordeaux are cultivated in a wide area stretching on both banks of the Garonne and Dordogne rivers and along the left bank of the Gironde estuary to the Atlantic Ocean. The climate benefits from the ocean's influence, producing mild winters and warm summers. Tradition, moderate climate and humidity, and a unique combination of vine, soil, and climate allow the creation of a diversity of wines.

Bordeaux wines are made from several grape varieties combined to provide different qualities. The best-known red grape varieties are Cabernet Sauvignon, Cabernet Franc, Malbec, Petit Verdot, and Merlot. The best-known white grape varieties are Sauvignon Blanc, Muscadelle, and Sémillon.

Bordeaux's red wines are generally delicate, light bodied, and dry, but they also may be full bodied. Bordeaux red is commonly called claret by the British. *Claret* is an anglicization of the Old French word *clairet,* meaning "wines made from red and white grapes combined," but the word *claret* is not found on any bottle label. Bordeaux whites are sometimes sweet, but not always. Bordeaux also produces some rosé wines. The quality of Bordeaux wines varies from ordinary to some of the best-known high-quality wines in the world. The price range is also just as extreme. Bordeaux wines are easy to recognize by the shape of their bottles, which are tall, slender, and high shouldered.

Any wine grown in the Bordeaux area, as long as it conforms to the relevant *appellation contrôlée,* may be labeled Bordeaux. However, to understand Bordeaux wines it is best to break them down into three main categories: the regional wines (mostly blended), the district wines (from a more precise geographical area), and the *château* wines (from a specific vineyard).

Bordeaux Regional Wines

Regional wines are most frequently labeled Bordeaux Rouge (red), Bordeaux Blanc (white), Bordeaux Rosé, Bordeaux Mousseux (sparkling), or simply Bordeaux Supérieur (superior, red or white). Note that Bordeaux Supérieur is not a superior quality wine; it is superior only because it contains about 1 percent more alcohol than do Bordeaux wines not labeled *supérieur.*

Wines labeled simply Bordeaux Rouge (or one of the other categories listed in the preceding paragraph) with no further description are normally not high quality, although they may still be agreeable to drink. Such wines are generally blended by a wine dealer or shipper who has selected them from different vineyards and bottled them under his own name. If the shipper is reliable, the wine will be good but not outstanding. A shipper's label will bear the word *négociant* followed by his name, or the label may bear the word *monopole* (literally meaning "a vineyard in single ownership" but also meaning "shipper" or "bottler") followed by the shipper's particular brand name for that wine. Some regional wines may be labeled with a specific district within the Bordeaux region, such as Médoc or Sauternes. Bordeaux's regional wines do have a consistent and dependable quality and style (without being very distinctive) and are also intended to be consumed without great aging. Regional wines make up about 75 percent of Bordeaux's total wine production.

Bordeaux District Wines

To find a better Bordeaux one must select from a specific Bordeaux district. There are more than thirty-five legally defined Bordeaux wine districts, most of them producing adequate wine. But only five of these districts are noted for quality wines: Médoc, Pomerol, St. Emilion (all three mainly producing red wines), Graves (producing both red and white wines), and Sauternes (noted particularly for its sweet white wines). These five districts are shown on the map of Bordeaux in Figure 3-4.

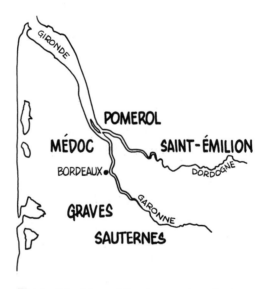

Figure 3-4 Map of Bordeaux wine districts.

A wine from Bordeaux labeled simply Appellation Contrôlée Bordeaux may be from anywhere in the Bordeaux region. But a wine labeled Appellation Contrôlée Sauternes will be from a vineyard within the Sauternes district and will usually be a better-quality wine.

Bordeaux Château Wines

If the wine is further labeled with the name of a *commune* or vineyard within a specific district, it will usually be one step higher in quality. Therefore, knowing the names of these five major Bordeaux districts and the villages or *communes* within those districts will enable one to identify the best wines of Bordeaux.

Traditionally, an individual vineyard in Bordeaux is referred to as a *château,* which, literally translated, means "castle." Although castles are seldom found at these vineyards, there may be large country houses. Today, more loosely translated, the word means an estate or vineyard. If the word *château* appears on the label, one can usually be sure that the wine is a Bordeaux. However, the word *château* may sometimes be replaced with the word *domaine* or *clos.* Note, though, that if a wine is labeled *château,* one can be sure that it is an authentic wine (in regard to where it is produced) but have no guarantee of its quality. However, the *château*-labeled wines of Bordeaux are generally among the finest that the region has to offer.

Médoc

The Médoc district produces some of the best red wines of France. Médoc reds have a fine ruby color, an exceptional bouquet, and an extremely delicate flavor. Being tannic, they are often astringent when young but are very good keeping wines that mature and round out with age.

A wine bottle labeled Médoc, rather than just Bordeaux, will generally be a good wine, and its quality can be guaranteed if it carries a reputable shipper's name. But quality also can be refined even further within the Médoc district. Médoc itself has two subdistricts, Haut Médoc and Médoc, and the better wines come from the Haut Médoc district. The Haut Médoc district is subdivided into many *communes* (village municipalities). Four of the more prestigious of these communes are Margaux, Pauillac, St. Estèphe, and St. Julien.

Thus, a label stating that a wine is a Bordeaux is a good start; a label stating Médoc is even better. But a label stating St. Julien (a commune within the Haut Médoc district of the Bordeaux wine-producing region) is better still, as long as its label still bears the words *appellation contrôlée.* There is only one more step that one can go. The greatest of the Médoc wines bear on their label the name of the individual vineyard or *château* within the commune where the wine was produced.

It was in the Médoc that the custom began of selling the best wines from an estate, vinified separately, under the name of the *château* from which they came. The wine brokers, who were also tasting specialists and arbitrators in commercial transactions, soon began calling these wines by the collective name of *crus classés* (classified growths). Of incomparable quality in a good vintage year, the *crus classés* wines—owing to their particular soils and to the grapes selected by the proprietors—are invariably of excellent quality, even in a reputedly light vintage year. The *château* wines of Médoc have a consistently high quality and character year after year. If a crop should be bad, which rarely happens, the vigneron might sell the wine to a dealer to be blended rather than have his reputation spoiled by bottling it under his *château* name.

A committee of Bordeaux wine merchants first graded the Médoc *château* wines more than a hundred years ago, basing their rank on the price that people were willing to pay for them at that time. Even though many decades have passed since that first grading, the prices that people are willing to pay today prove that the wines' comparative quality has changed little in more than one hundred years.

The grading system for the *crus classés* is numerical. Top-quality wines are given the name *premier cru* (literally, "first growth" or, more loosely, "top quality"). Only five Bordeaux wines fit into the *premier cru* category, and four of these are from Médoc (see Table 3-1). The fifth *premier cru* wine, Haut Brion, is from the Graves *appellation* district, discussed later in this chapter.

After the *premier cru* wines come the *deuxième cru* (second growth), down to the fifth. But even a fifth-growth Médoc wine is far from a low-quality wine; it just is not ranked as high as those in the higher (lower-numbered) growths.

The wines in these various growths are listed in Table 3-2. Some lists rank the wines in order of the author's grading of quality. But because quality is always very subjective, this table lists them in alphabetical order.

Situated between the classified growths and the "common" growths of Médoc are wines known as *crus bourgeois*. These wines come from excellent estates in the region originally owned by the bourgeois class of merchants and shippers. Because each growth possesses basic qualities specific to the

Table 3-1 The *premier cru* wines of Médoc.

Wine	*Commune Appellation*
Château Lafite–Rothschild	Pauillac
Château La Tour	Pauillac
Château Margaux	Margaux
Château Mouton–Rothschild	Pauillac

Table 3-2   The *crus classés* wines of Médoc.

Deuxième Cru—Second Growth	Commune Appellation
Château Brane-Cantenac	Margaux
Château Cos d'Estournel	St. Estèphe
Château Ducru-Beaucaillou	St. Julien
Château Durfort-Vivens	Margaux
Château Gruaud-Larose	St. Julien
Château Lascombes	Margaux
Château Léoville-Barton	St. Julien
Château Léoville-Las-Cases	St. Julien
Château Léoville-Poyferré	St. Julien
Château Montrose	St. Estèphe
Château Pichon-Longueville	Pauillac
Château Pichon-Longueville-Lalande	Pauillac
Château Rauzan-Gassies	Margaux
Château Rauzan-Ségla	Margaux

Troisième Cru—Third Growth	
Château Boyd-Cantenac	Margaux
Château Calon-Ségur	St. Estèphe
Château Cantenac-Brown	Margaux
Château Desmirail	Margaux
Château Ferrière	Margaux
Château Giscours	Margaux
Château d'Issan	Margaux
Château Kirwan	Margaux
Château Lagrange	St. Julien
Château La Lagune	Haut Médoc
Château Langoa	St. Julien
Château Malescot-Saint-Exupéry	Margaux
Château Marquis d'Alesme-Becker	Margaux
Château Palmer	Margaux

Quatrième Cru—Fourth Growth	
Château Beychevelle	St. Julien
Château Branaire-Ducru	St. Julien
Château Duhart-Milon	Pauillac
Château La Tour–Carnet	Haut Médoc
Château Marquis-de-Terme	Margaux
Château Pouget	Margaux
Château Prieuré-Lichine	Margaux
Château Rochet	St. Estèphe
Château Saint-Pierre	St. Julien
Château Talbot	St. Julien

Table 3-2 *(cont.)*

Table 3-2 *(cont.)*

Cinquième Cru—Fifth Growth	Commune Appellation
Château Batailley	Pauillac
Château Belgrave	Haut Médoc
Château Camensac	Haut Médoc
Château Cantemerle	Haut Médoc
Château Clerc-Milon	Pauillac
Château Cos-Labory	St. Estèphe
Château Croizet-Bages	Pauillac
Château Dauzac	Margaux
Château Grand-Puy-Ducasse	Pauillac
Château Grand-Puy-Lacoste	Pauillac
Château Haut-Bages-Libéral	Pauillac
Château Haut-Batailley	Pauillac
Château Lynch-Bages	Pauillac
Château Lynch-Moussas	Pauillac
Château Mouton-Baron-Philippe	Pauillac
Château Pédesclaux	Pauillac
Château Pontet-Canet	Pauillac
Château du-Tertre	Margaux

locality in which it is produced, these *crus bourgeois* constitute a logical extension of the *crus classés*, without being as expensive. For these wines the words *cru bourgeois* will appear on the label. Some of the more common are

Château Bel-Air–Marquis d'Aligre
Château Chasse-Spleen
Château Fourcas-Dupre
Château Fourcas-Hostein
Château Phélan Ségur
Château Siran

Although no white *appellation contrôlée* Médoc wines are produced, there are nevertheless white Médoc wines produced that may be labeled Appellation Contrôlée Bordeaux Supérieur.

Graves

Graves is a district known for its gravelly soil. Although the Graves district is noted for its *premier cru* Château Haut Brion (mentioned earlier as one of only five Bordeaux wines that are given this prestigious classification), its other red wines are also noted for their quality. They have a deep, dark ruby color and a well-developed bouquet. These wines are fuller bodied than those of Médoc, but without as much finesse. Graves also produces a sweet white wine that is simply labeled Graves or Graves Supérieur.

The most famous red growths are to be found in the northern part of the district. As is the case with the Médocs, they are excellent keeping wines. They were classified in 1953, except for the *premier cru* Château Haut Brion which was classified in 1855. Red Graves *crus classés* (classified growths) are

Château Bouscaut
Château Carbonnieux
Château de Fieuzal
Château Haut-Bailly
Château La Mission–Haut Brion
Château La Tour–Haut Brion
Château La Tour–Martillac
Château Malartic-Lagravière
Château Olivier
Château Pape-Clément
Château Smith–Haut-Lafite
Domaine de Chevalier

The best of Graves's white wines are produced in the southern part of the district. These wines range from very sweet to extremely dry, and they may have the right to be labeled Graves Supérieur if they contain 12 percent or more alcohol. Like all dry white Bordeaux wines, Graves should be served cool if mature and dry, colder if young, and chilled if sweet. White *crus classés* are

Château Bouscaut
Château Carbonnieux
Château Couhins
Château Haut-Brion
Château La Tour–Martillac
Château Laville–Haut-Brion
Château Malartic-Lagravière
Château Olivier
Domaine de Chevalier

Pomerol

Pomerol is a relatively small Bordeaux district primarily producing red wines that are sometimes referred to as the Burgundies of Bordeaux. There are no official *cru classés* wines in Pomerol. However, one of the best-known quality wines is Château Pétrus. Other well-known wines are

Château Gazin
Château La Conseillante
Château l'Evangile
Château Lafleur
Château La Fleur–Pétrus
Château La Tour Pomerol
Château Petit-Village
Château Trotanoy
Vieux-Château Certan

St.-Émilion

St.-Émilion produces more wine than Médoc does. Much of it is simply labeled St.-Émilion. St.-Émilion wines are characterized by their fullness. They all are red wines with a deep, dark, true (not blood) red. The best of them are the peers of the greatest Médoc and Graves reds, although there are fewer of them. In general they have a higher alcohol content than do the other Bordeaux wines. A lengthy maturation period is desirable, particularly in excellent growth years. St.-Émilion has both *premier grands crus* (first great growths) and *grands crus* (great growths). These wines were first classified in 1955 and then reclassified in 1986. They are listed in Table 3-3.

Sauternes

The fifth well-known Bordeaux district is Sauternes, most famous for its white wines. The wines from this district are naturally sweet, with a golden robe that turns to amber in a mature wine, with a bouquet hinting of honey and acacia. Because of their sweetness, Sauternes wines need to be well chilled before serving.

The very sweet Sauternes are uniquely made: The grapes are allowed to ripen until they reach the stage of *pourriture noble* (noble rot). At this stage the filaments of molds on the grape's skin penetrate it and draw off the water from inside. Only the shriveled, moldy grapes are picked—by hand, when they are just at the right stage. The grapevines are checked several times to make sure that grapes that are not ready remain on the vines to catch more sunlight. This selective picking may take several weeks, and as a result, the remaining juice in the grapes is more concentrated and has a sugar content as high as 40 percent (about three times more than normal grape juice). The most outstanding of these wines is Château d'Yquem, which, like other sweet Sauternes, is extremely rich and sweet in flavor and almost gold in color. Indeed, Château d'Yquem is classified as the only *premier grand cru* wine of Sauternes.

The sweet wines of Sauternes may be kept indefinitely and, when aged,

Table 3-3 The *premiers grands crus* and *grands crus* wines of St.-Émilion.

Premiers Grands Crus	Grands Crus
Château Ausone	Château L'Angélus
Château Beauséjour	Château Balestard-la-Tonnelle
Château Belair	Château Cadet-Piola
Château Berliquet	Château Canon-La-Gaffelière
Château Canon	Château Cap de Mourlin
Château Cheval Blanc	Château Corbin
Château Figeac	Château Corbin-Michotte
Château La Gaffelière	Château Curé-Bon
Château Magdelaine	Château Dassault
Château Pavie	Château Fonroque
Château Trottevieille	Château Grand-Barrail-Lamarzelle-Figeac
Clos Fourtet	Château Grand-Corbin
	Château La Clotte
	Château La Dominique
	Château Lamarzelle
	Château Larcis-Ducasse
	Château La Tour-Figeac
	Château Pavie-Macquin
	Château Ripeau
	Château Soutard
	Château Tertre-Daugey
	Château Trimoulet
	Château Troplong Mondot
	Château Villemaurine
	Château Yon-Figeac
	Clos des Jacobins

have a sort of bitter aftertaste which makes them a suitable accompaniment for many dishes. They can also be served as an aperitif and with dessert or cheese (in particular with Roquefort).

Within Sauternes is the commune of Barsac. Barsac wines are in fact Sauternes wines, but they have the right to be labeled Appellation Contrôlée Barsac. Indeed, some of them use both words: Sauternes and Barsac.

The wines of Sauternes and Barsac (in addition to the *premier grand cru* Château d'Yquem) are classified as *premier cru* and *deuxième cru* wines. They were classified in 1855 along with the Médoc wines and are listed in Table 3-4.

BURGUNDY

Burgundy (Bourgogne in French) is a narrow strip about seventy-five miles long in the middle of eastern France, stretching southeast of Paris from Dijon to Lyons. Burgundy's reputation is based on its red wines, which are

Table 3-4 The *premiers crus* and *deuxièmes crus* wines of Sauternes.

Premier Cru	Deuxième Cru
Château Coutet	Château d'Arche
Château Climens	Château Broustet
Château Guiraud	Château Caillou
Château La Tour–Blanche	Château Doisy-Daëne
Château Lafaurie-Peyraguey	Château Doisy-Védrines
Château Rabaud-Promis	Château Filhot
Château de Rayne-Vigneau	Château Lamothe
Château Rieussec	Château de Malle
Château Sigalas-Rabaud	Château de Myrat
Château Suduiraut	Château Nairac
Clos Haut-Peyraguey	Château Romer
	Château Suau

smooth, robust, and full bodied, and on its whites, which are refined and distinguished. Burgundy's red wines challenge the wines of Bordeaux in color and alcoholic strength, but they differ from them in bouquet, flavor, and style or personality. This difference is not so much one of quality as of character. However, although the white wines of Burgundy cannot compare as favorably to the rich whites of the Sauternes district of Bordeaux, some of the drier whites are considered some of the finest in the world (for example, Chablis).

Whereas Bordeaux produces its great wines by blending several grapes, most Burgundy wines are made from a single grape variety. Almost all red Burgundy wines are made from Pinot Noir grapes, although Gamay grapes are sometimes used, notably in the wines from the Beaujolais district. Some red wines are made from a combination of both grapes, in which case they will be labeled Bourgogne Passe-tout-grains. The white wines of Burgundy are made primarily from the very aromatic Chardonnay grapes, as well as from the Aligotés.

Some consider red Burgundy wine to be too heavy and indelicate, particularly if it is to be consumed in a hot climate. Those in colder climates do not agree, which is why Burgundy has always been popular in England and other countries of Northern Europe. But many Burgundy wines are also delicate and seem to taste less dry than do the dry wines of Bordeaux.

Quality Burgundy wines generally reach their prime sooner than do those of Bordeaux. Nevertheless, they can have a long life if allowed to stay in the bottle. The shape of the Burgundy bottle differs from that of Bordeaux, having a more traditional shape than the high-shouldered Bordeaux bottle (see Figure 3-3).

Burgundy produces only about 50 percent as much wine as Bordeaux does, and thus it is usually more expensive than that of Bordeaux.

Burgundy Wine Identification

One of the problems of identifying Burgundy wines is that the vineyards are not usually individually owned, as those in Bordeaux are. Burgundy wines also do not usually use the word *château* on their label, and for this reason their quality may be a little more difficult to discern. In Burgundy the word *domaine* or *clos* is used to indicate that the wine is estate bottled. But a vineyard in Burgundy may be shared among dozens of different own- ers, each using his own label with the vineyard's name on it. As a result, two bottles with the same vineyard name may contain two completely dif- ferent qualities of wine.

Another complication is that a wine producer may also own a share in several different vineyards that may be either close to one another or geo- graphically distant, in different villages. This protects the grape grower from the vagaries of weather that may strike one vineyard and not another, but it also means that a wine is unlikely to be produced from a single vineyard.

To find a quality Burgundy wine, one must know the names of the major villages and also the names of the *grand cru* wines from them, while still paying attention to the name of the grower or shipper on the label. This is particularly true in the case of blended wines (which the majority of those from Burgundy are today), because the growers who produce specific wines may still sell them to big shipping firms who will do the blending in order to produce a wine of consistent, dependable quality. In such cases the wine label will usually state *mis en bouteilles dans nos caves* (bottled in our cellars), a statement that has little meaning, as all the wines in Burgundy are bottled in cellars. Further, if the bottler is not the vineyard owner, it is likely that this statement is made to imply to the purchaser that the bottler is the estate owner, even though the wine is not estate, or *domaine,* bottled.

If the growers have bottled their own wines themselves, this will be in- dicated on the label by terms such as *mis au domaine, mis en bouteille au do- maine* (bottled at the winery), or *mis en bouteille à la propriété* (bottled at the estate). Sometimes, on exported wines, the label will simply state in English, "Estate bottled." For identification purposes these wines are the equivalent of the *château*-bottled wines of Bordeaux.

Classification of Burgundy Wines

Burgundy wines fall into three classifications. The best of these are the *grands crus,* or great growths. *Grands crus* wines are outstanding and have on their label only the name of the vineyard, such as Clos de Tart (from the village of Morey–St. Denis), although sometimes, for reasons of prestige, the name of the village is attached. There are only about thirty such wines.

Next in line are the *premiers crus,* or first growths. *Premiers crus* are usually labeled with the name of the village followed by the name of the vineyard.

For example, Pommard–Le Clos Blanc. Finally there are the village wines made from any vineyard within that village, such as Pommard or Volnay.

With a knowledge of Burgundy's geography, one can identify the major village names and be assured that a particular village-labeled wine will be good. If another name follows the name of the village, the wine is likely to be even better. And if one can learn the thirty or so *grands crus* wines, then one can identify the best.

There are five Burgundy region wine districts: Côte d'Or, Chalonnais, Mâconnais, Beaujolais, and Chablis, which are identified in Figure 3-5.

Côte d'Or

The supreme Burgundy wines come from the Côte d'Or district which stretches for about thirty miles in a narrow strip south of the city of Dijon. This district produces only about 15 percent of all the wines made in Burgundy, but the villages and vineyards most famous for high-quality wines are located here. The Côte d'Or is itself divided into two parts: the Côte de Nuits (immediately south of Dijon), which is famous for its red wines, and the Côte de Beaune (somewhat farther south) which, although famous for its white wines, produces many more reds than whites.

Some of the great red wine vineyards are found in the Côte de Nuits, whose villages, from north to south, along with their *grands crus* and *premiers crus* red wines, are listed in Table 3-5.

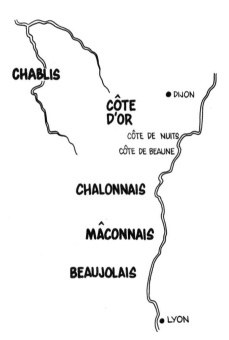

Figure 3-5 Map of Burgundy wine districts.

Table 3-5 The *grands crus* and *premiers crus* wines of Côte de Nuits.

Village	Grands Crus	Premiers Crus
Fixin		Clos de la Perrière
		Clos du Chapitre
		Les Arvelets
		Les Hervelets
Gevrey-Chambertin	Chambertin	Clos St. Jacques
	Chambertin–Clos de Bèze	Combe-au-Moine
	Chapelle-Chambertin	Les Cazetiers
	Charmes-Chambertin	Varoilles
	Griotte-Chambertin	
	Latricières-Chambertin	
	Mazis-Chambertin	
	Mazoyères-Chambertin	
	Ruchottes-Chambertin	
Morey-Saint-Denis	Bonnes Mares	Clos Bussière
	Clos de la Roche	Clos des Lambrays
	Clos de Tart	
	Clos Saint-Denis	
Chambolle-Musigny	Bonnes Mares	Les Amoureuses
	Clos de Tart	Les Charmes
	Musigny	
Vougeot	Clos de Vougeot	
Flagey-Echézeaux	Echézeaux	
	Grands-Echézeaux	
Vosne-Romanée	La Romanée	Aux Brûlées
	La Tâche	Les Beaumonts
	Richebourg	Clos des Réas
	Romanée-Conti	La Grande Rue
	Romanée-Saint-Vivant	Les Gaudichots
		Les Malconsorts
		Les Suchots
Nuits-Saint-Georges		Aux Boudots
		Aux Perdrix
		Aux Thorey
		Clos de la Marée
		Clos des Corvées
		La Richemone
		Les Cailles
		Les Didiers
		Les Porrets
		Les Pruliers
		Les Saint-Georges
		Les Vaucrains

Table 3-6 The *grands crus* red and white wines of Côte de Beaune.

Village Name	Red Wines	White Wines
Aloxe-Corton	Le Corton	Charlemagne Corton-Charlemagne
Puligny-Montrachet		Bâtard Montrachet Bienvenue-Bâtard-Montrachet Chevalier-Montrachet Montrachet
Chassagne-Montrachet		Bâtard-Montrachet Criots-Bâtard-Montrachet Montrachet

The Côte de Beaune produces some great white wines and also some impressive red wines. The villages in the Côte de Beaune, along with their *grands crus* red and white wines, are listed in Table 3-6, and the *premiers crus* red and white wines of the Côte de Beaune are listed in Table 3-7. The reason that some of these villages have hyphenated names is that they have adopted the name of their best vineyard as part of their name (after the

Table 3-7 The *premiers crus* red and white wines of Côte de Beaune.

Village Names	Red Wines	White Wines
Aloxe-Corton	Corton Bressandes Corton Clos du Roi Corton Les Meix Corton Maréchaudes Corton Renardes	
Pernand Vergelesses	Iles des Vergelesses	
Savigny-les-Beaune	La Dominode Les Jarrons Les Lavières Les Marconnets Les Vergelesses	
Beaune	Clos du Roi Les Avaux Les Bressandes Les Cent Vignes Les Clos des Mouches Les Fèves Les Grèves Les Marconnets	Les Clos des Mouches

Table 3-7 *(cont.)*

Village Names	Red Wines	White Wines
Pommard	La Platière	
	Le Clos Blanc	
	Les Chaponnières	
	Les Epenots	
	Les Pézerolles	
	Les Rugiens	
Volnay	Clos des Ducs	
	Le Clos des Chênes	
	Les Caillerets	
	Les Champans	
	Les Fremiets	
	Santenots	
Monthélie	Les Champs Fuillots	
Auxey-Duresses	Clos du Val	
	Les Duresses	
Meursault		Blagny
		Charmes
		La Goutte d'Or
		Les Genevrières
		Les Perrières
		Poruzot
		Santenots
Puligny-Montrachet		Clovaillon
		Le Champ Canet
		Les Caillerets
		Les Chalumeaux
		Les Combettes
		Les Folatières
		Les Pucelles
		Les Referts
Chassagne-Montrachet	Clos de la Boudriotte	Les Caillerets
	Clos Saint-Jean	Les Chenevottes
	La Maltroie	Les Ruchottes
	Les Caillerets	Morgeot
	Morgeot	
Santenay	Clos Tavannes	
	Gravières	

hyphen). A Burgundy bottle label may list only one of these hyphenated village names as its origin, without further estate identification. For example, a bottle labeled only Gevrey-Chambertin is an ordinary Gevrey village wine (allowed to use the name Gevrey-Chambertin) and probably contains no Chambertin vineyard wine.

Chalonnais

The wines of Chalonnais (sometimes referred to as the Côte Chalonnaise) are not well known outside France, but they still are very good. Some of the best-known names are Givry, Mercurey, and Rully (for reds and whites) and Bouzeron and Montagny (for whites).

Mâconnais

Mâconnais is sometimes referred to as the Côte Mâconnaise. The Mâcon district produces red, white, and some rosé wines. The red is from Gamay grapes, and the white from the Chardonnays. Generally the Mâconnais whites are better and generally less expensive than are the whites of the Côte de Beaune. Perhaps the best-known wine from Mâconnais is Pouilly-Fuissé, a pale golden wine that can be consumed while still young and is excellent with fish or poultry. A neighbor of Pouilly-Fuissé is Pouilly-Vinzelles. Other names are Pouilly-Loché, Saint Véran, as well as Mâcon, Mâcon Supérieur, and Mâcon-Villages.

Beaujolais

Beaujolais is a vast area that produces a great deal of wine of widely different qualities. Although part of southern Burgundy, some people consider Beaujolais to be almost a separate wine-producing region.

Beaujolais is probably one of the best-known French wine names in North America. One of the reasons for this is the immense publicity that surrounds its name each year in November, with the introduction of the Beaujolais Nouveau (sometimes known as Beaujolais Primeur), a light, fresh, delicate, and fruity wine often improved by being served slightly chilled. As a result of this publicity, and the related demand for Beaujolais wines, their prices have risen considerably in the last few years.

How did *nouveau* fever begin? In the 1950s the producers of Beaujolais had a surplus of newly fermented wine and no market for it, so they decided to promote a race to see who could reach Paris first with the wine. Restaurants in cities around the world now compete in their own locality to see who can become the first each year to obtain and offer their customers the new imported Beaujolais. This has become one of the most successful wine-marketing ideas in history; indeed, many other wine-producing countries have copied the idea with their own new and fruity young wines.

Many people think all Beaujolais wines are alike, but there is a vast variation in their quality and taste, and so a Beaujolais wine should be selected with care and knowledge. Most Beaujolais wines are made from Gamay grapes—which grow well in the region's sandy, granite-based soil—rather than from the Pinot Noir grapes used for other Burgundies. Beaujolais wines also have a short vatting period to minimize the amount of tannin. For these reasons most Beaujolais wines are somewhat less robust than are other red Burgundies.

Some people, particularly those in warmer climates, prefer to drink their Beaujolais slightly chilled. Beaujolais can also be consumed when quite young and will not improve much if it is more than three years old. Indeed, Beaujolais Nouveau is marketed and consumed a few weeks after the grapes are harvested and as soon after bottling as it can be distributed to the consumer. In any case, it is meant to be consumed within a few months.

Some of the other, non-*nouveau*, Beaujolais wines shipped to North America are intended to stay longer in the bottle and, for that reason (to give them some "staying" power), are heavier-bodied and fuller-flavored wines, while still retaining the delicacy for which Beaujolais wines are renowned.

There are nine red *grands crus* Beaujolais wines:

Brouilly
Chénas
Chiroubles
Côte de Brouilly
Fleurie
Juliénas
Morgon
Moulin-à-Vent
St. Amour

Some of these nine great wines are not labeled with the word Beaujolais (although they will probably still have the word *cru* on the label), and so it pays to have these nine names in mind when purchasing a quality Beaujolais.

Somewhat lower in quality are the wines labeled Beaujolais-Villages (with the name of a village seldom appearing on the label). Next in line is Beaujolais Supérieur, and then ordinary Beaujolais. The only difference between Beaujolais Supérieur and Beaujolais is that the former contains about 1 percent more alcohol, without any difference in quality.

Although Beaujolais is known for its red wines, the Beaujolais region also produces some white wines and some sparkling red and white wines.

Sometimes the name of a specific vineyard may appear on the label of a Beaujolais bottle, but this vineyard name is not as important to identifying product quality as is the name of a vineyard on a bottle of Bordeaux.

Chablis

Northwest of the Côte d'Or is the town and district of Chablis. Although the district of Chablis is geographically a part of the Burgundy wine region, its wines are often thought of separately. The very dry white wines of Chablis are world famous and are considered a particularly suitable accompaniment to oysters, fish, and white meat. They are free of both sweetness and acidity. Chablis wines are often a yellowish color with a greenish tinge.

Chablis is classified under four headings: *grand cru* Chablis (or more simply *grand* Chablis), *premier cru* Chablis, Chablis, and *petit* Chablis (a lighter-bodied Chablis intended to be consumed very young, within a year).

Grand Chablis is produced in only seven vineyards, but it is not necessary to remember these names, as the words *grand cru* or *grand* will appear on the label. Nonetheless the seven vineyards are

Blanchots
Bougros
Les Clos
Les Grenouilles
Les Preuses
Valmur
Vaudésir

One can be fairly certain that a *premier cru* Chablis will also be excellent, although the other two classifications—albeit still good—will not be of such high quality. Some of the best *premier cru* names are

Chapelot
Côte de Fontenay
Fourchaume
Mont-de-Milieu
Montée de Tonnerre
Vaucoupin
Vaulorent

Many countries in the world produce a wine labeled *chablis* (and it is not illegal for them to do this), but it is far from the true Chablis.

Other French Regions

In addition to Bordeaux and Burgundy, other regions worthy of note are Côtes-du-Rhone, the Loire Valley, Alsace, Jura, Provence, Languedoc-Roussillon, the Southwest, and Savoy.

CÔTES-DU-RHÔNE

The Côtes-du-Rhône is the Rhone River Valley located southeast of Paris and extending 125 miles south from Lyons to Avignon. The best of its wines come from the southern part of the valley near the ancient walled city of Avignon. Côtes-du-Rhône wines are generally rich and hearty, with a higher alcohol content than that of most French wines. Ninety percent of these wines are red; the rest are whites and some rosés. The red grapes used are Syrah, Grenache Noir, and Cinsault, and the white grapes are Viognier, Clairette, and Picpoul.

Côtes-du-Rhône wines are very consistent, as the hot, steady climate varies little from one year to the next. Indeed, the extreme heat of the Rhone Valley is not suitable for growing many of the finest grape varieties, and for this reason many different varieties are used, often in the same wine. These wines are best if they are allowed to age for a few years before bottling, and the best of them are not bottled until they are five years old.

One of the great characteristics of the Rhone Valley wines is their stability and keeping quality, as well as their attractive color and distinctive bouquet. They will last for years without loss of personality. Wines from this area—whether white, rosé, or red—are given the general appellation Côtes-du-Rhône. If the wine is labeled Côtes du Rhône–Villages, then it will generally be of a higher quality than the general appellation.

One of the best-known Côtes-du-Rhône wines is Châteauneuf-du-Pape, made from a blend of grapes (anywhere from six to as many as a dozen different types). It is made in both a red and a white variety, although it is best known for its red. Although Châteauneuf-du-Pape is seldom an outstanding wine, it can usually be relied on for its consistent quality from year to year. Other well-known wines are Côte Rôtie (red), Hermitage (red and white), Clairette de Die (white), Condrieu (white), and Château Grillet (white).

The Rhone Valley is also the home of Tavel, France's best rosé. Some rosés are made by mixing red wine with white wine, but in Tavel the red grapes are pressed and the skins later removed from the must as soon as it reaches the desired shade of pink. The result is a sharp, full-bodied, dry rosé.

Other better-known Côtes-du-Rhône wines are

Coteaux du Tricastin (red and rosé)
Côtes du Ventoux (red and rosé)
Crozes-Hermitage (red and white)
Cornas (red)
Lirac (rosé)
St. Joseph (red and white)
St. Péray (white)

LOIRE VALLEY

South of Paris and west of Burgundy is the Loire Valley, which takes its name from the majestic Loire River which flows gently westward to the Atlantic through the numerous vineyards that border its banks. It may be the most beautiful wine region of France and is popular with tourists, who visit it to view its historic castles. It produces crisp white and golden sweet dessert wines, along with fine sparkling wines, and superb rosés that are light, fruity, and just slightly sweet. It also produces a few reds. The white grapes used are Muscadet, Chenin Blanc, and Sauvignon Blanc, and the red grapes are Cabernet Sauvignon, and Cabernet Franc.

Very few of the Loire wines are sold under the name of the grower or his estate; most of them are sold under the *appellation contrôlée* of the district or village. Bad vintages are seldom seen in the Loire Valley, and so it is less important to know the vintage date than it is for other French wines. Indeed, many of the Loire wines are sold without any vintage date. Many of them are best when young.

One of the best-known Loire Valley wines is Anjou. Although it is produced in both white and red dry and sparkling varieties, the best Anjou wines are the rosés. Indeed, Anjou is a leading French wine region for rosé wines. None of the Anjou rosés is dry. Cabernet d'Anjou is also a rosé wine and is a little less sweet than the Anjou rosé.

Muscadet is a dry Loire Valley wine whose flavor is lightly musky and now is a popular alternative to Chablis and is much less expensive. Oddly, this wine is not typical of French wines, in that it is named after the Muscadet grape rather than the location of its production. A bottle labeled Muscadet Sur Lie indicates that the wine was bottled without racking (or being transferred to another container), that is, directly from the fermenting vat while still sitting on its lees or natural deposits.

Pouilly Fumé (not to be confused with Pouilly-Fuissé from the Mâconnais district of Burgundy) is sometimes called Blanc Fumé (meaning white smoke) because of the misty blue dust that the grapes give off in harvest time. Blanc Fumé is the name of the grape, and the name Pouilly Fumé is an exception to French wines, as both the village name (Pouilly) and the grape name (Fumé) appear on the label.

Other well-known Loire Valley wines are

Bourgueil—Red.
Chinon—Red.
Gros Plant du Pays Nantais—Red or white.
Mountlouis—Wines similar to Vouvray and also available as *vins mousseux* (sparkling wines).
Sancerre—Available in both white and rosé.
Saumur—Both still and *mousseux* reds, whites, and rosés.

Touraine—Red, white, and rosé still and sparkling wines.

Vouvray—White. Vouvray is also particularly well known for its *vin mousseux*.

ALSACE

Alsace, along with the area where Champagne is produced, is the most northerly wine region in France, extending along the edge of the Alsatian plains at the foothills of the Vosges Mountains from Mulhouse to Strasbourg where the Rhine River separates Germany from France. This area is sheltered from the influence of the sea and has a great deal of sunshine with very little rain, a combination that is particularly beneficial to ripening grapes. Alsace is the biggest producer of *appellation contrôlée* white wines after Bordeaux and Champagne. Indeed, well over 95 percent of all wines produced in Alsace are white.

The wines of Alsace were not well known until after World War I, which ended its fifty-year German occupation. The wines of Alsace are similar to the wines of the Moselle district in Germany. They are made from the same grapes, are marketed in the same tall, tapering, elegant green bottles (known as *flutes d'Alsace* in France), and are light and fresh, even though they have not gained the reputation enjoyed by the Moselle wines. One reason is that while Alsace was part of the German Empire (a period during which European wines were only just getting back on their feet from the phylloxera infestation), the Alsace region was planted with inferior grapes—perhaps so that its wines would not compete directly with the Moselle wines of Germany. They were also primarily blended wines, many of which were used to produce *Schaumwein* (German sparkling wine).

After 1918, when the French regained Alsace, they replanted the vineyards with better vines. But there was another setback during World War II when the Germans again occupied Alsace, and so the French had to begin all over again after 1945.

The better wines of Alsace are made from Sylvaner, Riesling, and Gewürztraminer grapes, although other grapes are also used, such as Muscat, Pinot, or Traminer. The official appellation of these wines is Alsace or Vin d'Alsace and is usually and traditionally followed on the label by the grape variety (of which 100 percent must be used) and the producer's name. Sometimes the name of the village of origin follows the grape name, such as Riesling de Ribeauville, and some of the very best quality wines are allowed to be labeled Alsace Grand Cru.

Alsatian wines are generally bottled within a year of harvest. They are fermented until they are dry, which differentiates them from German wines, which generally tend to be a bit sweet. Alsace wines are therefore more fully flavored, with more body and alcohol than their German counterparts.

For example, wine made from Gewürztraminer grapes has a sharp, spicy bouquet and a pungent taste (appropriately, the German word *Gewürz* means "spicy").

JURA

The Jura region is east of Burgundy between Beaune and Geneva. Production in the Jura wine region is fairly low, which means that these wines are not very well known by the general public. This is a pity, for this region produces a unique wine known as *vin jaune* (yellow wine), resulting from storing the fermented wine in cool cellars in vats that previously contained other *vin jaune* whose old yeast cells form a veil of yeast on the surface of the wine. The wine is thereby protected from excessive oxidation and so turns a unique yellow color and has a flavor unlike any other wine produced in France. The major one is Château Chalon. Three other notable Jura wines are Etoile, Arbois, and Côtes-du-Jura.

Another specialty of this region is *vin de pailles* (straw wine), so named because it used to be made from grapes that were dried for two months on straw. Today straw is not used; the grapes are simply hung up to dry before they are pressed and fermented. As a result of the sugar concentration, this is a very sweet wine.

PROVENCE

Most of the wines from the region of Provence (south of the Rhone River and stretching east along the Mediterranean coast) are labeled Côtes de Provence. However, one of the better-known ones is Cassis, a full-flavored white wine that is used locally with the *bouillabaisse* made there. Do not confuse the wine name Cassis with the French crème de cassis—a sweet, black currant–flavored syrup used with some desserts and in certain cocktails (such as Kir). Other wine names are Palette (red and white) and Bandol (red and rosé).

LANGUEDOC-ROUSSILLON

Sweeping westward from the Rhone River to the Spanish border at the foot of the Pyrenees and bounded on the south by the Mediterranean, the region of Languedoc-Roussillon (also known as the Midi) occupies more than a third of France's total vineyard area and produces about 40 percent of all French wine.

Some wines names from this region are

Blanquette de Limoux (sparkling)
Corbières
Costières du Gard
Coteaux du Languedoc
Faugères
Fitou
Minervois
Muscat de Frontignan
St. Chinian

SOUTHWEST

The southwest corner of France also produces some notable wines. Names to look for are

Bergerac
Cahors
Gaillac
Madiran
Monbazillac
Montravel

SAVOY

The Savoy region is located at the foothills of the Alps along various rivers and overlooking Lake Geneva (Lac Leman is its French name). One of Savoy's best wines is the dry white Crépy. Savoy also produces Seyssel, a sparkling wine.

OTHER FRENCH WINES

There are hundreds, if not thousands, of other French wines that, even if they have no claim to distinction, are thirst quenching and satisfying. However, most of these wines are consumed in France by the local population living near the vineyards where the wines are produced.

CHAMPAGNE

One last major wine-producing region of France is Champagne, where the world-famous sparkling wines of that name are made. Because these wines are so special, they will be described in a separate chapter.

DISCUSSION QUESTIONS

1. What disease almost wiped out the European wine industry in the nineteenth century? How was the industry saved?

2. What does the acronym AOC stand for? VDQS? Apart from AOC and VDQS wines, what two other qualities of French wine are defined by the country's wine laws?

3. What are the seven general requirements for labeling a bottle of French wine to be exported?

4. Define the terms *château* and *négociant* when used on a French wine bottle label.

5. Excluding Champagne, name five major French wine-producing regions.

6. What name do the British often use to refer to Bordeaux wines, and what is its origin?

7. What are the five districts in the Bordeaux region noted for their high-quality wines?

8. What does the term *cru classé* mean in regard to Bordeaux wines?

9. What five wines are designated as *premiers crus* in the Bordeaux region? From which districts within Bordeaux do they come?

10. What does the term *crus bourgeois* mean in regard to Médoc wines?

11. What does the term *pourriture noble* mean in regard to Sauternes wines? Which wine in Sauternes is known for its *pourriture noble?*

12. Except for the Beaujolais district of Burgundy (where mostly Gamay grapes are used), most other Burgundy red wines are made from which grape?

13. Why are Burgundy wines more difficult to identify than, for example, those of Bordeaux?

14. What does the term *mis en bouteilles dans nos caves* mean, and what does it signify on a label of Burgundy wine?

15. What do the terms *mis au domaine, mis en bouteille au domaine,* and *mis en bouteille à la propriété* mean, and what do they signify on a label of Burgundy wine?

16. The Côte d'Or is one of the five Burgundy wine districts. What are the Côte d'Or's two subdistricts?

17. Excluding the Côte d'Or, what are the other four Burgundy region wine districts?

18. In which Burgundy district is Pouilly-Fuissé produced?

19. Name five red *grands crus* Beaujolais wines.

20. Name the extremely dry white Burgundy wine that is a good accompaniment to fish and shellfish.

21. Which French wine region produces Châteauneuf-du-Pape?

22. What region produces Anjou?

23. Why is Pouilly Fumé sometimes named Blanc Fumé? In which region is it produced?
24. In what region are Sancerre, Vouvray, and Saumur produced?
25. Why were the wines of Alsace not well known before World War I?
26. Name the three kinds of grapes from which the best Alsatian wines are made.

4

Wines of Germany

CHAPTER OBJECTIVES

After studying this chapter the reader should be able to

- Discuss the situation of Germany's northerly location for grape wine production and the type of grapes used there.
- List the Rhine region's five wine-producing areas.
- Identify German wine names such as Hock, Liebfraumilch, Moseltaler, Steinwein, and Eiswein.
- Describe how Rhine wine bottles differ from those of Moselle.
- List the three quality categories of German wine, and define the five descriptive words, such as *Kabinett*, used with the top-quality wines.
- Define the word *Edelfäule*.
- Define terms used on German wine bottle labels such as *Einzellage*, *Erzeugerabfüllung*, and *Halbtrocken*.
- Explain the term *Amtliche Prüfungsnummer* that is placed on the labels of German quality wines.

INTRODUCTION

Germany does not make much wine, with production only about 10 percent of either France's or Italy's and only about 1 percent of the world's total. Nor is wine the major national alcoholic beverage of choice as it is in those two countries. Beer is the national drink of Germany. However, Germany does produce wine from one of the major vines in the world, the Riesling. In addition, Sylvaner and Müller-Thurgau and limited amounts of Traminer, Rulander, and Gewürztraminer grapes are also used. Although in earlier times most of Germany's wine was red, today it is almost entirely white, and this white wine is unique among the world's wines for its flowery bouquet and fine balance between acidity and sweetness.

The wines of Germany are produced primarily in the valleys of the Rhine (Rhein in German) and Moselle (Mosel in German) rivers, bordering Belgium, Luxembourg, and France on the west and Switzerland to the south. These two river valleys are the most northerly wine areas in Europe, along with the Alsace and Champagne regions of France. Because of this northern location, the summers are relatively short, and crops can be damaged by early frosts. The vines are planted on the steep riverbanks. Because of the shortage of sun the grapes are not able to ripen as well as they can in more southerly climates, and so in poorer years sugar often has to be added to the grape must in order to increase the wine's alcoholic content and counterbalance the acidity. The added sugar makes the wine more drinkable, without oversweetening it and without adding to or detracting from the wine's bouquet.

Some of the best German wines are produced from overripe grapes, a condition that concentrates the grape sugar and natural flavor. (It is the degree of ripeness that forms the basis of West Germany's wine laws, to be discussed later in the chapter.) Because of their sweetness, German wines are best consumed on their own or with dessert, but not with any strongly flavored foods.

Eleven Regions

Eleven regions *(bestimmten Anbaugebiete)* fall within the *Qualitätswein* (quality-wine) categories, which are shown in Figure 4-1:

Ahr
Baden
Bergstrasse
Franken (Franconia)
Mittelrhein
Mosel-Saar-Ruwer
Nahe

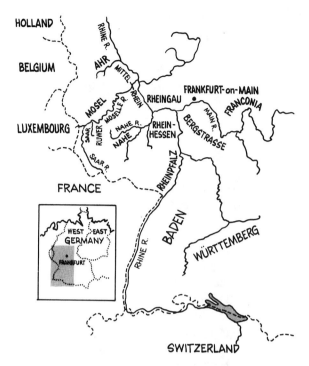

Figure 4-1   Map of German wine-producing regions.

Rheingau
Rheinhessen
Rheinpfalz
Württemberg

of which Rheingau, Rheinhessen, Rheinpfalz, Mittelrhein, Nahe, and Mosel-Saar-Ruwer, plus perhaps Franken (Franconia), are the most important. For a *Qualitätswein* the name of one of these regions must appear on the label. Within each region are two or more districts, with thirty-four districts in total. Each district has several villages or parishes forming a geological and climatic unit, and each village has several vineyards. In total there are about 1,400 wine villages (*Gemeinde*) and 2,600 vineyards (*Einzellagen*) whose names may appear on quality-wine labels.

RHINE WINES

Five of the eleven major wine-producing regions lie in the Rhine River area: Rheingau, Rheinhessen, Rheinpfalz, Mittelrhein, and Nahe, of which the first three are the most important.

The Rhine wines (as well as the other German wines) all are made from the same varieties of grape—Riesling (which is considered to produce the very best German wines), Sylvaner, and Müller-Thurgau (a cross between Riesling and Sylvaner). Rhine wines are elegantly light, dry, and slightly sweet. Wines produced from Riesling grapes in other parts of the world do not seem to be able to duplicate the elegance of the German wines.

Rheingau

Some of the better-known villages in the Rheingau, which lies on the east side of the Rhine River along the twenty-five or so miles between the towns of Wiesbaden and Rudesheim, are

Eltville
Erbach
Geisenheim
Hattenheim
Hochheim
Johannisberg
Oestrich
Rauenthal
Rudesheim
Winkel

In the 1800s one of the well-known wines consumed by the British was from the village of Hochheim (actually on the Main River but still considered to be part of Rheingau). The British had become acquainted with this wine at the spas in Hessen and so began to use the word *Hock* (an anglicized abbreviation of the word Hochheim) to describe all German Rhine wines.

Rheinhessen

The Rheinhessen is on the west bank of the Rhine south of the Rheingau region and roughly between the towns of Mainz and Worms. Well-known villages are

Alsheim
Bingen
Bodenheim
Nackenheim
Nierstein
Oppenheim

One of the better-known wines from the Rheinhessen is Liebfraumilch. Although many people think that Liebfraumilch is a wine from a specific village, it is not. Rather, Liebfraumilch is an invented name and can refer to any wine from this region. It is frequently a blend of lower-quality wines that can vary considerably in both quality and price. The quality of a Liebfraumilch can best be judged by the name of a reputable shipper.

Rheinpfalz (Palatinate)

The Rheinpfalz is sometimes referred to as the Palatinate. This area is also on the west bank of the Rhine south of Rheinhessen but is more protected from cold winds than is Rheinhessen and has somewhat more sunshine. For this reason, some Rheinpfalz wines are very rich and sweet. Some of the village names are

Deidesheim
Dürkheim
Forst
Ruppertsberg
Speyer
Wackenheim

Nahe

Besides the three main Rhine areas there is the less well-known area of the Nahe, a tributary of the Rhine. Three important village names on the Nahe are

Bad Kreuznach
Niederhausen
Schloss Böckelheim

Mittelrhein

Finally, the Mittelrhein is the most northerly of the eleven German grape-growing districts.

MOSELLE WINES

Another of the major, quality wine–producing regions is the Mosel-Saar-Ruwer, made up of the Mosel (Moselle in English) River and its two tributaries, the Saar and the Ruwer. The Moselle River Valley lies to the west of the Rhine, joining it at Koblenz, and produces slightly less sweet wines than those of the Rhine. Moselle wines are quite low in alcohol (as low as 10 percent). A unique feature of the Moselle vineyards is the steepness of the river valley slopes (those that face north get almost no sun). These vineyards are layered with slate which is broken up in the winter into small pieces that, in the summer, store heat from the sun and radiate it back at night. The best-known Moselle River villages are

Bernkastel
Graach
Piesport
Trittenheim
Urzig
Wehlen
Zeltingen

Saar and Ruwer

As is the case with the Rhine, the Moselle River also has some tributaries, the Saar and the Ruwer, that produce excellent wines. Well-known Saar villages are

Ayl
Kanzem
Ockfel
Wiltingen

and some of the Ruwer villages are

Eitelsbach
Grunhaus
Kasel

Note that all the wines from any of the three river areas (the Moselle, the Saar, and the Ruwer) will bear the same quality-wine region label identification: Mosel-Saar-Ruwer.

The Moselle region also has its generic equivalent to the Rhine's Liebfraumilch: Moseltaler, a dry, crisp wine quite distinct from the sweeter Liebfraumilch. In earlier days the generic wine of the Moselle was named Moselblümchen (meaning little flower of the Moselle), but this has now been replaced in the North American market with the easier-to-pronounce Moseltaler.

The easiest way to differentiate Moselle wines from Rhine wines is by the color of the bottle. Both come in a tall, fluted, elegant bottle similar to that for French wines produced in Alsace, but the Rhine wine bottles are brown, whereas Moselle bottles are green (just like those of Alsace). This differentiation can be useful in remembering the major difference between the two wines—the brown bottle of the Rhine representing the wine's rich, full flavor and the green of Moselle representing the wine's paler color and fresh delicate flavor.

FRANCONIA (FRANKEN)

One other important wine-producing region in Germany is that of Franconia (Franken in German), east of Frankfurt along the Main River. The wines produced here are much drier with a less intense bouquet than those of either Rhine or Moselle. These wines are sometimes referred to as *Steinwein* and are shipped in a flat-sided, gourd-shaped bottle (a sort of stumpy flagon) known as a *Bocksbeutel*. The wines of Franconia are often drier and more similar to French wines than are the sweeter wines from the Rhine and the Moselle. Some village names are

Eschendorf
Randersacker
Retzbach
Stetten
Würzburg

OTHER REGIONS

Less important German regions are Ahr (the main region for red wine), Baden (stretching along the Black Forest from Heidelberg to Lake Constance), Bergstrasse (the smallest region), and Württemberg (known for its reds and rosés).

WINE LAWS

West Germany also has well-established wine laws, which identify three major legal categories: *Qualitätswein mit Prädikat, Qualitätswein bestimmter Anbaugebiete,* and *Deutscher Tafelwein.*

Qualitätswein mit Prädikat

Qualitätswein mit Prädikat (frequently abbreviated to Q.m.P.) means a quality wine with special attributes—in other words, the best German wine. No sugar is allowed to be added to the must when making this wine. These top-quality German wines are similar in status to the AOC wines of France and usually contain on their label one of the following five words:

Kabinett
Spätlese
Auslese
Beerenauslese
Trockenbeerenauslese

Kabinett is the first (lowest) level among the five *Prädikat* wines. The grapes are picked at the normal time, generally in October, which is later than most other grapes are picked in Europe, owing to the longer ripening time needed because of the northerly location.

Spätlese means "late picked" or "gathered" (two to three weeks after normal harvest time). These grapes will be fully ripe and produce a wine somewhat sweeter and richer than a *Kabinett* wine from the same vineyard.

Auslese means "selected picking" or "gathering." It refers to a slightly higher quality wine made from fully ripened grapes handpicked from ripened bunches and producing a fuller-bodied, sweeter wine than *Spätlese*.

Beerenauslese means "selected overripe grapes," again handpicked from overripe bunches producing a high-quality wine that is even fuller and sweeter than *Auslese*. *Beerenauslese* wines are made only in very good years.

Trockenbeerenauslese means "selected dried grapes." With their concentrated sugar, these grapes produce the highest-quality German wines. These raisinlike grapes have what is called *Edelfäule* in German, equivalent to the French *pourriture noble* (noble rot) used to produce some Sauternes wines. *Trockenbeerenauslese* wines are made only in exceptionally good years.

If a label contains one of these five words, it must have no sugar added; that is, it is 100 percent natural. If none of these five words appears on the label, the wine has probably been produced from a normal harvesting and will therefore be quite dry or, if sweet, will have had sugar added.

In good sunny years, German wine producers will make several pickings from the same vineyard, each subsequent picking producing a fuller and richer wine. Each picking also costs more, not only because of the extra labor but also because of the higher risk of frost that would prevent the very best wine, the *Trockenbeerenauslese,* from being produced.

An unusual German Q.m.P. wine is Eiswein. For this wine, the grapes are allowed to ripen to their full extent and also to partially freeze, owing to the low temperatures while still on the vine. Eiswein is considered to be a German wine specialty. It was first produced in desperation when grape growers did not want to discard a grape crop that was frost damaged. Such grapes need to be pressed quickly before the ice crystals thaw.

One of the drawbacks to Eiswein is its high acidity, which can be three times the level of standard German wines. Another problem is the difficulty in getting the must to ferment, as it is cold and concentrated. Normal yeasts do not work, and so special strains of yeast have to be used. Eiswein may be made only when the conditions are right—perhaps only in three years out of ten. For this reason, little of this wine is produced, and it is very expensive. Because it has a highly flavored, sugary and acidic content, it is usually consumed at the end of a meal, much like a liqueur or cordial.

Qualitätswein bestimmter Anbaugebiete

Qualitätswein bestimmter Anbaugebiete (frequently abbreviated Q.b.A.) means a quality wine from a controlled growing district. This is the next level down of German quality wines; they are best when young. Q.b.A. wines are good-quality wines whose natural sugar content is not high enough for them to achieve Q.m.P. status, and so sugar may be added.

Deutscher Tafelwein

Deutscher Tafelwein means "German table wine," and it is a lower-quality wine, which is usually locally consumed and seldom exported. The designation *Deutscher Tafelwein* is given to wines labeled with only a broad regional appellation such as Rhein (Rhine) or Mosel (Moselle), as long as the wine is produced from grapes grown in that region. If the label says only Tafelwein, then it is most likely a blend of wines produced outside the country, to which sugar may have been added.

BOTTLE LABELS

German wine bottle labels sometimes discourage people from trying the wines, particularly because there are many more important wine-producing villages with which one needs to be familiar in Germany than in, for example, the Burgundy region of France. Many of the German village vineyards are owned by several different vintners, and in some years these vintners produce several different wines from the same vineyard from successive gatherings of grapes in various stages of ripeness.

Although German wine labels at first seem more confusing than do the labels on wine bottles of other countries, this is simply because the labels carry more information about the wine, and so they actually provide more precise descriptions of the wines. The information on the label includes not only the grape's regional origin, the year the wine was made, and the vintner's name, but also facts about the grape-growing conditions and method used to make the wine. The following comments concerning German wine bottle labels pertain to the two top-quality wines: *Qualitätswein mit Prädikat* (Q.m.P.) and *Qualitätswein bestimmter Anbaugebiete* (Q.b.A.).

Name of Region

The first item to appear on the wine bottle label is the name of one of the eleven delimited or controlled regions (such as Rheingau or Mosel-Saar-Ruwer) established by German wine law.

Year

The next item on the label is the year the wine was made. However, remember that German vineyards are quite far to the north, and so get less sun than do those in France. Thus there are fewer really great years for German wine than for French, and even good years for French wine do not necessarily mean good years for German wine. Reasonably good wines are produced in Germany every year, but weather conditions inevitably influence the results, especially regarding the quality wines.

Village and Vineyard Names

The next item on the label states the name of the village where the grapes were grown, followed by the name of the vineyard. For example, Niersteiner Schlossberg indicates that the grapes are from the Schlossberg vineyard in the village of Nierstein. Note that the village name takes on an extra "er," in much the same way that a person from New York becomes a New Yorker.

The most specific origin of a wine—as is the case in most wine-producing countries—is the name of the individual vineyard, known as *Einzellage* in German. If a wine does not list a vineyard, it is likely to be a blended wine without any special quality—although a label with a vineyard name is no guarantee of quality.

However, there is an exception to this village–vineyard rule. Some German wines are so outstanding that only the vineyard name appears on the label and no village identification is needed. Some of these vineyard-only names are

Maximin Grünhaus (Mosel-Saar-Ruwer region)
Scharzhofberg (Mosel-Saar-Ruwer region)
Schloss Johannisberg (Rheingau region)
Schloss Vollrads (Rheingau region)
Steinberg (Rheingau region)

There are hundreds of vineyard names in Germany, and so it is difficult, if not impossible, for consumers to know them all. To make it easier, German laws have established an appellation known as a *Grosslage* (vineyard collective), made up of a number of neighboring vineyards, although care must be taken that the name of the *Grosslage* (which often uses one of the local village names) is not confused with the wines of the individual vineyards within it. In total there are currently 152 recognized collectives.

A further simplification is the use of the word *Bereich* (district) on the label. For example, if the wine is labeled Bereich Nierstein, this will refer to a district wine of the Rheinhessen region that uses the village name Nierstein to represent the district. Do not confuse these district appellations with village names.

Grape Name

After the village and vineyard names (when they appear) usually follows the name of the grape used. For the finest wines of Germany, this will be Riesling, as that is the best German grape. If the grape name does not appear, it is because of one of two reasons. First, it is an easily recognized wine that is assumed to be made with Riesling grapes, or second, it is a wine not made from Riesling grapes but from some other (such as Sylvaner), and the wine maker does not wish to draw attention to the fact that Riesling has not been used!

If the wine is a Q.m.P., the grape name may be followed by one of five words, discussed earlier, stating the ripeness or sweetness of the grapes when picked.

Shipper

The next item to appear on a German wine label is the name of the producer or producers. Most vineyards in Germany (just as in the Burgundy region of France) are owned by several different proprietors, and one proprietor may have a share in several different vineyards. If a proprietor bottles a wine on his own estate, the label will state *Erzeugerabfüllung* (bottled by the producer or grower), *Aus eigenem Lesegut* (from the producer's own harvest), or *Abfüller* (bottler) followed by the producer's or proprietor's name. The astute consumer must thus know the names of the best producers as well as the best vineyards.

There is one more complication. A well-known proprietor producing wine from a well-known vineyard may produce two or more different wines from that vineyard. In other words, a producer will give each barrel a separate label, as he believes the wine's characteristics differ from barrel to barrel.

A.P. Number

One other requirement of German wine law is that the labels of *Qualitäts-wein* (either Q.m.P. or Q.b.A.) bottles show the certification number, or *Amt-liche Prüfungsnummer* (official test number), usually abbreviated to A.P. Nr. followed by an actual number. In order for a producer to obtain this num-ber, each lot of wine must have been approved by sample quality control testing and tasting by a regional board that certifies that it lives up to its type's style and quality.

Wine Category

Finally, the label will state the wine category, such as *Qualitätswein mit Prä-dikat* (followed by one of the harvest descriptive words, such as *Kabinett*) or *Qualitätswein bestimmter Anbaugebiete*. Note that the authorities allow Q.b.A. wines to be simply labeled *Qualitätswein*.

Illustration

Figure 4-2 illustrates a typical German quality-wine bottle label. Note that the label lists the wine category as *Qualitätswein*, indicating that it is a Q.b.A. quality wine and not a Q.m.P.

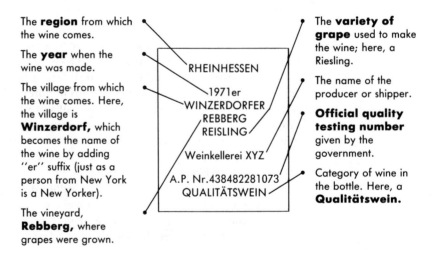

Figure 4-2 Typical German wine bottle label.

Other Terms

There are two relatively new types of better-quality *Tafelwein,* known as *Landwein* (country wine) now being produced in Germany by some of the estates along the Rhine and Moselle rivers. These wines are *Trocken* (dry) or *Halbtrocken* (half or medium dry) and have less residual sugar than do other German wines. These terms are official government designations.

Many German wines are produced by cooperatives made up of many different grape growers. For instance, cooperatives produce much of the wines from Franconia. On a German wine label the words *Winzergenossenschaft* or *Winzerverein* mean a wine grower's cooperative. If the word *Hochgewächs* appears on the label, it means that the wine is made from grapes grown high on the hills rather than on the lower valley slopes.

Some other German words to know are

Keller—Wine cellar.
Kellerei—Winery.
Roseewein—Rosé wine.
Weinbaugebiet—Viticultural region.
Weingut—Wine estate.
Weinkellerei—Wine cellar.

DISCUSSION QUESTIONS

1. Does the fact that Germany's wine-growing districts are so far north create problems? Explain. In what way can adding sugar to the wine overcome these problems? Why?
2. List the five Rhine wine-producing areas.
3. What is the most important grape variety used in producing German wines? Name two other types of grapes used.
4. What word do the British often use to describe Rhine wines generically?
5. What is Liebfraumilch, and in which wine-growing region of Germany is it produced?
6. What is Moseltaler, and in which German wine-growing region is it produced?
7. How do the bottles for Rhine wines differ from those for Moselle wines?
8. In which German wine-growing district is *Steinwein* produced? Describe the type of bottle used for this wine.
9. List the three major categories of German quality wines.
10. What words describing the condition of the grapes when harvested

appear on the labels of the top-quality German wines? Discuss three of them.

11. What is the German equivalent of the French *pourriture noble?* Describe what this means.

12. What is *Eiswein?*

13. Define *Einzellage, Grosslage,* and *Bereich.*

14. Define *Erzeugerabfüllung, Aus eigenem Lesegut,* and *Abfüller.*

15. What does *Amtliche Prüfungsnummer* mean on a German wine bottle label?

16. What do the terms *Trocken* and *Halbtrocken* mean on a German wine bottle label?

5

Wines of Italy

CHAPTER OBJECTIVES

After studying this chapter the reader should be able to

- Discuss wine production in Italy in general.
- Describe an Italian wine *consorzio,* define the acronyms DOC and DOCG, and list the six DOCG wines.
- Explain where wines such as Valtellina are produced.
- Explain why wine labels are sometimes worded in German in the Adige Valley area of Italy.
- Describe the major wines produced in districts such as Veneto, Tuscany, and Sicily.
- Explain the origin of the wine name Est! Est!! Est!!! and to what the wine name Lacryma Christi refers.
- Define Italian wine label terms such as *abboccato, bianco, dolce, rosato, rosso,* and *spumante.*

INTRODUCTION

Italy's vineyards are some of the oldest in Europe, save for those in Greece. Italy produces more wine and more varieties of wine than does any other country in the world. Indeed, together, Italy and France produce annually about half of all the wine in the world. However, Italy—a country half the size of France and, because of its mountains, possessing a far smaller area suitable for vine growing—is more noted for the quantity than the quality of its wine, even though it does produce many quality wines. These quality wines range from sweet to dry (both white and red), from sparkling to table, and from hearty to light and delicate.

Vines are grown in each of Italy's twenty provinces, yielding a tremendous variety of moderately priced wines as well as some extremely fine quality wines. About 60 percent of Italy's wines are red, the remainder white. Italy's red wines are better known, probably because of their mature taste, due to their long aging in the cask before bottling.

Many quality Italian wines are never seen beyond the country's borders, as they do not travel well. One should not compare Italian wines of medium quality and price with the fine, high-quality single-vineyard wines of France. Rather, most good-quality Italian wines are the equivalent of a French district or village wine entitled to a French *appellation contrôlée* designation. Nor should Italian wines be compared in taste or bouquet with French wines.

In general, Italy produces bigger and fuller red wines than those produced in France, as well as some delicate reds and quality dry whites. It is estimated that Italy produces as many as four thousand different wines.

Grape Versus Village Name

The wines of Italy are not classified as they are in France and Germany, with a clear delineation from region to district, to village, and to vineyard. In fact, very few Italian wines are given individual vineyard names, and vineyards are not classified as they are in Bordeaux, with its listing of wines of various qualities of *crus* or growths.

Italian wine names can even be confusing, as some are known by the grapes from which they are made (such as Barbera), others by the name of the village or district (such as Barbaresco), and some by both the grapes and the village or district name. Some are even labeled with names that do not pertain to either the grapes or the location of origin. Further, some wines are given the same name, even though one may be dry, another sweet, and a third sparkling. Therefore, knowing the geography of Italy, unlike the cases of France and Germany, is not always helpful in recognizing a good-quality wine. One recent trend in Italy has been the introduction of some French grape varieties such as Cabernet Sauvignon, Chardonnay,

Merlot, and Sauvignon Blanc. The product of these grapes is blended with wine from local grapes to create new wines. Many of the best producers are also now bottling their wines on their own estates with a single vineyard name.

Wine Cooperatives

Italian wine making has changed dramatically in recent times, particularly because many small growers have joined to form local cooperatives. In fact, cooperatives today produce about half of Italy's wine. The cooperative or association is known as a *consorzio* or *cantina sociale* (cooperative cellar), and each has its own seal that it uses on its label. Perhaps one of the best known is the one used for Chianti Classico: a black rooster on a gold background. A bottle label for a cooperative is illustrated in Figure 5-1.

WINE LAWS

In the mid-1960s, the Italian government passed stricter wine laws known as *denominazione di origine controllata* (denomination of controlled origin) similar to the *appellation contrôlée* laws of France. Among other things, these laws specify the geographical limits of each appellation, the grape varieties that may be used, the maximum yield that may be produced per hectare, and the minimum alcohol content of the wine. In addition, unlike the wine laws of France and Germany, the Italian laws specify the minimum amount of aging of certain wines. Finally, they classify the wines into four groups.

Velletri

Denominazione di origine controllata

White Wine

Produced in the original zone and bottled by

CONSORZIO PRODUTTORI VINI DI VELLETRI
V.le OBERDAN n. 113—VELLETRI—ITALIA

1 Litre   *Produce of Italy*   11.5% alc./vol.

Figure 5-1   Italian DOC wine cooperative *(consorzio)* bottle label.

Denominazione di Origine Controllata e Garantita

Denominazione di origine controllata e garantita (often abbreviated to DOCG) means "controlled and guaranteed denomination." This category is reserved for outstanding wines whose quality is guaranteed by a committee of experts. These wines, Italy's most prestigious, are the following:

Albana di Romagno
Barbaresco
Barolo
Brunello di Montalcino
Chianti
Vino Nobile di Montepulciano

Except for Albana di Romagno, they all are red.

Denominazione di Origine Controllata

Denominazione di origine controllata (often abbreviated to DOC) means "controlled denomination." The DOC designation certifies that the wine is made from grapes grown in a defined production zone and complies with specific quality levels. The DOC laws for many regions also allow a wine made from grapes grown in a special zone within that region to be labeled Classico (such as in Chianti Classico). If a wine is also labeled *superiore* (superior), it will have a slightly higher alcohol content and will have been aged a bit longer.

In Europe, Italian DOC wine bottle labels bear the additional acronym VQPRD, for *vino di qualità prodotto in regione di denominazione* (quality wine produced in a denominated region), which is a European Common Market requirement.

Vino Tipico

Vino tipico (typical wine) is a type of wine that in France would be labeled *vin de table*. These wines are made from an established grape variety but are not up to DOC quality standards.

Vino da Tavola

Vino da tavola (table wine) includes wines that are excluded from the other categories for quality reasons or because an unapproved grape variety was used in their manufacture. But some of these wines—though not entitled to DOC labeling—may equal or surpass the quality of some DOC wines. Often these are wines whose DOC status has not yet been codified or is pending because they are a relatively new type of wine.

ITALIAN WINE REGIONS

A region or province in Italy is both a political and cultural division with its own identity, customs, and traditions. The numbers in parentheses for the following regions key the region to the map of Italy shown in Figure 5-2. Generally the numbers move from west to east and from north to south.

Valle d'Aosta or Aosta Valley (1)

In the very northwest of Italy is the small district of the Aosta Valley. The region's best-known wines are the full-bodied red Donnaz (made from Nebbiolo grapes) and Enfer d'Arvier (made from Petit Rouge grapes).

Figure 5-2   Map of Italy.

Piedmont (2)

Immediately to the south of the Aosta Valley is the Piedmont region, whose capital is Turin. Italy's best and most varied wines are produced in this region. The two best known are the robust reds: Barolo (a DOCG wine and one of the great red wines of Italy made from Nebbiolo grapes) and Barbaresco (also a DOCG wine and made from Nebbiolo grapes). Barbaresco is considered somewhat superior to Barolo, as it is slightly less robust. If a Barolo is labeled *riserva,* it must be at least four years old, and if labeled *riserva speciale,* five years old. A third well-known wine made from Nebbiolo grapes is Gattinara. Five other villages around Gattinara also produce quality red wines: Ghemme, Boca, Fara, Sizzano, and Lessona. Other Nebbiolo grape wines named after a village are Carema and Spanna.

The Barbera grapes are much more common in Piedmont than are the Nebbiolo grapes. Many wines made from Barbera grapes are labeled with both the grape and the village, such as Barbera d'Alba and Barbera d'Asti.

From the Moscato (Muscat) grapes comes the famous delicate and somewhat sweet sparkling white wine Asti Spumante. Another important white Piedmont wine is Cortese di Gavi (made from Cortese grapes).

Other red grape varieties are Grignolino, Dolcetto, and Freisa. The labels of wines made from these grapes also usually give the place name, such as Grignolino d'Asti, Dolcetto d'Alba, and Freisa di Chieri.

Liguria (3)

Liguria is a narrow coastal strip along the Italian Riviera where Genoa is located. Liguria produces relatively little wine, but two kinds are fairly well known: Cinqueterre (a dry white) and Dolceacqua (a dry red wine sometimes known as Rossese di Dolceacqua).

Lombardy (4)

Lombardy is a major wine-growing district in the center of the very north of Italy; its capital is Milan. In the Valtellina Alps 2,500 feet above sea level northeast of Milan, the Nebbiolo grapes are grown and produce a hardy red wine named Valtellina. This area also produces a dry wine higher in alcohol than the Valtellina labeled Sfursat or Sforzato. The subdistricts of Sassella, Grumello, Inferno, and Valgella also produce red wines.

Other grapes grown in Lombardy are the Pinot and Riesling which produce such white wines as Franciacorta Pinot. Franciacorta Rosso (red) is made from another variety of grapes.

From the Lombardy bank of Lake Garda comes a very pale red wine labeled Riviera del Garda Rosso. If it is labeled Riviera del Garda Chiaretto, it will be a rosé. Also coming from this area is a delicate white wine named Lugana.

Trentino-Alto Adige or the Adige Valley (5)

In northeast Italy, immediately south of the Tyrol region of Austria, is the district known as the Adige Valley. The major cities here are Trento, Bolzano, and Merano. The Teroldego grape gives its name to a full-bodied red wine called Teroldego Rotaliano. Other grape-named wines are Merlot (such as Merlot del Trentino), Cabernet (Trentino Cabernet), Pinot, Moscato, and Riesling, as well as a rosé Casteller.

Surprising to many visitors to Italy is that in the upper part of the Trentino valley, as it narrows toward Bolzano, German is the main language. Until 1919, this region was part of Austria (and indeed the Austrians still refer to it as South Tyrol). Many of the wines are still bottled with labels bearing German terminology and script, as illustrated in Figure 5-3. The red wines produced here are Caldaro (Kalterer in German), Lago di Caldaro (Kaltersee in German), Santa Maddalena (St. Magdalener in German), and a white wine, Terlano (Terlaner in German).

Veneto (6)

Situated between Lake Gardo and the Po and Piave rivers in northeastern Italy is the region of Veneto, with Venice its main city, located on the Adriatic coast. The Veneto region is best known for its two great red wines, Valpolicella and Bardolino, which are fresh and light bodied, with Valpolicella having somewhat more body than Bardolino. Recioto della Valpoli-

Figure 5-3   Italian wine bottle label in German script from Adige Valley.

cella has more alcohol and flavor than does Valpolicella and may be slightly sweet with a hint of sparkle. But if it is labeled Recioto della Valpolicella Amarone, it will have been fermented to a dry wine. Recioto wine is made from the *recie* ("ears," or the outermost grapes on a bunch and thus the ones receiving the most sunshine) which are left to dry before being crushed.

Soave, produced in Veneto, is perhaps Italy's most famous white wine.

Some of the grapes grown in this area after which wines are named are Cabernet, Merlot, Pinot, and Tocai, with wine names such as Cabernet di Pramaggiore, Merlot del Piave, and Tocai di Lison. Prosecco grapes are used to make both still and sparkling wines.

Friuli-Venezia Giulia (7)

Another district in northeast Italy is Friuli-Venezia Giulia, whose wines are usually labeled with varietal names such as Cabernet, Merlot, Pinot Nero, Riesling, Sylvaner, Sauvignon, Traminer, and Pinot Grigio. However, six wine-producing subregions also lend their names to wines: Colli Orientale di Friuli, Grave del Friuli, Collio Goriziano (or simply Collio), Isonzo, Latisana, and Aquileia. Sometimes these names are combined with a grape name, such as Cabernet di Latisana (red).

Emilia Romagna (8)

In north central Italy is the large district of Emilia-Romagna, a great culinary center, with Bologna its major city. This district produces four important wines named after grapes: Lambrusco (a semisparkling, somewhat sweet red, one of the better known being Lambrusco di Sorbara), Sangiovese, such as Sangiovese di Romagna (a red made from Sangiovese grapes, which are also used to make Chianti), Trebbiano (white), and Albana (white), as well as Albana di Romagno—one of the six DOCG wines.

Tuscany (9)

Farther south again is Tuscany, in central Italy, where Florence and Siena are located. Tuscany is best known for its Chianti, a wine that is best drunk when young, as it does not age well. The Chianti wines from Italy should not be confused with the generic word *chianti* used to describe certain wines from California. Italian Chianti is made primarily with Sangiovese grapes, sometimes supplemented with Canaiolo Nero, for their aroma and delicacy.

In earlier times Chianti was made with a blend of red and white grapes to soften the hard tannin of the red grapes. Today the vintners make a soft and fresh Chianti without adding white grapes, which thin the wine. Also gradually being abandoned is the practice (known as *governo*) of adding dried grapes to stimulate a second fermentation, so as to increase the wine's alcohol content and character. In earlier times a white Chianti was also produced, but no longer.

Italian Chianti has become one of the best-known Italian red wines simply because so much of it has been produced and because it was exported in a wicker-covered *fiasco*. This bottle design was special not only for its appearance but also because it held more wine with less contact with the glass surface and with its small amount of air than did any other design of bottle. This preserved the freshness of the young wine. This bottle design and straw mantle were a useful marketing device that caught the public's imagination and became symbolic of Italy. Today, most quality Chianti is exported in a standard Bordeaux-type bottle.

Young Chianti wine, although not resembling young Beaujolais, is intended to be enjoyed in the same way, while it is still fresh and fruity. This wine does not age well, although other Chiantis are intended to be aged.

Chianti quality can vary greatly, as some wines are bottled within a year after harvest, whereas others are aged in wood for two or three years and can age further in the bottle for several years after that. A Chianti may be labeled Vecchio (meaning old) if it is at least two years old or Riserva if it is at least three years old. These three years may be in cask or be a combination of cask and bottle aging.

Some of the best Chianti is known as Chianti Classico, one of the few wines entitled to the DOCG designation. The word *classico* means that the wine was produced in a restricted zone within a general DOC area. This special zone is usually central and by implication—and also generally in practice—produces the best wine in that area. The best of all Chiantis is Chianti Classico Riserva, an excellent Chianti that is aged in oak casks for three to six years before it is bottled.

Although Chianti is the best-known wine of Tuscany, other quality wines are Brunello di Montalcino (DOCG red), Vino Nobile di Montepulciano (also a DOCG red), Vernaccia di San Gimignano (white), Vin Santo (white), Tignanello (red), Solaia (red), Galestro (white) and Pomino (white).

Marches (10)

Marches is an Adriatic coastal region, with Ancona its main city. In Marches, Verdicchio grapes are used for most wines, the best known of which is Verdicchio del Castelli di Jesi, a dry white wine. Another white wine made here is Bianchello del Metauro. Good red wines made in this area are Rosso Conero and Rosso Piceno (both from Sangiovese grapes).

Umbria (11)

Between Florence and Rome is the region of Umbria, and produced here is its white wine Orvieto (named after the walled town perched on a massive rock out of which are carved the cellars where the wine matures). If Orvieto is labeled Secco, it will be dry, and if labeled Abboccato, it will be semisweet. Near Assisi is produced both the red and white Torgiano wine. Other wines are Sagrantino and Montefalco.

Latium (12)

Latium is the region where Rome is located. From this region white Frascati is produced and is made in both a *secco* (dry) and an *abboccato* (semisweet) style. Other wines from this region are Colli Albani, Colli Lanuvini, and Marino (all white wines).

Est! Est!! Est!!! di Montefiascone, a white wine similar to Frascati, is also produced here. Its unusual name has a story: The steward of a twelfth-century German bishop was traveling to Rome ahead of his master to mark the inns where good wine could be found. On the doors of these inns he was to chalk *Est* (meaning "this is it"), but at Montefiascone he was so enthusiastic about the wine he chalked Est! Est!! Est!!!

Some grape varieties used in Latium are Trebbiano (white) and Sangiovese and Merlot (reds) that have names such as Merlot di Aprilia.

Abruzzo (13) and Molise (14)

East of Latium are the two regions of Abruzzo and Molise, on the Adriatic coast. Some pleasant wines are produced here such as Montepulciano d'Abruzzo (red), Trebbiano d'Abruzzo (white), Biferno (red and white), and Pentro (red and white).

Campania (15)

In southwest Italy is Campania, with Naples its chief city. Among the wines for which this district is famous are the reds and whites of Ischia (an island off the coast) and Lacryma Christi (tears of Christ), grown on the slopes of the volcano Vesuvius and with bottle labels distinguished by the words *del Vesuvio*. Lacryma Christi is made as a red, a white, and a rosé, with the white (both still and sparkling) the best known.

Other wines from this district are Greco di Tufo (white), Taurasi (red), and Fiano di Avellino (white).

Apulia (16)

Apulia is a long, narrow district than runs along the Adriatic right down to the heel of Italy. A well-known wine from this district is Castel del Monte (white, red, and rosé). The rosé is considered to be one of the country's most important rosés. Other wines from this district are San Severo (white and red) and Locorotondo (white).

Basilicata (17)

Between the heel and the toe of Italy is Basilicata, with its extinct volcano Vulture on whose slopes grows the unusual Aglianico grape that produces the dry red wine Aglianico del Vulture. The white wine of this region is Asprino.

Calabria (18)

Calabria is the toe of Italy, with its best-known wine Ciro (red, white, and rosé) made from Gaglioppo grapes. Other red wines are Donnici, Pollino, and Savuto.

Sardegna or Sardinia (19)

Sardinia is an island off the west coast of Italy across the Tyrrhenian Sea. Its most unusual wine is Vernaccia di Oristano (a dry and bitter aperitif wine). Others are Cannonau di Sardegna (red and rosé) and Monica di Sardegna (red).

Sicily (20)

Finally there is Sicily, a huge island off the toe of Italy, most famous for its fortified dessert wine Marsala, which is often used as a cooking ingredient. (Dessert wines are discussed in Chapter 8.) Sicily is also famous for Mount Etna, after which Etna wine (red and white) is named. Other wines produced in Sicily are Alcamo, Faro, Corvo, Ragaleali, Faustus, and Cerasuolo di Vittoria.

ITALIAN WINE TERMS

The following are the translations of terms sometimes found on Italian wine bottle labels:

Abboccato—Semisweet.

Amabile—Semisweet.

Annata—Vintage year.

Asciutto—Dry.

Azienda agraria or *azienda agricola*—Farm or agricultural holding.

Bianco—White.

Cantina—Cellar.

Cantina sociale—Cooperative cellar.

Casa vinicola—Winery.

Classico—From a special inner district of a DOC zone.

Consorzio—Consortium or cooperative.

Dolce—Sweet.

Fattoria—Estate.

Frizzante—Lightly sparkling.

Imbottigliato—Bottled.

Liquoroso—A sweet wine, sometimes fortified with grape spirit.

Recioto—Wine made from partly dried grapes.

Riserva or *riserva speciale*—Aged for a specific length of time in cask or bottle before being released to the market.

Rosato—Rosé.

Rosso—Red.

Secco—Dry.

Spumante—Sparkling.

Superiore—Superior in alcohol content.

Tenuta—Estate, farm, or agricultural holding.

Vecchio—Old.

DISCUSSION QUESTIONS

1. Briefly discuss wine production in Italy.
2. Explain the confusion that can arise in the way that Italian wines are named.
3. What is an Italian wine *consorzio?*
4. What do the acronyms DOC and DOCG stand for? List the six DOCG wines.
5. Name the two best-known robust red wines produced from Nebbiolo grapes in the district of Piedmont.
6. What is the quality sparkling white wine made from Moscato (Muscat) grapes in Piedmont?
7. In what district are Valtellina, Sassella, Grumello, and Inferno all produced?
8. Why do some Adige Valley wine bottle labels contain German words?

9. For what two well-known red wines and one white wine is Veneto famous?

10. Although Tuscany produces many wines, it is well known for what particular one?

11. Which well-known white wine is named after a walled town perched on a massive rock out of which are carved the cellars where the wine matures?

12. Explain how Est! Est!! Est!!! di Montefiascone wine was named.

13. What does the name Lacryma Christi mean?

14. Sicily is famous for its production of what dessert wine?

15. What do the following Italian wine bottle label terms mean? *Abboccato, bianco, dolce, rosato, rosso, spumante.*

6

Wines of the United States

CHAPTER OBJECTIVES

After studying this chapter the reader should be able to

- Discuss the effect that Prohibition had on the U.S. wine industry.
- Explain why U.S. wines have improved considerably in the last thirty years.
- Explain the technological and other manufacturing factors that differentiate U.S. from most European wine making.
- Discuss how wines are generally named in the United States.
- Discuss wine production in the northeastern United States.
- Discuss wine production in California.
- List five of the most common grapes used to make California red wines, and five to make white wines.
- Discuss the labeling of California wines and explain the specific terms used.

INTRODUCTION

The United States has two major wine regions. The first is centered in the state of New York but spreads into other states as far away as Ohio, Indiana, Michigan, Wisconsin, and Oklahoma, and even north across the Canadian border into the Niagara peninsula. The climate in these areas is rugged, and so sturdy North American vines such as the Concord and the Catawba have been traditionally used. The wines they produce are often described as "foxy" flavored.

The other region is centered in California but spreads as far north as Oregon and Washington and even into British Columbia in Canada. Here the climate is far milder, and so the European *vitis vinifera* is used. The wines produced by this vine can rival and even outdo their European cousins. The best of the wines comes from the northern part of California close to San Francisco.

A Short History

Grapevines were introduced into California by Spanish missionaries in the mid-1600s. The vines were mainly from France and Germany: Pinot Noir and Gamay vines from Burgundy and the Cabernet Sauvignon from Bordeaux for the reds; and the Pinot Blanc and Pinot Chardonnay from Burgundy and the Sémillon and Sauvignon Blanc from Bordeaux, as well as the Sylvaner, Traminer, and Riesling from Germany for the whites.

By the 1830s European immigrants had established the first commercial vineyards, and the industry was blossoming by the late 1800s and early 1900s. Then in 1919 the industry suffered a terrible setback under Prohibition, which put most of the wineries out of business and ordered the high-quality grape wine vines to be replaced with varieties intended to produce only table grapes and raisins.

Repeal of Prohibition

When Prohibition was repealed in 1933, the commercial wine industry had to start all over again. Not only did the land have to be replanted with wine grapevines, but the equipment also had to be replaced and skilled personnel trained. Worst of all was that the general public knew very little about wines—a situation that has taken several decades to correct. In contrast with wine making in many European countries, which dates back hundreds of years, California's wine industry since its new start is only about fifty years old.

In the early years of the industry's rebirth, most of the wines produced in California were cheaper fortified wines such as port and sherry, and it was not until the mid-1970s that regular table wines constituted more than 50 percent of California's wine production. When grapevines were planted that produced higher-quality wines, U.S. consumers began to be more discriminating, probably because of their exposure to better wines in their travels to Europe. The resulting demand encouraged the opening of many new, small wineries in California that specialized in only a limited number of table wines. (Before this, the wineries felt compelled to produce every type of wine, from fortified to table to sparkling.) Today there are an estimated six hundred wineries in California.

Only in the past decade or so have some of the excellent and varied wines of California attracted world attention. In that same period California has been recognized as a major wine grape–growing district with its own types of grapes and wines. However, it has taken time to achieve this status. New vines take three years to bear fruit, and the best need another three more years to mature. Add to that the time for experiments to ferment, produce, and test the new wine (plus experiments to see whether a new type of vine will produce just enough grapes—and no more, as too many can produce a poor wine)—and it can take ten years from start to finish. Indeed, so young today is California's wine industry that many of the newer vines are not yet mature and have still to produce their best quality of grape.

Temperature-controlled Fermentation

One of the major developments in U.S. wine making in the last two decades is the use of stainless steel, temperature-controlled fermentation tanks. These tanks allow wineries to ferment white wines more slowly at lower temperatures, a procedure that allows the wine to retain more of its fruit flavor and remain more delicate. In the case of red wines, fermentation can be carried out at higher temperatures, so as to make their flavor more pronounced.

Another technological improvement is the use of microfiltration to clarify the wines before bottling. Microfiltration removes all yeast and bacteria particles, resulting in "cleaner" wines. Older processes still use pasteurization to kill these bacteria in the bottle, which produces a somewhat cooked flavor in the wine, or else sulfur is added to the wine, which gives it an acrid taste.

Wine-making Freedom

U.S. wine makers have much more freedom in wine making than do European vintners. U.S. vintners can decide where to grow their grapes, which vines to plant, and when to take out old varieties or add new ones, or where to buy grapes to mix with their own. When aging wine they can decide how long the wine will be aged in wooden casks and even what kind of casks to use. They can also decide whether or not to clarify wines before bottling and which method to use to do this. All these variables offer choices and challenges to the wine makers, but they also can lead to confusion for the consumers, as the wines produced from an individual winery may not be consistent in quality from year to year.

California wine makers can also create "designer" wines, by finding out what the public wants and then producing it. This is how wine coolers were developed. Vintners can also regraft their vines to produce grapes that are a blend of two types. Even though the strict European wine laws do protect consumers from unscrupulous wine makers, those same laws are also restrictive in regard to changing, experimenting, and even marketing. In the United States, growers can produce according to their customers' dictates, and there is no tradition holding them back.

WINE NAMES

U.S. wines have three different names: generic, varietal, and brand.

Generic Wines

A generically named wine is one that bears the name of a European type, such as burgundy, chianti, chablis, or rhine. This terminology has traditionally been used since the early U.S. wine makers tried to imitate European wines, even though the resemblance was slight. Generic wines in the United States really have more in common with one another, and it is unfair to compare them with their European counterparts whose names they use.

These generically labeled wines account today for most of the table wine sold in the United States, a situation analogous to that in Europe, although the European countries generally have government standards of quality that can be identified on bottle labels. But this is not the case in the United States, and therefore consumers have little to guide them in discerning from a label what a wine might be like. Indeed, some wineries market the same wine in different bottles, with merely a change in generic labeling. This means that a bottle labeled chablis in the United States may be either a dry or a sweet wine, whereas a Chablis from the Burgundy region of France is always extremely dry.

Similarly, a Sauternes wine from the French Bordeaux region is a naturally sweet wine, whereas a California sauterne probably had grape concentrate added when it was bottled, in order to sweeten it. (Note also that French Sauternes has an "s" at the end of its spelling; the U.S. sauterne does not.) U.S. law does state, though, that generically named wines must include the place of origin on the bottle label, such as California chablis, which distinguishes them from their European counterparts.

Generic wines are often suitable as house or table wines or for use in wine cocktails or coolers. They may not keep well when opened. Red wines should be used within a day or so after opened, and whites within two or three days. Generic wines are often sold in large containers and are sometimes referred to as *jug wines*.

Varietal Wines

Today there is a trend away from giving U.S. wines a generic label and instead naming them after the grape variety (thus the word *varietal*) used to make them. A varietal wine is one in which 75 percent or more of a single grape predominates. In comparison, in France a varietally named wine must contain 100 percent of that grape, and in Germany 85 percent. Typical grape varieties used in the United States are Chenin Blanc, Zinfandel, Pinot Noir, Chardonnay, and Cabernet Sauvignon.

A varietal wine will generally be moderately priced, although higher than a generic wine, but a varietal name is no guarantee of quality, and even among wines with the same varietal name there can be a large divergence of flavors. But it is among varietals that the best California wines are now found, as knowledgeable consumers have discovered. Some of the best exceed the 75 percent minimum of the single-grape requirement, and some even contain 100 percent of the named grape that gives the wine its particular character.

Brand-Name Wines

Generally the very best quality U.S. wines are those that carry a specific brand name. These are sometimes referred to as *proprietary wines*. Brand-name wines are those whose name is confined to a particular vineyard or shipper who is willing to stand behind the wine's quality.

By law, brand-name wines must also state the class or type of wine, and although the brand name is emphasized on the label, it may actually be a varietal wine. For example, a label stating "Chateau Blanc—a California white burgundy wine made entirely from Pinot Blanc grapes" is referring to a varietal wine.

THE NORTHEAST

The earliest settlers in the eastern United States discovered native vines growing wild along much of the Atlantic coast. Attempts to cross them with imported European *vitis vinifera* varieties in the seventeenth and eighteenth centuries were not successful because of disease and very cold winter temperatures that the *vitis vinifera* could not withstand. Thus the native vines (notably Catawba and Concord of the *vitis labrusca* type) have generally been used in the east. They have a distinctive flavor and give the wines made from them a pungent aroma often described as *foxy,* which some people do not like. These labrusca vines have also been cultivated in other states, such as Oregon and Washington, and in other countries, such as Canada and Brazil.

However, the northeast has been using some vinifera vines (primarily in the Finger Lakes area of New York) since a method was found in the 1950s to help them survive the cold winters. American-French hybrids are also used.

Most of the eastern U.S. wine production is in New York State, but only a small proportion of all table wine produced in the United States is from New York, as most of its grapes are used to produce sherry, port, and sparkling wine. There are four recognized wine regions in New York State: Erie-Chautauqua (along the shoreline of Lake Erie), Finger Lakes (in the center of the state), Hudson River, and Long Island.

A wine labeled New York State may contain as much as 25 percent of wine from outside the state (such as from California). This blending helps mellow the harsher taste of the labrusca vine. If the label says American, rather than New York State, then more than 25 percent of the content is from wine from outside the state.

THE CALIFORNIA DISTRICTS

About two-thirds of all wines consumed in the United States are produced in California. Although many people still think of California as a single grape-growing district with uniform climate and conditions, this is not the case. The grape-growing districts are quite diverse, in the same way that the Bordeaux and Burgundy regions of France, though in the same country, differ. And just as in Bordeaux and Burgundy (as well as in many other European wine grape–growing areas), vintners have discovered that different areas lend themselves better to some grape varieties than do others.

For example, the hotter areas in southern California are similar to the grape-growing districts of southern Spain or North Africa (such as Algeria), whereas the cooler areas in northern California are as cool as the most northerly grape-growing areas (such as Alsace in France, and the German regions). In addition, there are many varieties of soil, and the different combinations of climate and soil produce many kinds of wines. California's greatest advantage is its relatively consistent climate which means that chaptalization (or the addition of sugar) during fermentation is not necessary and, in fact, is illegal, as sugar levels in the mature grapes are the same from year to year. This also means that the quality of wine is consistent.

In very broad terms, California's wine districts can be categorized geographically as coastal areas or central valley areas. However, within each of these areas are several subdistricts, as shown in Figure 6-1.

Coastal Areas

The coastal area embraces the north coast counties, San Francisco Bay area, the north central coast, the south central coast, and southern California.

The north coast counties (Mendocino, Sonoma, and Napa) are immediately north of San Francisco. The finest wines of California are grown primarily in this and the San Francisco Bay area. The vineyards are located on the slopes of valleys where the climate is stable from year to year; rainfall is not extreme; sunshine is plentiful; frost is rare; and soil drainage is well suited to high-quality wine production. Mendocino is the most northerly county and has a moderate climate that produces high-quality red and white

Figure 6-1 Map of California's wine-producing regions.

wines. Sonoma and Napa are parallel to each other and are separated by the Mayacamas Mountains. The Sonoma Valley has a moderate climate somewhat similar to that of Burgundy. Sonoma County has three other wine grape–producing areas: the Russian River Valley, with a climate cooler than that of the Sonoma Valley, and the Dry Creek and the Alexander valleys, with a climate similar to that of the Bordeaux region. Napa County is considered to be California's top-quality wine-producing area, which includes the finest Cabernet Sauvignons in the United States.

South of the three north coast counties is the San Francisco Bay area, with its counties of Alameda, Santa Clara, and Santa Cruz. Within Alameda County is the Livermore Valley, noted for its white Sauvignon Blanc wines and its sweeter Sauternes-type dessert wines.

The north central coast embraces the counties of San Benito and Monterey, and the south central coast includes the counties of San Luis Obispo and Santa Barbara.

Central Valley Region

The other major California area is the widespread and hot inland region which contains three viticultural areas: the central valley, the Sacramento Valley, and the San Joaquin Valley. This region stretches some two hundred miles north from Bakersfield, and most of California's vineyards planted in the last twenty years are in this inner valley. The wines from this valley, because it is so much hotter, tend to have less individuality and character than do the varietals produced in the cooler coastal regions. These "southern" grapes are used primarily for bulk (jug) wines, as well as sweet dessert and fortified wines.

The Sierra Foothills area is a relatively small hilly area (embracing the counties of Amador, El Dorado, and Calaveras) with a higher altitude than that of the central valley. It thus has a cooler climate which allows for a wider range of grape types.

American Viticultural Areas

Traditionally, California vineyards have been referred to by their county names, but recently more specific geographic names have been used, which are known as American viticultural areas (AVAs). These are similar to the French appellations of origin. The AVAs are administered by the government through the Bureau of Alcohol, Tobacco, and Firearms, and the AVA names can be listed on the label.

California Grapes

The best California wines are the dry reds, some of which are excellent, made from the Cabernet Sauvignon grapes (also used in the Bordeaux region of France, as well as in Italy, Argentina, Chile, and Australia for their best wines). Another well-known grape variety used is the Pinot Noir, found also in the Burgundy and Champagne districts of France. Other major red grape varieties used in California are Gamay Beaujolais, Napa Gamay (also known as Gamay Noir), Barbera, Merlot, Zinfandel—a grape native to and grown only in California—and Petite Sirah. Less well known varieties are Charbono, Grignolio, Carignane, Carnelia, Carmine, and Centurio.

For white wines the grape most commonly used is the Chardonnay, famous in the Chablis and Champagne regions of France. On some labels the Chardonnay is called Pinot Chardonnay. Other white wine grapes are the Folle Blanche, Chenin Blanc, Sauvignon Blanc, Pinot Blanc, Sémillon, Riesling (sometimes labeled Riesling-Sylvaner or Franken Riesling; other varieties are Grey Riesling and Emerald Riesling), Gewürztraminer, French Colombard, Moscato di Canelli, Green Hungaria, and Flora.

Even California's lower-priced, lower-quality wines are as good as or better than many wines of equal price produced elsewhere in the world. Many of California's best wines are produced in the smaller wineries and in small quantities.

CALIFORNIA WINE LABELS

In many ways California wines are easier to understand than many of their European cousins. Labeling descriptions are minimal, but still informative. Although California wine labels do sometimes indicate their specific place of origin (for example, Sonoma Valley Pinot Noir or Napa Valley Chablis), the place of origin is no guarantee of quality. In Europe the soil, grapes, and production methods must meet rigidly controlled, government-approved standards in order for an area to use a place-of-origin name distinguishing the wine's special character. In California there is less correlation between place of origin and the wine's character.

Geographic Origin

California wine labels require an indication of the geographic origin. That is, for a wine to be labeled simply California, 100 percent of the grapes must be from the state. If the origin is more specific, such as Sonoma County, at least 75 percent of the grapes must be grown in that county.

Sometimes more than one county is listed; as many as three are allowed as long as the corresponding percentages of grape origin are shown by county. If the label shows an inner region, such as Alexander Valley (or another official American viticultural area), at least 85 percent of the grapes must be from that area.

Varietal Labeling

If the label has a varietal grape name, then 75 percent of the wine must be from the named grape. If used with a geographic appellation, the minimum required percentage of the named grape must come from the appellation area. A generically labeled wine has no requirements regarding the grape varieties used.

Estate Bottled

If a label states "Estate Bottled," then 100 percent of the grapes must have been grown by that winery, and the wine must have been bottled there.

Alcohol by Volume

The law allows a 1.5 percent variation on either side of the stated amount of alcohol by volume. Some labels also indicate (although this is not a legal requirement) residual sugar (unfermented grape sugar), total acid, and other items.

Vintage Dates

Vintage dates do not normally appear on U.S. wine labels, although there is a trend toward using the date of production. If the label contains a vintage date, 95 percent of the grapes used must have been harvested and crushed in that year in the region named on the label. The 5 percent tolerance allows for topping up wines that are aging in containers. Note also that just as the existence of a high-quality French Bordeaux vintage wine does not indicate that all French wines produced in that year are quality vintage wines, so too does a vintage-dated California wine from a particular valley not represent the quality of all California wines of that year.

Other Information

Some wine labels also list the vineyard or name of the grape grower and may contain the words *reserve, special reserve,* or *vintage selection* to indicate a better-quality wine.

If the label says "Produced and Bottled by . . ." it means that at least 75 percent of that wine was fermented by the winery named, whereas if it says "Made and Bottled by . . ." as little as 10 percent and as much as 74 percent may have been crushed and fermented by that winery, with the rest being bulk-blended wine. The terms "Perfected and Bottled by . . ." "Cellared and Bottled by . . ." or "Vinted and Bottled by . . ." do not require the bottler to have fermented any of the wine.

If a white wine is made from red or black grapes, it will be labeled Blanc de Noirs or with the name of the grape plus the word Blanc (white), such as Pinot Noir Blanc or Blanc de Pinot Noir. The term *blush* is sometimes used on labels, meaning that the wine is a rosé.

Late-Harvest Wines

Some California wines are made with shriveled grapes highly concentrated in sugar, known in Germany as *Edelfäule* or in France as *pourriture noble.* The labels of these bottles will state that the wines are Late Harvest or Selected Late Harvest. The label must also state the grapes' sugar content when harvested and the wine's residual sugar after fermentation. Obviously, the higher the residual sugar is, the sweeter the wine will be.

THE PACIFIC NORTHWEST

Wine making in the Pacific Northwest—Washington, Oregon, and Idaho—is relatively new, as the first *vitis vinifera* grapes were planted in Washington's Yakima Valley in the 1950s.

The climate of the Pacific Northwest differs from that of California in that the winters can be quite cold, but the summer growing season is warm with cool nights. As a result, the grapes (just like those in the more northerly regions of Europe) are high in acid, producing light, crisp, and somewhat tart wines similar to those of Alsace and Germany. The principal grapes used are Chardonnay, Riesling, and Gewürztraminer (for whites) and Pinot Noir (for reds).

SPARKLING WINES

The United States also makes effervescent or sparkling wine, but the label must state whether these wines are bottle fermented or produced by the bulk, or Charmat, process, in which the second fermentation occurs in glass-lined tanks. The difference between these two methods will be discussed in Chapter 9.

DISCUSSION QUESTIONS

1. What was the principal setback to the U.S. wine industry, and how did it recover?
2. Why have Americans begun to demand better-quality wines from their domestic wine industry?
3. What has been the major technological change in wine fermentation in the United States in the last two decades, and what effect has this had on the end product?
4. In what ways does the U.S. wine-making industry have more freedom than its European counterparts?
5. Describe the three ways of naming U.S. wines.
6. Describe the laws pertaining to U.S. wines' varietal wine grape content. How do they compare with France's and West Germany's laws?
7. What is the name of the native grapevine usually used in the northeast to make wine, and what are two types of its grapes?
8. A New York wine in a bottle labeled "Made in New York State" must contain what percentage of wine from that state? If the label says American rather than New York State, what does this mean?
9. What is the principal grapevine used in California?
10. What are California's two major wine-producing areas?
11. What does the acronym AVA stand for? Explain.
12. List five of the most common kinds of grapes used to make California red wines.
13. List five of the most common kinds of grapes used to make California white wines.
14. Discuss the geographic-origin labeling requirements for California wines.
15. Discuss the varietal-labeling requirements for California wines.
16. If a California wine bottle label says "Estate Bottled," what does this mean?

17. If a California wine bottle label says "Produced and Bottled by..." what does this mean? How does this differ from "Made and Bottled by..."?

18. What do the terms Late Harvest or Selected Late Harvest mean on the label of a bottle of California wine?

7

Wines of Spain, Portugal, and Other Countries

CHAPTER OBJECTIVES

After studying this chapter the reader should be able to

- Name the major wine-producing region in Spain and the fortified wine for which Spain is famous.
- Define the Portuguese *vinho verde* and name the fortified wine for which Portugal is famous.
- Explain why most wine produced in Algeria is exported rather than consumed there.
- Briefly discuss Austrian wines.
- Name the countries in which wines such as retsina and Tokay are produced.
- Describe saké and name its country of origin.
- Name the country that produces wines such as Fendant.

SPAIN

In wine production volume, Spain ranks third among the Western European countries, after Italy and France. Its production is about half the grape tonnage of Italy and two-thirds that of France. Although Spain's still wines are not considered among the finest in the world, their quality is improving with better production methods. The quality of Spanish wines may be unpredictable because the climate and soils do not seem to be able to produce wines of the quality of France's, despite the proximity of the two countries.

Rioja

Spain's best wines are from the Rioja region in the north, bordering the Ebro River (see Figure 7-1). Here, wine makers still use traditional wine-making methods: For example, the fermenting must of reds is kept in contact with the grape skins for a long period so that the wine will have a high tannin content and a rich red color. These wines are also often aged for a long time in the barrel. But most of Rioja's wine grapes are sold to shippers or are grown by cooperatives that sell them to shippers who produce blended wines. Thus there are few well-known individual vineyards in the Rioja, but the wines they produce are marketed under brand names or the proprietary names of individual shippers.

Rioja wines have four quality classifications:

1. *Gran Reserva* is the top quality and is used for wines aged for a minimum of three years in wood and then two in the bottle.
2. *Reserva* is the next quality and is aged two years in wood and one year in the bottle.

Figure 7-1 Map of Spain and Portugal.

3. *Vino de crianza* (literally, wine that has been "nursed," or aged) is aged for only one year in wood and only a few months in the bottle.
4. *Garantia de origen* (guarantee of its Rioja origin) is not aged in either wood or bottle.

Rioja wine is bottled in either Bordeaux-type bottles or Burgundy-type bottles.

La Mancha

The district of La Mancha in central Spain produces an abundance of both red and white wine, with its Valdepeñas one of the better known.

Catalonia

In northeast Spain near Barcelona, the area known as Catalonia produces red, white, and rosé wines.

Penedès

The area of Penedès (stretching from the Catalonian coastline between Barcelona and Tarragona north into the Pyrenées Mountains) is probably best known for its sparkling wines, although still wines are produced near the town of Vilafranca. Spain's best white wines are also produced in this area, as well as reds made from the French Cabernet grape variety.

Label Terms

Spanish wine bottle labels include such words as *tinto* (red), *blanco* (white), and *rosado* (rosé). Some specially aged wines are labeled *reserva* or *reserva especial*. If a wine label bears the word *reserva,* it generally means that the wine has been specially bottled by the shipper and is of a higher quality. The word *cosecha* on a label means vintage, but the vintage year has far less meaning than it might on a Bordeaux or Burgundy wine. Other Spanish label words are

Cepa—Grape variety.
Criado y embotellado por . . . —Grown and bottled by.
Denominación de origen—Officially regulated wine region.
Dulce—Sweet.
Espumoso—Sparkling.

Gaseoso—Sparkling.
Seco—Dry.
Vendimia—Vintage.
Vina—Vineyard.
Vino—Wine.

Sherry

Spain is also noted for its sherry, which is discussed in detail in Chapter 8.

PORTUGAL

Portugal's climate and geographic location—well to the south of France and west of Spain—are not conducive to the production of great wines (see Figure 7-1). Even so, Portugal makes a greater variety of wines than does any other country in the world and in sufficient quantity to meet its own domestic needs. Many of these wines are excellent, as Portugal's sunny climate gives its wine a high alcohol content and a full body. Some excellent reds, whites, and rosés are now produced there, and the government has introduced standards of wine production. These standards include a system of designating wines that is patterned after the French system, with the best wines labeled *designaçao de origem* (designation of origin). The majority of the grape growers are small-scale farmers, many of whom are members of cooperatives.

Vinho Verde

About 25 percent of all Portuguese wine is produced in the northern area immediately south of the Spanish border. These wines are labeled *vinho verde*, literally "green wine." Green in this context, however, refers to the youth of the wine and not its color, which can be a pale lemon (for the whites) or a light ruby (for the reds).

Douro and Dao

The Douro region is also in the northern mountains of Portugal and is famous for its port grapes, but it also produces an abundance of red and white table wine. The Dao region, in north central Portugal, produces the country's best red wines.

Other Regions

Other Portuguese wine regions are Bairrada (mostly reds), Bucelas (mostly whites), Colares (reds and whites), Carcavelos (best known for its fortified sweet wine), Setúbal (famous for its dessert wine Moscatel de Setúbal), and Algarve.

Rosé Wines

Two of Portugal's better-known rosé wines are Mateus and Faisca, both available as a still and a sparkling wine.

Label Terms

Quality Portuguese wines are labeled *garrafeira*, which means "specially selected" or a wine that the shipper feels is above average. This wine has been put aside by the vintner for further bottle aging. It must have aged for at least two years in wood, and several in the bottle. The label will indicate the vintage date, or *colheita*. Other Portuguese wine terms are

> *Branco*—White.
> *Clarete*—Light red wine.
> *Doce*—Sweet.
> *Engarrafado na origen*—Estate bottled.
> *Espumante*—Sparkling.
> *Maduro*—A descriptive term for any wine that is not a *vinho verde,* that is, a mature wine.
> *Quinta*—Estate or farm.
> *Rosado*—Rosé.
> *Seco*—Dry.
> *Tinto*—Red.
> *Vinha*—Vineyard.
> *Vinho de mesa*—Table wine.

Port and Madeira

Portugal is also noted for its port and Madeira, which are discussed in some detail in Chapter 8.

OTHER COUNTRIES

Many other countries around the world produce wines. Some of these are briefly discussed, in alphabetical order, in the following sections.

Algeria (and Other North African Countries)

Algeria's wines are mostly robust and red. Algeria's hot, dry climate is suited to producing low-acid wines that blend well with harsher wines (such as those from the French Midi region). Today a great deal is also exported in bottle as well. In the past, most of Algeria's wine was shipped in bulk to France and other European countries for blending. But in 1962 Algeria gained its independence from France, and since then its wine production and exports have declined considerably. Not much is consumed locally because Algeria is a Muslim country and Muslims do not drink alcoholic beverages. Today, most of Algeria's production is shipped to the Soviet Union. The other wine-producing countries in North Africa are Morocco, Tunisia, and Egypt.

Argentina

Only two countries in Latin America are noted for their wines: Argentina and Chile. Argentina is the fifth largest wine producer in the world, but little of its wine is shipped outside the country, as the Argentinians consume most of it themselves. Argentina's Italian and German immigrants introduced to the country their wine-making techniques. Most of the wine is produced in the Mendoza region west of Buenos Aires on the border with Chile, and most are labeled with generic and varietal names.

Australia

Australia also is a prolific wine producer, most of it being consumed domestically, although some is exported to North America. The country has more than four hundred wineries and a wine-making history that dates back to the end of the eighteenth century when the first penal settlers were sent there from England. Initially, fortified wines such as port and sherry formed the bulk of production, shipped back to England; only recently have table wines become popular. Many of these table wines today rival the best in Europe and cost far less.

As in California, Australia has a wide range of climates and soils, and vineyards may be as much as two thousand miles apart. The major wine-producing areas are on the east coast such as in the Hunter River Valley north of Sydney where Shiraz grapes—known as Hermitage in Australia—predominate in the production of red wines, although Cabernet and Pinot Noir are also used for reds. Riesling, Chardonnay, Sauvignon Blanc, and Traminer grapes are used for white wines. Although the Hunter Valley only produces about 5 percent of Australia's wine, these wines are generally considered to be of the highest quality. Other producing areas are the Barossa Valley, Clare Valley, and Coonawarra in South Australia, and the Swan Valley on the distant west coast near Perth.

Many Australian wines are blended and marketed with proprietory brand names or generic European names such as chablis or burgundy. Appellation systems are only just being introduced and often vary from state to state, but some regulations are standard. For example, varietally named wines must contain at least 80 percent of the specified grape; the region specified must have supplied a minimum of 80 percent of the grapes; and any vintage-labeled bottles must contain 100 percent wine from the year specified.

Austria

Austrian wines are produced from the same type of grapes as are German wines, and for that reason Austrian wines are similar, but do not quite match, the quality of the German ones. Austria's climate is more like that of Alsace than of Germany, which gives the grapes a fruitier flavor than their German-named equivalents. As in Germany, almost all the Austrian wine produced is white. Austrian wine laws and label descriptions are also in many ways identical to German ones.

The most commonly grown grape in Austria is the Grüner Veltliner (and one of Austria's best-known wines is named after it); other white wine grapes used are Müller-Thurgau, Rheinriesling, and Traminer. All the major wine-producing regions are in the eastern part of the country near Vienna, with the Burgenland area south of Vienna the main producing region. Austrian wine labels usually bear the name of the village of origin along with the grape variety used, although some Austrian wines are labeled with a proprietary brand name. *Ausbruch* is a word found on the labels of some sweet wines and can be used legally only for wines with a quality between that of a *Beerenauslese* and a *Trockenbeerenauslese*. Each November in Austria cloudy new wine, known as *heurige* wine, is commonly served in wine gardens and other drinking spots.

Austrian wines recently suffered a major international setback: Many of the wines are not naturally sweet, and so to counteract this, some shippers decided to help nature along by adding a dose of diethylene glycol, a toxic chemical used in antifreeze. When this was discovered, Austrian wines were temporarily removed from sale in many countries, but no doubt many consumers were permanently discouraged from buying these otherwise good wines.

Bulgaria

Bulgaria has the most advanced wine industry in Eastern Europe. The grapes used most commonly there are the traditional Gamza (red) and Misket (white). Other reds are Kadarka, Merlot, and Pamid. But Bulgaria's finest red wine is made from the Cabernet Sauvignon grape and is similar in style to a Bordeaux. Chardonnay grapes are also beginning to replace some of the native white grapes. Bulgaria's wine industry is state controlled, and the wines are exported through a company known as Vinimpex.

Canada

Wine is produced in three regions in Canada: British Columbia's Okanagan Valley in the west, Nova Scotia's Annapolis Valley in the east, and southern Ontario's Niagara peninsula. Both British Columbia's and Nova Scotia's wine regions are located at the northern extremity of the wine belt, although the Niagara Valley (where 80 percent of the country's wine is produced) is at a latitude similar to that of Bordeaux.

When Canada's wine industry started in the latter part of the nineteenth century, it used the sturdy *vitis labrusca* vine with grapes such as the Concord and Catawba. However, since the end of World War II, the industry, paralleling that in New York State, has been using French hybrids and special, cold-resistant *vinifera* vines such as Seyval Blanc, Verdelet, and Vidal for whites, and de Chaunac, Marechal Foch, and Baco Noir for reds. The *labrusca* grapes are mostly used today for sherry, port, and other dessert wines.

Chile

Along with Argentina, Chile is generally considered to produce the best wines in Latin America. Chile ranks twelfth in world wine production quantity. Wines were introduced into Chile by Spanish missionaries more than four hundred years ago, but commercial wine making really began at about the same time as in the United States, in the mid-nineteenth century. Chile's wine production, like Argentina's, gained from the influx of French, German, and Italian immigrants who brought their wine-making technology with them. Chile's wines are of special interest to wine connoisseurs because the vines escaped the devastation of the *phylloxera* infestation that destroyed most of the world's vineyards in the late 1800s.

Chile produces a wide variety of wines, which is not surprising, as the country stretches more than 2,500 miles from north to south between the Pacific Ocean and the Andes Mountains. This long strip of terrain also offers a wide variety of climates, producing three general types of wine: In the hotter north, rich wines, some of them fortified, are made; in the central part of the country (around the city of Santiago) white and red high-quality dry table wines are produced (some of which are similar to the wines of Bordeaux and Burgundy); and in the cooler southern part of the country more ordinary table wines are produced.

Some Chilean wines are marketed with generic names such as burgundy, and others, with grape varietal names such as Riesling. Today, the most common varieties are Cabernet Sauvignon, Sauvignon Blanc, Sémillon, Riesling, and Chardonnay.

Cyprus

Cyprus has produced wine since ancient Egyptian times. Its red and white wines are light and dry and are consumed locally as well as exported. Cyprus also produces sherry and sweet dessert wines, many of which are exported to Britain. Its best-known sweet wine is Commandaria.

Greece

Some of the world's earliest vines originated in Greece, perhaps as long ago as 1500 B.C. Greek history is full of written accounts of its ancient wine industry, and three thousand years ago the city of Athens thrived as a business center for exporting Greek wines throughout the entire Mediterranean. For that reason wine has always played a major role in Greek life.

One of Greece's wines that has a long history is retsina, a generic white wine unusually flavored with pine resin, which gives it a raw taste reminiscent of turpentine. The ancient Greeks mixed the resin with plaster to seal their storage containers known as amphorae. Retsina wine today is produced for consumption while it is still young and goes well with the traditional oily foods popular in that country. Retsina is also made as a red or a rosé, in which case it is labeled Kokinelli. Common retsina wines are Metaxas, Cambas, and Courtakis. Unresinated reds, whites, and rosés, both dry and sweet, are also made in Greece.

Greek wines may be generically labeled or may list the grape variety or village name. Greece was recently admitted to the European Economic Community, and since then the government has implemented quality control standards defining twenty-six wine appellations. Greece is also known for its anise-flavored aperitif made from a brandy base and known as Ouzo.

Hungary

The Romans introduced grapevines into Hungary about two thousand years ago. Today, most of Hungary's wine production is in the hands of state-owned agencies, although there are some private wineries. Wine exports are handled by the state company Monimpex.

Hungary is famous for a rich sweet white dessert wine known as Tokay (spelled Tokaji or Tokaj on some labels). It is made from the unique Furmint grape after the normal harvest. These grapes are allowed to develop the noble rot that produces the *pourriture noble* of the very sweet wines of France's Sauternes region. Hungary also produces a dry Tokay, which is the one generally exported. (The sweet versions may be labeled Tokay Aszu or Tokay Essencia.) Hungary's best-known red wine is a strong-flavored, robust one named Egri Bikaver (blood of the bull) made in the vineyards of the village of Eger. The wine is a deep red color, with a dry, slightly bitter flavor. Hungary also produces some sparkling wines.

Israel

Vines have been grown in Israel for almost as long as in Greece, but wine has been made commercially there for only about one hundred years. Many of Israel's wines are sweet sacramental ones that adhere to kosher laws. However, much of the wine production today emphasizes making wines for export. Although Israel does not produce a lot of wine, it does export a considerable amount to North America, most of them with the Carmel Winery's label.

Japan

One of Japan's most popular drinks is saké. Although made from fermented rice, rather than from grapes, saké is a colorless, slightly sweet product that has the flavor of a wine.

Mexico

Mexico is primarily a beer-consuming country. Even so, it has a long history of wine production, as it was the place where the first *vitis vinifera* vines were planted in North America in the sixteenth century. Although some local wine is produced for Mexican consumption, most of its grape production goes into the manufacture of brandy, which is more popular in Mexico than is the tequila for which Mexico is more famous abroad.

New Zealand

New Zealand's climate is cooler than that of its South Pacific neighbor Australia, and accordingly, its wines have their own identity. New Zealand is a small country, with only about three million inhabitants. It has about one hundred wineries, most of them small. Although some New Zealand wine is exported, most of it is consumed domestically.

Romania

The Balkan country Romania has a rapidly expanding wine industry, with many of these wines made sweet for export to the Soviet Union.

South Africa

The South African climate lends itself well to the production of quality wines, some of which are exported to North America. That country's Dutch settlers first planted vines there in the mid–seventeenth century. During and after the French Revolution the British turned to South Africa as a source of wines to replace those no longer available from France. This created a base for the local wine industry, whose vineyards now produce an abundance of table wines and brandies. South Africa also produces port and sherry, for which it was better known until it more recently began producing excellent table wines. The principal grapes used are Cabernet Sauvignon for reds, and Sauvignon Blanc, Chenin Blanc, and Chardonnay for whites. South Africa also has its own hybrid: Pinotage. Today the industry is controlled by the Kooperatieve Wijnbouwers Vereniging van Zuid-Afrika (KWV), which classifies the wines.

Soviet Union

Although the Soviet Union is most noted for its distilled spirit vodka (which is the country's most popular drink), it does produce an abundance of wines (many of them sweet, to suit its population's taste) and is the world's third-largest producer after Italy and France. Soviet wines probably are equal in quality to those of Spain, although not up to those of France, Germany, or Italy. Most of the wines are produced in the southern republics of Armenia, Azerbaijan, Georgia, Moldavia, Russia, and the Ukraine. Reds and whites, both sweet and dry, are produced, as well as a sparkling wine Kaffia, made in the Crimea. The Soviet Union is making a concerted effort to use more West European grape varieties, to make less sweet wines that might be more palatable to the export market.

Switzerland

Nearly all the wines produced in Switzerland are dry (unless the label states otherwise) and white, with none of them outstanding and none of really poor quality. Their dryness differentiates them from their nearby neighbor wines produced in France, Germany, Italy, and Austria. Most Swiss wines are produced in the French-speaking cantons or districts of Neuchâtel, Vaud, and Valais around Lac Leman (Lake Geneva). The majority of Swiss white wines are made from Chasselas grapes. The red wines are made from Pinot Noir and Gamay grapes. One of Switzerland's best-known whites is Fendant (made from grapes of that name). Another is Neuchâtel which is a natural complement to that famous Swiss cheese dish: fondue. A well-known red is Dôle, made from a blend of Pinot Noir and Gamay. Other Swiss wines are Dézaley, Saint-Saphorin, Aigle, and Yvorne.

Yugoslavia

Yugoslavia is the world's tenth-largest wine producer. Its wines, although light bodied, tend to be high in alcohol (as high as 14 percent). They have become popular abroad because of their relative low cost. Many of them are made by cooperatives similar to those in Italy. The white wines tend to be better than the reds and are often named after the grape variety used, such as Riesling, Sylvaner, and Traminer for whites (the same grape varieties used in Germany and in Alsace in France), and Gamay, Merlot, and Pinot Noir for reds. Wine labels usually list the grape variety used followed by the geographic origin where the wine was made.

DISCUSSION QUESTIONS

1. In what region are Spain's best wines produced?
2. Besides its still wine, Spain is noted for what fortified wine?
3. What does the Portuguese wine term *vinho verde* mean?
4. Besides its still wine, Portugal is noted for what fortified wine?
5. Why is most wine produced in Algeria exported and not consumed there?
6. Austrian wines are similar to the wines produced in what other European country?
7. Besides Argentina, what is Latin America's other major wine-producing country?
8. Where is retsina wine produced? What is its unique characteristic?
9. Where is Tokay produced, and what is that country's best-known red wine?

10. Saké is the most popular drink of what country? What is it made from?
11. What is the world's third-largest wine producer?
12. Fendant, Neuchâtel, and Dézaley are the names of dry white wines produced in what country?

8

Fortified Wines

CHAPTER OBJECTIVES

After studying this chapter the reader should be able to

- Differentiate between Italian and French vermouth and name two other aperitif wines from France.
- Explain the origin of the word *sherry*.
- Define the terms *flor* and *solera* in reference to sherry manufacture.
- Differentiate between a *fino* and an *oloroso* sherry and identify the sherry types Manzanilla and Amontillado.
- Explain the origin of port and differentiate between the two types.
- Define crusted port, ruby port, tawny port, and explain the meaning of the acronym LBV on a port bottle label.
- Identify the geographic origin of each of the dessert wines Madeira, Marsala, and Malaga.

INTRODUCTION

Fortified wines are still wines that are made in a normal way but then have extra alcohol added to them. This alcohol is added either to stop further fermentation and produce a sweet fortified wine or, after fermentation is complete, to produce a dry fortified wine. The alcohol added to produce a fortified wine is usually a distilled grape spirit such as brandy. Fortified wines can be broadly classified into two types: aperitif and dessert.

APERITIF WINES

Aperitif wines are named after the Latin word *apero* which means "to open," and appropriately these wines are often used as an opener or a drink before a meal. Aperitif wines are not only fortified but are often aromatized with herbs and other ingredients that are either soaked in the wine or added before bottling.

Vermouth

Probably the best-known aperitif wine is vermouth, which is named after the German word *wermut*, which means "wormwood." Wormwood is a shrub of the absinthe family and is one of the major flavoring ingredients used in vermouth. Vermouth itself is classified as either dry or sweet.

Dry vermouth is usually made from white wine, and sweet vermouth from red wine. Dry vermouth can be made anywhere, but that considered best is made in France, with brand names such as Noilly Prat. Dry vermouth can be consumed on its own, with or without ice and with or without a twist of lemon, but it is also an ingredient of the Martini cocktail.

Sweet vermouth also can be made anywhere, but that considered best is Italian, with brand names such as Martini (not to be confused with the Martini cocktail) and Cinzano. Sweet vermouth can also be consumed on its own but is also an ingredient of the Manhattan cocktail. In England it is used in a cocktail known as Gin and It (Gin and Italian vermouth).

Italian vermouth is traditionally thought of as dark (almost red) in color and sweet, whereas French vermouth is identified as pale and dry. However, both types are made in each country, as well as in many other countries.

Other Aperitif Wines

Another aperitif is Dubonnet, from France. Dubonnet can be made from either sweet red or white wine and is flavored with bitter bark and quinine.

It is usually served on the rocks. Other common aromatic aperitif wines are St. Raphael, Byrrh, and Lillet (all from France).

DESSERT WINES

Fortified dessert wines are generally sweet and are often consumed with a dessert or as an after-meal drink. But it is a mistake to call them dessert wines, as one of the most popular "dessert" wines is sherry, which is often drunk in either its dry or sweet form as a before-meal drink or aperitif. The dessert wines from Spain, Portugal, Madeira, Marsala, and Malaga are the most important. Originally, each of these wines was developed to suit the tastes of English people who, in their damp climate, relished a strong, robust-tasting wine. Much of the trade in these dessert wines is still in British hands.

Sherry

Sherry was originally made in Spain, although it can be made anywhere. In Shakespeare's day great amounts of sherry were imported into England from Spain. Sherry first arrived in England in the early sixteenth century and immediately became popular. Its fortification of additional alcohol stabilized it for travel, even when stored in casks. Indeed, sherry continued to age in those casks (whereas port, to be discussed in the next section, did not). In these earlier days sherry was known as *sack* (from the Spanish word *sacar* which means "to export"). In fact, a popular brand of sherry sold today is known as Dry Sack, whose bottle is actually wrapped in a small sack. Sack eventually became known as *sherris* (an anglicized form of the Spanish town of Jerez, in the Andalusian region in the southwest of the country, where the product was originally made) and then sherry.

Sherry is a blended wine, but the whole process of producing sherry is quite unusual. Palomino grapes for sherry are first laid out in the sun to dry or raisinize, which also concentrates their juice and sugar. After the grapes are pressed, gypsum (a calcinized essence of the white soil in which the grapes are grown) is added to the must to increase its acidity, after which the wine is left to ferment in casks. But the casks are not completely filled, thereby leaving the wine exposed to the air. As a result, the fermentation is slow, taking up to three months and resulting in a completely dry wine with no residual sugar. Further—and this is unique to sherry production—the vintner cannot tell what kind of wine will be produced until the fermentation is completely finished. That is, the wine in one cask may be completely different from the contents of a second cask that was filled with the same must produced from the same vineyard on the same day.

Another curious feature of sherry is that after fermentation is complete and the wine has been racked into new casks and the fermentation sediment left behind, a white, soft crust known as *flor* appears on its surface. This *flor* (actually a kind of fungus) is essential to making quality dry sherries and is what gives them their distinctive character. Sherry wines that develop a thick, heavy *flor* will turn into a type known as *fino* (fine), and those with little or no *flor* will produce a type known as *oloroso* (rich fragrance). Fino and oloroso are the two basic categories of sherry.

The sherry is then processed through the *solera* (base or foundation) system of maturing and blending. A *solera* is a series of casks stacked one on top of the other in a pyramid three or four casks high. The casks are connected to one another from top to bottom. The younger sherry is at the top, and the older at the bottom. As wine is drawn off at the bottom, the lower casks will be filled from those above, so that the sherry is continually blending with older sherries. All sherry is thus blended. The *solera* allows continuity of style year after year, and sometimes wine from more than one *solera* is blended to ensure this style. Sherry thus is never identified by vintage or vineyard.

The finished sherry is finally racked into fresh casks and fortified with Spanish brandy (sherry that has been distilled). Finos are raised to only 15 percent alcohol so as not to kill the *flor*. Olorosos are raised to 18 percent alcohol. This extra alcohol in the olorosos kills any remaining *flor* in the wine.

When the sherry is drawn from its final cask, it is absolutely free of sugar. It is then *fined* (clarified) to remove any remaining sediment and then sometimes blended further before its final bottling. In the case of oloroso, the sherry is sweetened with a heavy, sweet wine.

Finos (such as Tio Pepe and Amontillado) are generally pale, rich, and very dry. Finos are more natural wines, as they do not contain any added sweetener. There are different types of finos. For example, Manzanilla is a special type of extremely dry fino sherry made in the seacoast town of Sanlucar de Barrameda. Amontillado is a more nutty-flavored type of fino with a longer barrel age and thus a fuller body and, although consumed dry in Spain, is sometimes made sweeter for the North American market.

Olorosos are darker and heavier than finos. They can be medium dry (such as Aloroso sherry) or heavy and sweet (such as Brown, Cream, or Golden sherry). Olorosos are converted into heavier, creamier sherries by the addition of a special sweet wine in the last stage of blending. Amoroso is the name given to a golden-colored sherry that is between an Amontillado and a heavy cream sherry in both sweetness and color.

The best criterion for judging all sherries' quality is the name of the shipper.

The process described for making sherry is that used in Spain. But sherry has many imitations around the world (for example, South Africa, Australia, and the United States all produce good-quality sherries, but many of these producers do not make them in the same way as in Spain). Thus, wine labeled sherry that is not made in Spain is sometimes made by cooking neutral white wines to age them artificially in order to bypass the costly *solera* system of aging and blending. As a result, most of these sherries do not have the distinctive, nutty flavor of a good Spanish sherry.

As well as being a fine drink on its own or on ice, sherry can also be used in many different cocktails and is also a popular cooking alcohol (for example, consommé with sherry). Because sherry has a higher alcohol content than do other table wines, it will last longer when opened, although it can lose its special qualities if not used within a week or two. Olorosos will keep longer than finos will.

One other very special sherry is almacenista, a well-matured unblended sherry that has aged in its cask for decades. In the past almacenistas were frequently sold to big bottling houses when old quality sherry was needed to improve their top lines. But today, some of these almacenista sherries are exported and sold as a product in their own right as an extremely high quality sherry.

Port

Port constitutes only 5 percent of Portugal's total wine production, yet it is one of the most important wines produced there. Originally, port wine was shipped from Lisbon and Oporto (from whence its name was derived) for consumption in England. In fact, port was developed for the British market in the early eighteenth century when, for political reasons, it was cheaper for the British to import wines from Portugal rather than France. Strangely, the French today are bigger consumers of port than are the British.

Grapes from the port-making regions in Portugal are rich in sugar at harvesting time. As a result, the must may ferment too quickly in the hot climate of Portugal, leaving no sugar unfermented. Thus the addition of brandy during fermentation stops it and results in a wine with about 5 percent unfermented sugar and a little less than 20 percent alcohol. Such a strong wine needs extra time to mature.

There are basically two kinds of port: vintage and wood. Vintage port is considered to be the superior product. It normally contains a heavy sediment and thus needs careful handling in both storage and decanting before serving. Vintage port may require twenty years to reach its peak; thus little vintage port is produced. Crusted port is a type of vintage port that is one step down in quality. It is a blended wine, often made from a single grape harvest, that matures in the bottle after having been aged in wood for a few years. This aging in wood for a longer period than that for true vintage port actually speeds up its maturing. In the bottle this port forms a sediment (or crust) and as a result has to be carefully decanted.

Wood ports are fully matured in wood casks and spend only a short time in the bottle before being consumed. Most port produced and sold is wood port, of which there are two types: ruby and tawny. These ports are named after the color they acquire as a result of aging in wood. It can take as long as six to eight years for a ruby and twelve years for a tawny port to develop. Wood ports do not improve in the bottle and should be consumed within a few months.

Some types of port have on their labels the word *vintage,* even though they are not true vintage ports. One of these is known as LBV (for late-bottled vintage) port, which is bottled after only about five years in wood, with the year of bottling appearing on the label. Some of these LBV ports can be consumed immediately after bottling, although others will continue to improve for a few more years. LBV port has more or less replaced crusted port as a quality product.

Some port is labeled *port of the vintage.* This is not a vintage port but, rather, a tawny wood port from a specific year.

Port is invariably a sweet product, usually made from red grapes and therefore a dark wine. Port is essentially a dessert or after-dinner wine, as for most people it is too heavy as an aperitif, although it is popular in France as such. However, white port (made from white grapes) is light enough to drink before a meal. It can vary from dry to semisweet. Port goes especially well with fruit (peaches, pears, melons) and cheese.

Other Dessert Wines

Other dessert wines are Madeira, made on the Atlantic island of Madeira five hundred miles southwest of Lisbon. Light and dry Madeira wines are Sercial and Verdelho; rich and heavy ones are Bual (or Boal) and Malmsey. Their names come from the type of grape used. Like sherry, Madeira can be consumed as both an aperitif and a dessert wine. As is the case with port, the fermentation of Madeira traditionally was stopped by adding brandy to the still-fermenting must. But generally today, most Madeira is fermented out until dry, as is the case with sherry. Madeira is the longest lived of any wines: Bottles opened after one hundred years have revealed a still-excellent wine.

Two other dessert wines are Marsala and Malaga. Marsala is a fortified wine made in Sicily, which is fermented until dry and then fortified and sweetened. Malaga is made on the southern coast of Spain and is a sweet, fortified wine.

DISCUSSION QUESTIONS

1.   Describe and compare Italian and French vermouth.
2.   Name three French aperitif wines.

3. Explain the origin of the word *sherry*.
4. What is *flor,* and what is its role in sherry manufacture?
5. Differentiate between a *fino* and an *oloroso* sherry.
6. What is the *solera* system, and how is it used in making sherry?
7. What are Manzanilla and Amontillado?
8. Explain how port originated as a dessert wine.
9. What are the two basic types of port, and how do they differ?
10. What is a crusted port?
11. Differentiate between ruby and tawny ports.
12. What does the acronym LBV mean on a port bottle label?
13. What are Sercial, Bual, and Malmsey, and where are they made?
14. What are Marsala and Malaga, and where are they made?

9

Champagne and Sparkling Wines

CHAPTER OBJECTIVES

After studying this chapter the reader should be able to

- Discuss Dom Perignon's contribution to making Champagne.
- List the three grape varieties used in making Champagne and define the terms *blanc de blancs* and *blanc de noirs*.
- Discuss double fermentation and disgorging in regard to making Champagne.
- Explain the meaning of champagne label terms such as *brut* and others indicating the wine's dryness or sweetness.
- Differentiate between Cramant and crémant with reference to Champagne, and define the terms *mousseux* and *pétillant*.
- Name five well-known Champagne shippers.
- Explain the Charmat or bulk process of making sparkling wine.
- State where Schaumwein is made and explain the difference among Schaumwein, Sekt, and Perlwein.
- State where Spumante is made and explain the meaning of *frizzante*.

CHAMPAGNE

The province of Champagne is situated in the eastern Parisian basin, about ninety miles east of Paris near the towns of Äy, Reims, and Épernay. Only a few vineyards in this area have the right to the *appellation* Champagne. Champagne is blended and marketed almost exclusively by brand name of a bottler or shipper and is the only French *appellation* wine whose label does not need to contain the words *appellation contrôlée*. Although these shipping houses produce and sell almost exclusively Champagne, they usually own only a very small proportion of the vineyards, instead buying grapes in bulk from the growers and then manufacturing the wine.

Dom Perignon

The "discovery" of Champagne is frequently credited to Dom Perignon who was the cellar master at an abbey in the late seventeenth and early eighteenth centuries. It is often said that he first put the bubbles into wine to create Champagne, but in fact nature puts them there. What Dom Perignon did do was apply to wine the process that puts fizz into beer. The bubbles are the same: carbon dioxide, a by-product of fermentation.

It is quite easy to make a fizzy or effervescent wine. If the wine is bottled before the fermentation has stopped and the bottle is tightly stoppered, the carbon dioxide cannot escape until the bottle is opened. What Dom Perignon really discovered was a process of tightly stoppering the bottles with cork. Before that, the wine made in the Champagne region was bottled; the bottles were plugged with tow; and olive oil was dripped on the top to keep out vinegar spores that would spoil the wine. This wine was not Champagne (because the tow-stoppered bottles would not have kept the carbon dioxide in the bottles), and not even very good wine because of the area's northerly climate. Dom Perignon learned to cork the bottles and also how to improve the not-very-good locally produced wine by blending it and converting it into Champagne.

CHAMPAGNE MANUFACTURE

Champagne receives more care and attention in its manufacture than does any other wine in the world, and although as a result good champagne is expensive, it is generally no more so than a quality bottle of French Bordeaux or Burgundy.

Blending

Champagne is a blend of grapes from several areas, and as such its quality can be maintained from year to year. It is made only from white wine.

French law allows only three vine varieties to be used: Pinot Noir and Pinot Meunier (both red) and Chardonnay (white). If champagne is made solely from white grapes, it is entitled to be labeled Blanc de Blancs, and if it is made solely from red grapes, it may be labeled Blanc de Noirs. A champagne labeled Blanc de Blancs is made from white Chardonnay grapes and so will be a more delicate wine.

Some rosé champagne is also produced, in either of two ways. According to the traditional method, the skins of the red grapes are left with the must for a time to impart the required degree of color. Or the must may be mixed with a proportion of red still wine made from the traditional Champagne red grapes. This rosé champagne is light, dry, and generally more expensive than regular nonvintage champagne.

Champagne wine must is allowed to ferment in the normal way. When the fermentation has slowed, the wines are tasted by experts who determine what proportion of each batch of wine is to be blended to produce the right quantity and quality of personality of each of the different brands that a particular firm sells. Sometimes wine from earlier years is also blended in to achieve the right results.

The fermented and blended must is next poured into large vats fitted with automatic stirring devices. Fermenting agents are added, together with tannin and a liquid consisting of wine in which sugar has been dissolved. Stirring homogenizes the product. The wine is then racked off into bottles that are hermetically sealed.

Maturing

After bottling, the wine is placed in a cellar where it remains and matures for at least a year, and sometimes for two or three years. These Champagne cellars are deep, dark chalk caverns resulting from the mining of chalk by the ancient Romans. These cellars have a constant, cold temperature that is ideal for its purpose. Inside the bottles stored in the cellars a second fermentation occurs as the sugar added just before racking is transformed into alcohol and carbon dioxide. It is this formation of carbon dioxide in the bottle that gives champagne its traditional fizz when it is finally poured.

To prevent the bottles from exploding, owing to this second fermentation, they are made of thick glass and specially shaped with an indented bottom that strengthens the glass. In earlier times, when bottles were hand blown and the sugar dosage could not be precisely measured, bottles did explode frequently and so were a danger to those working in the cellars.

As the second fermentation is occurring, sediment deposits form in the bottles. So to help remove this sediment, the bottles are put in special racks with their necks pointed downward. Each day, every bottle is rapidly turned by one-eighth and given a slight shake so that this sediment is worked down into the neck of the bottle and does not flow upward and mix again with the wine. Traditionally this task was done by hand by specialists known as *remouers* (shakers) who could shake up to thirty thousand bottles a day. To-day, however, many champagne producers use machines that can twist and shake many bottles at the same time.

Disgorging

When the *remuage* (shaking) is completed, the bottle is *dégorgé* (disgorged); that is, the sediment is removed. To do this, the neck of the bottle is plunged into a brine bath at a temperature of $-20°$ C. This freezes the wine in the neck of the bottle, along with the sediment, into a lump of ice, which is forced out by the carbon dioxide pressure in the bottle as soon as the cork is removed.

The bottles are then immediately passed through a machine to replace the wine lost in disgorging with a small amount of excellent old champagne with some cane sugar dissolved in it. The bottles are then stoppered with a new cork, and the cork and bottleneck are covered with a wire muzzle to prevent the cork's being forced out by the pressure of the carbon dioxide still in the bottle. Champagne corks are also compacted to a very hard state before they are used, ensuring that no air can pass through and thus pre-venting the carbon dioxide from escaping. Finally, the bottles are labeled, and a foil metal cap is placed over the wire muzzle and neck.

TYPES OF CHAMPAGNE

The amount of sugar present determines the type of champagne (in order of sweetness):

Brut, nature, or *zéro*—Bone dry, less than 1 percent sugar.
Extra sec or *très sec*—Literally, extra dry but actually a bit sweeter than *brut,* with 1 to 2 percent sugar.
Sec—Literally, dry but actually slightly sweet, with about 3 percent sugar.
Demi-sec—Literally, half-dry but actually medium sweet, with about 5 percent sugar.
Doux or rich—Quite sweet.

The cheaper champagnes are the sweeter ones, as sugar is often used to hide a lack of quality. Because the champagne's relative sweetness is deter-mined only when disgorged bottles are topped up and the final cork is inserted, shippers are free to vary the sweetness of their champagne (de-spite the wording on the label) to make it conform to the demands of a particular market. For example, brut champagne will be better if some sweetening is added, as its quality will show through better.

Some shippers also sell a far more expensive nonvintage brut known as a *cuvée spéciale,* which is often aged longer (and thus costs more). Two other words may sometimes appear on a Champagne bottle label: Cramant and crémant. Cramant is the name of a town from which some Blanc de Blancs Champagne comes. Crémant, on the other hand, is a type of Champagne that is less effervescent or bubbly and is crackling rather than sparkling.

Some still wines (primarily white, but also some red and rosé) are also produced in the Champagne region of France and are labeled Coteaux Champenois. These wines are light bodied and—as is typical of wines produced from northern vineyards—quite high in acid.

Only Champagne made in France and using the process described is allowed to use the words French Champagne on the label. Champagne (sparkling wines) made anywhere else in the world may not use the word champagne by itself on the label. Instead, the bottles must state *"La méthode champenoise"* (champagne method), "Champagne fermented in this bottle," or "Champagne process." The labels must also describe the origin, such as California champagne.

Vintage Champagne

Nonvintage champagne makes up about 80 percent of all champagne made. By law, these champagnes must age for one year in the bottle. Although most champagne is blended—and often from the wines of more than one harvest in order to maintain its particular shipper's type—occasionally a vintage champagne is produced, in a particularly good grape-growing year. When this happens, only the grapes from that year are used and the champagne becomes a vintage one, with the date appearing on the bottle's label and the cork. These champagnes are still blends of many wines, but all from the same year.

The vintage years may also differ from one shipper to another, as the shippers do not always agree on the quality of the wines in any given year, and even a declared vintage champagne may contain some wine from another year in order to enhance its personality and maintain that shipper's style of champagne. However, in order to be declared a vintage champagne, it must be matured for a minimum of one year and then be aged in the bottle for a minimum of five more years.

Vintage champagnes have more personality, are richer and more full bodied, and age better. They also cost more than nonvintage champagnes do. Vintage champagnes can continue to improve for ten or a dozen years, but nonvintage champagne should be consumed when young. If it is kept for more than four or five years, its quality tends to decline.

Champagne?

In most other places in the world other than in the Champagne region of France, the second fermentation of champagne is not carried out in the bottle, as it is a lengthy and labor-intensive (therefore costly) process. Instead, the refermentation is done in large containers; this is known as the Charmat, tank, or bulk process. The refermented wine is then bottled under pressure to retain its carbon dioxide fizz. This method allows the champagne to be produced in a few weeks. Accordingly this type of champagne is less expensive and is considered by some to be of lower quality and to have only a short period of fizz or effervescence once it is poured. But some people argue that it is not an inferior product, because the larger surface area and the more vigorous mixing of the ingredients guarantee a better quality; the temperature of the glass-lined tanks can be better controlled; and new filtration processes are superior to disgorging by hand. In any case, no champagne, however made, can be better than the grapes from which it is made.

An alternative method to the Charmat process is to carry out refermentation using the champagne process and then to transfer the finished champagne to a new bottle, minus its sediment. The label will read "Fermented in bottle" (note that it does not state "Fermented in this bottle"!).

When a sparkling wine is produced in a region of France other than Champagne, it is described as *mousseux* (foamy), regardless of which method is used to make it. A great deal of both red and white *vin mousseux* is made in France, including the regions of Bordeaux and Burgundy. If these wines are bottle fermented in an appellation-controlled region, they may legally be labeled *crémant,* as in Crémant de Bourgogne (sparkling wine from Burgundy). Some sparkling wines in France may be described as *pétillant* rather than *mousseux,* which means that the wine is only slightly sparkling, or what we might refer to as crackling in a North American wine.

Champagne Shippers

Because the process of making champagne is complicated, few individual vineyard operators do it themselves. Rather, most sell their grapes to manufacturers, or shippers, who contract with many vineyard operators (as well as possibly owning some of their own vineyards) and can produce a consistent quality from year to year. The largest shipper of Champagne is Moët et Chandon (makers of Dom Perignon Champagne), which produces 24 million bottles annually. The names of the other better-known shippers, in alphabetical order, are

Ayala
Bollinger
Canard-Duchêne
Charbaut
Deutz & Geldermann
Heidsieck, Charles

Henriot
Krug
Lanson
Laurent-Perrier
Mercier
Mumm
Perrier-Jouët
Piper-Heidsieck
Pol Roger
Pommery et Greno
Roederer, Louis
Ruinart
Taittinger
Veuve-Clicquot

GERMAN SCHAUMWEIN

The generic term for German sparkling wines is *Schaumwein;* sparkling wines with this word on their label are most likely made from French or Italian grapes. However, if the label states Qualitätsschaumwein, it must be made with 100 percent German grapes. If the label says Sekt, rather than Schaumwein, it can have been made from either locally grown or imported grapes, but it must have been made by secondary fermentation in the bottle.

Although the Germans were about a hundred years behind the French in first making champagne, their product initially was better accepted abroad than in Germany. The producers were often to blame for this, as they decorated their bottles with French labels that allowed them to sell the products at higher prices.

Schaumwein, though of high quality, is different from French Champagne. French Champagne is the ultimate in lightness, whereas Schaumwein, particularly when made from Riesling grapes, with their strong bouquet and powerful flavor, is a more robust product that equals French Champagne in quality but with which it should not be compared, as it is a different product.

More Schaumwein is made today in Germany than Champagne is made in France. Even wine from other countries is often imported into Germany to make it. One well-known brand name is Henkell Trocken; others are Söhnlein Brillant, Rüttgers Club, Faber Krönung, Kupferberg Gold, and Deinhard Kabinett.

Note that if Schaumwein is made from a wine from one of Germany's eleven controlled wine regions, 100 percent of the product must come from wine made in that region, and the bottle label must also contain an *Amtliche Prüfungsnummer* (official examination number). Indeed, even some of the well-known brand-name types contain hardly any German wines, the reason being that German wines are too expensive; Sekt makers can obtain all the wine they need much more cheaply from France and Italy. The description Deutscher Sekt (German Sekt)—which for many years misled consumers into believing the product contained only German wine—now may legally be used only for wines produced entirely in the controlled regions. Note also that the German equivalent of a crackling wine, or a *vin pétillant* in France, is labeled *Perlwein.*

SPARKLING WINES OF OTHER COUNTRIES

The sparkling wines of Italy are labeled *Spumante,* such as the well-known Asti Spumante (sparkling wine from the village of Asti in northern Italy), and are made from the aromatic Moscato (Muscat) grapes. Italian Spumante is invariably made by the Charmat process and usually contains less than 10 percent alcohol but also as much as 8 percent sugar.

A dry Italian sparkling wine will be labeled *brut, brut riserva,* or *brut nature.* If the wine is bottle fermented, its label will also state *"Metodo Champenois"* or *"Fermentazione Naturale in Bottiglia."* The Italian equivalent of crackling is *frizzante.*

Spain also produces an abundance of sparkling wines, primarily from the Penedes region, with the best of them made by the champagne method. If they are made with this method, they will be labeled *Cava.* One of the best-known Spanish producers is Codorniu. In Portugal, sparkling wines are labeled *Espumante.*

The United States also produces most of the sparkling wine consumed in North America. The word champagne can legally be used to describe U.S.-produced sparkling wines as long as it is preceded by the name of origin, such as California champagne. Most U.S. champagne is made by the Charmat bulk process, which must be stated on the label.

DISCUSSION QUESTIONS

1. Discuss Dom Perignon's contribution to making Champagne.
2. What are the three grape varieties legally allowed to be used in French Champagne?
3. What do Blanc de Blancs and Blanc de Noirs mean on a label of a bottle of champagne?
4. What is unique about the fermentation of champagne?
5. Describe the method of disgorging and what it achieves.
6. Explain what *brut, extra sec, sec,* and *demi-sec* mean on a bottle of champagne.
7. Why are the least expensive champagnes usually also the sweetest ones?

8. Differentiate between the words Cramant and crémant on a bottle of Champagne.
9. List five of the better-known French Champagne shippers.
10. Explain the Charmat, tank, or bulk process of manufacturing sparkling wine.
11. Differentiate between the words *mousseux* and *pétillant* with reference to sparkling wine.
12. What are Schaumwein, Sekt, and Perlwein?
13. What is the Italian word for a sparkling wine? What does the word *frizzante* on the label of an Italian sparkling-wine bottle mean?

10

Wine Storage and Service

CHAPTER OBJECTIVES

After studying this chapter the reader should be able to

- Discuss the proper conditions for wine storage and the proper temperatures for serving various types of wine.
- Explain the process of decanting.
- Discuss the role of glassware in serving wine and describe the advantages of an all-purpose wineglass.
- List the seven steps in opening a corked bottle of still wine.
- Explain the proper procedures for opening and pouring sparkling wines and discuss the pros and cons of the two main types of sparkling wineglass.
- Discuss the placement of wineglasses in a table setting.
- Describe how a wine bottle should be held when pouring wine and how full wineglasses should be filled.
- List the general rules for which wine to serve with which food and cite an appropriate type of wine to serve with certain foods.

WINE STORAGE

Wine storage can create some problems, particularly for quality wines. Red wines should be stored at 55° F (13° C) and white wines at 40° F (5° C). If cold storage cannot be provided for white wine, it should be stored with red wine and then cooled just before serving.

If wine bottles are cork stoppered, they should be stored on their side, as this will keep the cork moist and prevent air from making contact through the cork with the wine and possibly spoiling it. With corked wines, avoid very dry storage, as this encourages corks to dry out; in other words, a humid atmosphere is desirable. Consider using proper wine racks that allow correct storage of bottles on their sides. Wine space is often wasted when proper storage racks are not used.

Fortified wines do not need to be stored on their sides, as they have had distilled spirit added to them, which helps prevent spoilage.

It is important to handle high-quality aged red wines carefully, as they often develop a sediment that will cloud the wine if it is roughly handled. Storing such bottles on their sides also allows any sediment to gather in such a way that pouring is made easier once the bottles are opened. Even those quality wines that do improve in the bottle should be used before the quality begins to deteriorate. Red wines generally last longer than do white wines.

Wine that is purchased in large bulk glass or plastic containers (jug wine) and used for house wine may have been pasteurized. Pasteurization is a process of heating the wine and then cooling it, after it has been bottled and stoppered. This process kills any living organisms that may have been in the wine, and it will lengthen the shelf life of such wines but will not prevent deterioration once containers have been opened.

Wine Preparation

Before wine can be served, it must first be prepared for service, that is, brought to the temperature at which it will taste its best. It should be raised to this temperature as slowly as possible. The temperature of a wine at the time it is served is extremely important, but there are only guidelines for this, and no hard and fast rules, as so much depends on the wine itself, the food with which it is served, and local climatic conditions. But one generally can say that white wines are better served cold, and red wines at, or slightly below, room temperature. A cold wine does not mean, however, very cold or nearly frozen: Wine that is too cold numbs the tongue and makes it difficult, if not impossible, to appreciate its finer qualities.

White, Sparkling, and Rosé Wines

Dry and young white wines, as well as sparkling and rosé wines, require no special preparation before service other than placing them in a cool room, or in the refrigerator for a couple of hours, but no longer. If they are to be cooled in an ice bucket, then fifteen minutes at the most should be sufficient. The ice in this bucket should be shaved, rather than cubed, as this allows the ice to fit more snugly around the bottle.

Semisweet or sweet wines should be cooled a little longer, but they should never be fully chilled. The colder a wine is, the more difficult it will be to detect its flavor. Indeed, some restaurants will purposely overchill a poor-quality white wine to cover up its defects.

White wines are best at a temperature of 40° to 55° F (4° to 13° C)—the lower temperature for the sweeter ones, and the higher for the drier ones.

Rosé wines are best between 45° and 55° F (7° and 13° C)—the lower temperature for the sweeter ones, and the higher for the drier ones.

Champagne and other sparkling wines should be served at temperatures between 40° and 45° F (4° and 7° C). Again, the lower temperature is for the sweeter ones, and the higher for the drier ones. A dry champagne chilled too much will lose its aroma.

Red Wines

Young red wines should be brought up from the cellar, if they are stored in one, at least an hour before being served. They should be served somewhat cooled. In fact, light red wines often taste better if cooled below room temperature, particularly in the summer.

Red wines should be served at a temperature of 50° to 65° F (10° to 18° C)—the lower temperature for young and fruity reds such as Beaujolais Nouveau and the higher for quality mature reds. The oft-cited rule of serving red wine at room temperature was started when most people, particularly in Europe, lived in houses whose temperature was much lower than the 68° to 70° F (20° to 21° C) to which we are accustomed today. In today's centrally heated buildings, red wines, even mature ones, should not be raised to 70° F (21° C); a better temperature is about 65° F (18° C). Some fine, complex red wines may taste flat if served too warm, that is, above 70° F; however, such a fine red wine should never be chilled, as this will cause it to taste bitter.

Handling Mature Red Wines

Mature red wines need a lot of attention and care. While maturing, they become slightly paler and more tawny and deposit tannic matter on the side of the horizontally stored bottle. This deposit must not be disturbed by rough handling, and so wine is best moved from the cellar or other storage area in a wicker wine basket, such as that illustrated in Figure 10-1.

Wine bottles that contain a deposit may even need to be decanted, to separate the wine from its deposit, although some say that these wines are best not decanted. Any wine that requires decanting must be kept in its wicker basket while the cork is drawn. The bottle should not move, as this will stir up the sediment and create an unpalatable-looking wine. Decanting is pouring the wine very gently, while holding it carefully in its basket, into another container, such as a crystal decanter. Decanting should stop when the sediment begins to enter the neck of the bottle.

Those in favor of decanting say it has the advantage of facilitating serving, eliminating the tannic matter deposit, and aiding the oxidation of the wine through exposure to air, thus helping its bouquet develop. Its disadvantages are that if the decanting is inept, the oxidation can be too great, and a very old wine may be spoiled.

WINE SERVICE

Wine seems to taste better if served in a fine glass. In fact, glass is preferable to silver, pewter, plastic, or almost any other product. And clear glass allows the color of the wine to be appreciated best. Thinner glass also seems to show wine to its best advantage. A standard size of wineglass holds between three and five ounces of wine when properly filled. This means that the glass itself should hold about six to eight ounces. Properly filled means half to two-thirds full and not topped up to the brim. Although tradition calls for special wineglasses with some specific wines (as is the case with cham-

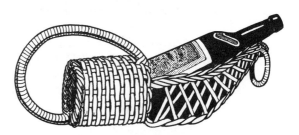

Figure 10-1   Wicker wine basket.

pagne), most restaurants today use a standard-shaped, all-purpose wineglass, such as that illustrated in Figure 10-2.

The standard wineglass has an elongated bowl that is narrower at the top
than at the bottom. This shape helps concentrate the wine's aroma and also
allows it to be used for sparkling wines if special sparkling wineglasses are
not available. The fairly long stem of the standard glass encourages its being
held here and not around the bowl, which would warm up the wine unnecessarily. This type of glass does the wine justice and is economical, for
a restaurant using this type of glass does not have to carry a large inventory
of several different shapes and sizes.

Needless to say, glasses and any wine-pouring containers, such as decanters, should be free of all odors that might otherwise affect the wine. If
wineglasses are not drip dried after being washed and rinsed, they should be
dried with a lint-free towel.

Opening Still-Wine Bottles

Some people believe that a red wine should be opened an hour or so before
it is to be served. This is referred to as allowing it to breathe and is supposed to release the wine's bouquet. However, when a wine bottle is opened,
only a very small amount of the wine's surface is actually exposed to the
air, and it is unlikely that this small amount will have much effect on the
wine's bouquet, even if it is allowed to breathe for several hours. Indeed,
it would probably be preferable to pour the wine into another container,
such as a decanter or carafe, before serving it.

When bringing a bottle of wine to the table in a restaurant, the server
should first present the bottle to the person who ordered the wine. This is
done by holding the body of the bottle from below, with the label facing

Figure 10-2   All-purpose wineglass.

the host, so that he or she can read it, ensure that it is what was ordered, and approve it for opening and service.

The key to opening corked wine bottles is the quality of the corkscrew. In restaurants the favored tool is a three-part one that contains a knife, a corkscrew, and a lever, as shown in Figure 10-3. The corkscrew part should be made with a flat cutting edge and not with a round wire that will not firmly grip the cork. The seven steps in opening a wine bottle are as follows:

1. The metal cap covering the cork and neck of the bottle should be cut *below* the top of the bottle's neck, and not flush with the cork. This is particularly important if the metal covering is made of lead. Cutting below the top of the bottle ensures none of the wine will come into contact with the metal while the wine is being poured.
2. Once this metal capsule has been cut and the top portion removed, the neck and top of the bottle should be wiped with a clean napkin. This ensures that no mold (which is harmless, even if unsightly) or dirt will fall into the bottle when the cork is being removed.
3. The corkscrew should then be inserted, by first placing its pointed tip slightly off the center of the top of the cork, so that the corkscrew's worm is centered over the middle of the cork, and then pushed and turned at the same time. The point of the corkscrew should not be screwed in so far that it appears below the bottom of the cork. If this happens, pieces of the cork will fall into the wine and end up floating in the wineglasses when the wine is poured.
4. Once the corkscrew is fully inserted, the lever part of the corkscrew is placed on the lip of the top of the bottle.
5. The cork should be drawn slowly and steadily without jerking it.
6. After the cork has been removed, the inside lip of the bottle should be wiped with a napkin to remove any remaining traces of cork.

Figure 10-3   Waiter's corkscrew.

7. Finally, the cork should be removed from the corkscrew and pre-sented to the host so that he or she can look at it and smell it for freshness if desired.

Sparkling Wine

Champagne or sparkling wine bottles should also not be roughly handled before opening, as this will only agitate the wine and cause it to gush out when the cork is removed. Most people, because they learned from watching movies or television, do not open sparkling wine bottles correctly. The proper way, after removing the foil and wire wrapping, is to hold the bottle at a 45° angle and grasp the cork firmly in one hand (preferably in the left hand for a right-handed person, and vice versa for a left-handed person) while twisting the bottle away from the cork with the other hand. The cork should come out easily. If it does not, thumb pressure should be used to start easing the cork out of the bottle. If this is done, when the cork is removed slowly (and without a loud pop!), more of the wine will be exposed to air and will not foam out under pressure and be wasted. After the cork is removed, the bottle should continue to be held at an angle for a few seconds before first pouring the wine. This time lapse helps equalize the pressure between the wine in the bottle and the air surrounding the bottleneck.

Pouring Sparkling Wine

For serving sparkling wine it is not a good idea to use stemmed glasses with a wide shallow saucer shape (see Figure 10-4), as they will expose too much of the wine to air and cause the bubbles to dissipate faster. The best type of glass is a tall, narrow, tulip- or flute-shaped one that narrows to a point where it joins the stem and helps contain the bubbles. (This type of glass is also illustrated in Figure 10-4.)

Finally, when pouring sparkling wine, at first pour only a little into the glass. This will foam up from the escaping bubbles and then subside. Then, when more wine is added, it will no longer foam and will retain its bubbles far longer.

After the glasses have been filled, the bottle should be returned to the ice bucket, which will help preserve the effervescence.

Serving Wine

In serving wine there is a ritual that calls for one person to taste the wine before it is served to the others. This tradition is a carryover from the days

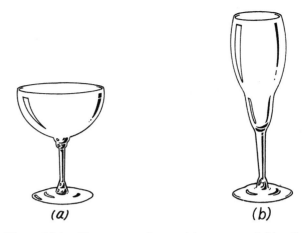

Figure 10-4   Champagne glasses: (a) saucer and (b) tulip.

when wine-making practices could lead to spoilage of the wine, as could a long sea voyage, and so it was better to have one person taste the wine and declare it fit to drink before everybody else's glass was filled. Today, spoilage is rare; indeed, it can often be detected by smelling the cork before the wine is even poured from the bottle, or by looking at and smelling the wine in the glass without needing to taste it. A good wine should be clear and not cloudy. Holding it up to a light will indicate if there is anything in it that there should not be, such as pieces of cork, sediment, or even dust from an unclean glass. The wine should smell fresh and fruity, and not musty. Swirling the wine in the glass before tasting it will also release its aroma or bouquet.

It is the host who should be given the task of tasting the wine, and the server should pour only a little wine into the host's glass for this purpose. After it has been approved, the remaining members of the party may have their glasses filled, and finally the host's glass is filled. Some guidelines for serving wine are the following:

- Wineglasses should be located right above the table setting's knife. If several wines are to be served, one with each course, then the glass to be used first should be located closest to the server. Traditionally, if glasses of two different sizes are used, the smaller one is usually used for white wine, and the larger one for red wine. If two reds are being served for two different courses, the larger glass should be used for the finer of the two wines.
- The wine should be served before the dish it is to accompany, or with the dish, but never afterward.
- All wines should be served from the right of the guest if possible, with the wine bottle held in the server's right hand.
- Glasses should not be lifted from the table to be filled.
- For pouring, a wine bottle should be grasped around its middle,

and not by the neck or by the base, as the middle is where the point of balance is. To help hold the bottle steady while pouring, the index finger can be pointed forward to the neck of the bottle. If a bottle is held by its neck or base, it will be much more difficult to hold it steady.

- Wine should not be poured from too great a height or with the neck of the bottle resting on the rim of the glass. Pour from a height of about two to three inches.
- Glasses should not be filled to the brim. If the wineglass is small, fill it two-thirds full. If it is large, fill it half-full. In either case, there should be enough room in the glass for the taster to swirl the wine to speed the release of its bouquet.
- As each glass is filled, the bottle should be given a slight twist to the right as it is raised. This will help ensure that any remaining drops of wine on the bottle's lip will not fall on the table but will run around the lip and then back inside the bottle's neck as the bottle is brought upright.

WINE AND FOOD

Although there are some general rules concerning which wines are best with which food, on some occasions these rules are not valid. For example, one rule is that white wine goes best with fish and white meat (such as veal, pork, and chicken) and red wine with red meat (such as lamb and beef). However, *coq au vin* (chicken in a red wine sauce) is best served with a red wine that complements the wine used in the sauce. And even a red Beaujolais, Valpolicella, or Chianti can complement a richly sauced veal scalloppine. In other words, the richer the dish is, the richer the wine should be. A peasant dish calls for a country wine, an aristocratic dish for a distinguished wine.

The rule that white wine should not be served with red meats has validity because the acidity of some white wines contradicts the sweetness of those meats. And the rule that white wine should be served with most fish is a good one, as some fish contain oils that can cause a red wine to taste acidic.

There are also some foods with which one should not serve wine; Chinese food is a good example. Tea or beer are preferable with such spicy foods. Similarly, strongly flavored foods such as a curry or a barbecued dish would make a wine useless as a complement. For these foods, beer, cider, tea, or even fruit juice works best. In other words, strong food, spices, and herbs will overpower a good wine and cause it to taste bland or even sharp. For this same reason a salad dressing containing vinegar or lemon juice; or a dish with a heavy garlic, mustard, Tabasco, Worcestershire, or soy sauce flavor can ruin a delicate wine. For these dishes a hearty red goes best. Other strong foods whose flavor a delicate wine cannot overcome are artichokes, smoked salmon, and strong fresh herbs.

Desserts containing cream, eggs, bananas, and especially chocolate are not good companions to most wines, other than perhaps champagne or sparkling wine.

Another general wine rule is that if more than one wine is to be served during a meal, white should be served before red, light before hearty or robust, young before old, and dry before sweet. However, this is only a general rule that can be broken; for example, a fortified sweet wine, a Sauternes, or a German *Auslese* wine may be served with dessert. Sparkling wine is often suggested as the one wine that can be served throughout a meal. However, sparkling wine does not complement all food; for example, a rich red meat. Wines should be chosen to complement the food with which they are to be served, and in a restaurant, the diner's choice takes precedence over any general rules.

General Guidelines

Some general guidelines are

- Soups—Dry sherry, full-bodied dry white, or light red.
- Appetizers—White or rosé dry and light wine, dry sherry, or champagne.
- Seafood—Light, dry white wine.
- Fish—Dry or medium-dry white.
- Fish in a rich sauce—White wine with body and flavor.
- Roast beef or lamb—Full-bodied red.
- Roast veal—Light red or full-bodied white.
- Grilled meats—Light, delicate red wine.
- Roast ham or pork—Dry or medium-dry white or rosé.
- Game—Full-bodied red.
- Stew—Full-bodied red.
- Pasta—Robust red or full-bodied white.
- Poultry—Full-bodied white or light red.
- Sweet desserts—Sweet white or semisweet sparkling.
- Strong cheese—Full-bodied red or, with a blue cheese such as Roquefort or Gorgonzola, a sweet white.
- Mild cheese—Medium-bodied wine (red, white, or rosé), or a fortified wine such as port or sherry.
- Fruit—Sweet or semisweet white or sparkling wine, or port.

WINE MENUS

Wine menus usually list wines by country of origin or type (such as red, white, rosé, and sparkling). Alongside each type the dryness of the wine may be indicated by number (for example, zero for a dry wine, with the highest number for the sweetest ones). The wine list may also contain a short descriptive phrase for each wine, including the origin of the wine and its year of vintage. Such descriptions should be clearly worded and useful to the consumer. Needless to say, they should also be true.

A recent trend is for restaurants to group the wines on their wine lists by grape variety, rather than by country of origin, because the best grape names (Chardonnay, Cabernet Sauvignon, and Pinot Noir, to name three) are often more indicative of the wine taste than is geographic origin. Some restaurants' menus suggest alongside each food a wine that would complement it, and specialty wine bars do the reverse; that is, the wine menu suggests a food item that would be a good accompaniment to that wine.

Many restaurants list their wines with a bin or cellar number. This is useful for two reasons. First, there will less likely be any misunderstanding if diners order by number rather than by name. Second, the foreign names of some wines are difficult for some diners to pronounce correctly, and thus allowing them to order by number avoids their embarrassment from mispronunciation.

DISCUSSION QUESTIONS

1. Describe the proper storage of wine.
2. What are the proper temperatures for serving various types of wine?
3. Explain how certain types of red wine are decanted.
4. Discuss the role of glassware in serving wine and describe the advantages of an all-purpose wineglass.
5. List the seven steps in opening a corked bottle of still wine.
6. Describe how sparkling wine bottles should be correctly opened.
7. Discuss the pros and cons of various types of glasses for sparkling wine.
8. How should sparkling wine be correctly poured?
9. What is the correct placement of wineglasses on a table setting?
10. How should a wine bottle be held while pouring?
11. How much wine should be poured into various types of glasses, and why?
12. Discuss the general rules governing the best wines to be served with various foods.
13. For each of the following, list an appropriate type of wine: seafood, roast beef, pasta, poultry, fruit.

11

Beer

CHAPTER OBJECTIVES

After studying this chapter the reader should be able to

- Explain the derivation of the English word *pub*.
- Compare the alcohol content of beer with that of wine and distilled spirits and convert alcohol by weight to alcohol by volume, and vice versa.
- List the four basic ingredients of beer and explain the role of each in the manufacture of beer.
- Differentiate between beer adjuncts and beer additives.
- Contrast the manufacture of ale with that of lager beer and name some of each type of these two beers.
- Explain the meaning of *wort, lagering,* and *krausening*.
- Discuss both the pasteurization of beer and beer storage requirements.
- Explain what "tapping" draft beer means.
- Describe how a glass of draft beer should be properly dispensed.

INTRODUCTION

Beer is an alcoholic beverage made by brewing and fermenting malted barley, and sometimes other cereals, with hops added to flavor and stabilize it.

Beer is one of the oldest alcoholic beverages and was well known in ancient Egypt. In those early times it was brewed for private consumption in households and monasteries; not until the late Middle Ages did it become a commercial product. In England, beer-drinking establishments were known as public houses (subsequently abbreviated to pub). In earlier times few people could read, which is why pubs were identified (as many still are today) by their pictorial signs such as the King's Head or the Red Rooster.

In North America, the Native Americans made a kind of beer from corn and birch tree sap, but brewing as we know it did not start until the mid-1800s when European immigrants brought their beer-making skills to the United States and made cities such as St. Louis, Milwaukee, and Cincinnati famous for their quality beers. Today, beer is made in almost every country in the world, but certain countries (notably England, West Germany, and the United States) are especially famous for their beers.

An interesting fact about beer is that countries that are well known for their beer are generally not noted for their wines or else do not produce wines. Accordingly, countries that do produce quality wines do not generally produce good beer in their wine-growing districts, and vice versa. Even though beers from around the world have markedly different contents and flavors, the brewing processes do not differ significantly.

Until recently, beer was often considered the blue-collar workers' drink, whereas those with money drank wine and spirits. Today, however, with the move toward moderation in alcoholic beverages, beer is now accepted as a sophisticated beverage even for those who can afford more expensive drinks. The alcohol content of beer generally ranges from 4 percent to 8 percent by volume, whereas wine can be from 8 percent to 15 percent, and distilled spirits from 40 percent to 50 percent. The United States federal government does not allow beer labels to state the alcohol content, but wine and liquor (distilled spirits) labels must. Care thus should be taken when a beer's alcohol percentage is shown or known, as in some jurisdictions it is specified by weight rather than volume. Alcohol by weight is only 80 percent of alcohol by volume. In other words, a 4 percent beer by weight is 5 percent by volume. An easy way to convert alcohol weight into alcohol volume is to multiply the weight percentage by 1.25.

BEER INGREDIENTS

Four main ingredients are used to make beer: water, grain, hops, and yeast. Some breweries also use other ingredients, known as *additives*.

Water

Water constitutes about 90 percent of beer volume. To most brewers, water quality is therefore of paramount importance. Indeed, some beers are marketed with the emphasis on the quality of their water. Nonetheless, the quality of water used in some beer types is not suitable for others. For example, the water used in making ale may not be suitable for making lager. (The difference between ale and lager is discussed later.)

Grain

For hundreds of years the grain traditionally used for making beer has been barley. Just as different grapes are used to make different wines, so different varieties of barley are used to make different beers. But beer can also be made from other grains, such as wheat, and grain extracts may be used in some cheaper beers. Barley, however, provides the best beer. The barley is first malted, by steeping it in water until it begins to sprout or germinate. This turns the starch in the grain into soluble sugar, which is later fermented by the addition of yeast. After the malt has sprouted, it is heated to stop the process. For some beers, it is then roasted, as roasting turns the malt dark and thus provides a darker color for some beers.

The malted grain, now commonly referred to as malt, is mixed with other cereals (such as rice or corn) which are frequently referred to as *adjuncts*. The more adjuncts that are used, the less expensive the beer will be to make, as barley malt is quite expensive. Also, the more adjuncts that are added, the lighter the body and flavor of the beer will be. Some breweries use as much as 35 percent adjuncts. However, some countries, notably West Germany, do not allow any adjuncts to be used, which is one of the reasons that German beers are considered to be some of the best in the world.

Hops

Hops are the dried flowers of the hop vine. Some of the best hops are grown in Europe, as they tend to be more flavorful than North American hops. Hops provide the characteristic bitterness found in beer, but they also act as an antiseptic during the brewing process. Hop tannins also help clarify and preserve the beer. Different varieties of hops are added at different stages of beer making to produce a particular beer.

Yeast

Yeast is what encourages the beer to ferment, a process that produces alcohol and carbon dioxide. Unlike the fermentation of still wine, when beer is fermented, the carbon dioxide is not allowed to escape. Rather, the carbon dioxide is retained and reintroduced in the beer at a later stage, and it is what provides the carbonation or fizz in beer. Most breweries develop their own strains of yeast to produce the particular character of their beer. There are hundreds of different types of yeast, and each imparts a specific flavor.

Additives

Many breweries use additives in the final product. Again, in West Germany—where beer is considered a food rather than an alcoholic beverage—the government has had a law since 1906 known as the *Reinheitsgebot* or "purity command" that only malt, hops, water, and yeast may be used to make beer. This also means that no foreign beer can be sold in Germany if it contains additives. Even though the European Court of Justice ruled in 1987 that this law created an illegal restraint of trade, it is likely that the Germans will continue to demand that their domestically produced beer remain "pure" and to make it very difficult for imported foreign beers containing additives to compete.

When government-approved additives are used, they do such things as aid the conversion of starch into sugar, adjust the color of the beer, prevent cloudiness, stabilize the beer foam or "head," and prolong the beer's shelf life.

LAGER VERSUS ALE

It is the yeast that most distinguishes the type of beer produced. There are two types of fermentation using yeast—bottom fermentation and top fermentation. Bottom fermentation produces lager, and top fermentation, ale.

Lager

With bottom fermentation the yeast settles to the bottom of the fermenting tank after it has finished its work. Most beer is bottom fermented and is known as *lager*. The word *lager* is from the German word for "resting" or "storing." Lager beer is generally aged for several weeks, and in some cases for months, to clear it of sediment and to make it smoother and more mellow. Lager is usually lighter bodied and less alcoholic than ale is.

Pilsner, light, malt, and bock all are types of lager. *Pilsner* beer (Pilsen-Urquell) originated and is still made in the town of Pilsen, Czechoslovakia, but today the term pilsner is used generically to describe a lively, mild, and thirst-quenching type of beer. The bottle label may or may not use the descriptive term pilsner. The authentic Pilsen-Urquell beer has more body and flavor than does its North American counterpart.

Light lagers are similar to pilsner beers but are lower in alcohol, carbohydrates, and calories and are more expensive to produce (because the manufacturing runs make only small quantities).

Malt beers are lagers with a higher alcohol content than that of pilsners. The malt from which they are made is dark toasted, and so the beer has a caramel color and taste.

Bock beers are also made from dark-toasted malt and are dark, rich, and heavy lagers, again with a caramel flavor.

More expensive lagers (the premium or superpremium brands) have more body and taste than do regular lagers, and thus a higher price tag. Some European examples are Heineken (Netherlands), Tuborg and Carlsberg (Denmark), Three Crowns (Sweden), and St. Pauli Girl (West Germany).

Ale

Ale is top fermented. When the yeast has finished its job, it rises to the top of the liquid rather than settling to the bottom. Ale yeasts also must be warmed to at least 59° F (15° C) before they can act on the beer. In earlier days this created a problem in the summer when the temperature could not be controlled and rose so high that fermentation could not be stopped, and so the ale often spoiled. Then, brewers in southern Germany discovered that if they stored their beers in Alpine caves, the yeasts "went to sleep" and sank to the bottom of the fermenting tanks, and so the beer was preserved for as long as it was kept there. Later, the Germans developed strains of yeast that carried out their task at the bottom of the tanks to begin with, and it was these bottom-fermented beers that became known as lagers. Today, of course, with refrigeration, brewers are able to control the temperature of brewing at all stages.

Ale normally requires less aging than lager does and can be sold within days after its fermentation is complete. Generally, ale has a more defined taste and a stronger hop flavor than lager does. Some ales also have a higher alcohol content.

Two variations of ale are stout and porter. *Stout* has a high hop content and a strong malt taste. The malt used for stout is also first roasted, which gives this beer its very dark color. One of the best-known stouts is Guinness, made in Ireland. Although Guinness is consumed as a beer in Europe, in North America it is probably best known as an ingredient of the Black Velvet cocktail (50 percent Guinness and 50 percent champagne).

Porter is similar to stout but has a milder hop flavor, although it is higher in alcohol content; indeed, it can be as much as 6 to 7 percent alcohol by volume. Porter was the favored drink of London's Covent Garden porters—thus its name.

To remember which process of fermentation produces which of the two types of beer, note that A for ale is at the top of the alphabet and produces top-fermented beer, whereas L for lager is much lower down in the alphabet, for bottom fermentation.

BEER MANUFACTURING

There are four major steps in beer manufacturing: mashing, brewing, fermenting, and lagering. For many beers there is also a fifth step: pasteurizing.

Mashing

In mashing, the malt is ground to a grist, and hot water is added. If any adjuncts such as corn or rice are used, they too are added at this point and cooked for several hours. As a result, the malt enzymes are broken down into starch and then into sugar. After cooking, the spent grain is strained out, and the resulting liquid is known as *wort*.

Brewing

Hops are now added to the wort, and the mixture is boiled for another hour or two. The wort is then cooled (for ale) or chilled (for lager).

Fermenting

Yeast is then added to the cooled or chilled wort. The yeast converts the sugar in the wort into alcohol and carbon dioxide. The carbon dioxide gas is collected and stored under pressure so that it can be added back at a later point. This *fermentation* process can take a week or more, with lagers generally requiring a longer fementation period than ales do.

Lagering

After the fermentation is complete, the beer is then aged, or *lagered*. Note that the word *lagered* is used for both lager- and ale-type beers. Lagering takes place at temperatures close to freezing, although some further, slow fermentation may occur. This lagering matures the beer and mellows its flavor. Ales mature very quickly, but lager beers may require weeks or even months. Lagering is done in stainless steel or glass-lined tanks (wood cannot be used, as any air contact through the wood would spoil the maturing beer). When the beer is mature, the carbon dioxide is reintroduced, and the beer is put into barrels, kegs (half-barrels), bottles, or cans.

Some beers use the *krausening* process for introducing carbon dioxide into the beer. This word derives from the German word *Krausen,* which means "froth." With krausening, additional, newly fermented wort is introduced into the beer before it is put into the maturing or lagering tanks. This produces a second fermentation and a natural carbonation in the beer.

Pasteurizing

Pasteurizing is the process of heating the beer in its final container to 140° to 150° F (60° to 65° C) for at least twenty minutes. Pasteurizing kills any bacteria in the beer as well as any remaining yeast, which might allow the fermentation to continue, thereby exploding the bottles or cans. Pasteurizing to kill bacteria was discovered by the French scientist Louis Pasteur and was used for beer sterilization long before it was applied to milk.

Barrel and keg beers (often called *draft* or *tap* beer) are generally not pasteurized, which is why many people believe that these beers taste better. However, unpasteurized beer must be kept refrigerated until used to maintain its quality. If it is warmed and then refrigerated again, it will lose some of its quality and become "bruised." Unpasteurized beer can also continue to ferment, which is why it is usually shipped and stored in metal containers constructed to withstand pressure. Some canned or bottled beer, however, is not pasteurized. Instead, it is very finely filtered to remove any remaining yeast and other impurities and is shipped, and must be stored, under constant refrigeration.

BEER STORAGE

Beer drinkers expect to be served a quality product, and to maintain this quality, beer must be stored properly.

Bottled and Canned Beer

Most bottled and canned beer is pasteurized to lengthen its shelf life and so does not have to be refrigerated until shortly before it is needed. However, it should always be kept below 70° F (21° C) and preferably in a dark room. Canned beer and bottled beer can be kept without refrigeration for about three months. Under refrigeration, canned beer can be kept four months, and bottled beer six months.

Beer should never be frozen, for when thawed, it will precipitate unsightly solids. Also, if beer is refrigerated for too long or is handled too roughly, it may gush when poured.

Bright light can also cause beer to deteriorate, which is why bottled beer is put into dark brown or green bottles. Sunlight can be particularly damaging, and beer served in a glass in bright sunlight will begin to deteriorate in minutes.

Because of its perishability, canned and bottled beer stocks should be properly rotated to ensure that the beer purchased first is sold first. If any unpasteurized canned or bottled beer is carried, it should be handled in the same way that keg beer is (see the next section).

Keg (Draft) Beer

Keg (or draft) beer is not pasteurized and so must be kept refrigerated (at 36° to 38° F, or 2° to 3° C) at all times; otherwise, the active yeasts will continue to work and to produce more alcohol and carbon dioxide. If this continues unchecked, the beer will sour, and the kegs could explode. But even refrigerated keg beer has only a two-week shelf life, and therefore kegs should be properly rotated so that those purchased first are used first.

Because keg beer needs constant refrigeration, it may be necessary to provide a separate storage area for it. This storage area should be close to the bar, as keg beer must be tapped (opened) in storage and travel through lines to the bar, and it is preferable to have shorter rather than longer lines.

Draft beer kegs must be tapped when ready for serving. *Tapping* is a process of opening the kegs under carbon dioxide pressure. The carbon dioxide containers must not be kept in the refrigerator, as the carbon dioxide must be at room temperature. Tapping maintains the beer carbonation and also provides the propulsion to move the beer from the barrel to the dispensing tap. Different beer types may need separate carbon dioxide supplies with different pressure amounts. If the pressure is too high, the beer will come out of the tap frothy and wild. But if the pressure is too low, the beer will be flat, as a result of lost carbonation. Draft beer thus requires constant monitoring of thermometers and carbon dioxide pressure gauges. These instruments need to be checked from time to time to be sure they indicate correct temperatures and pressures.

Draft beer kegs should not be stored in a food refrigerator, as the frequent opening and closing of the refrigerator door makes it difficult to maintain the beer's proper storage temperature. And if draft beer warms up even a few degrees, it can turn cloudy or even sour. By the same token, if the temperature is allowed to fall below freezing, the beer also may spoil, as the water in the beer will freeze and will separate from the still-unfrozen alcohol. A good safety measure is to have more than one thermometer in the storage area to compare with each other.

The lines from the kegs to the taps need to be flushed at the end of each day's service. Flushing is a simple process of disconnecting the lines that run from the kegs to the dispensing taps and reconnecting them to water faucets with a special connector that normally is provided when the beer-dispensing system is installed. Water should be flushed through the lines until it runs clear, and then the lines should be left filled with water between closing each day and opening the following day so that they do not dry out.

To start service the following day, fresh water should be run through the lines for a few moments before reconnecting the lines to the beer kegs. Then the beer tap should be opened to allow the beer to flow through the lines, to push out any remaining water ahead of it, until the beer starts flowing out of the tap. Keg valves and taps must be washed and cleaned at the end of each week. Cleanliness is paramount in draft beer service.

Common Draft Beer Problems

The following are some common problems that can arise in dispensing draft beer:

Flat Beer

- Beer storage temperature is too cold.
- Beer-dispensing lines are too cold.
- Air pressure is insufficient.
- Glasses are greasy.
- Air is leaking from kegs, tapping connectors, valves, or pressure lines.
- Air pressure was inadvertently turned off overnight.
- Beer has been exposed to drafts (air conditioners, open windows).
- Lines are obstructed.
- Beer is drawn too far ahead before serving.

Wild Beer (Excessive Foaming)

- Beer storage temperatures are too high.
- Beer is warming up too much in the lines.
- Dispensing pressure is too high.
- Lines are too long or are badly insulated.
- Lines are kinked or twisted.

- Dispensing tap is badly operated or beer is poorly dispensed into glasses.

Cloudy Beer

- Beer is stale, owing to improper stock rotation.
- Beer has been previously frozen or stored at too low a temperature.
- Lines and coils are unclean.
- Valves are defective.
- Beer is dispensed through a partly open faucet.

Unpalatable Beer

- There is stale, foul, or greasy air in the lines.
- Air pressure is incorrect.
- Lines and coils are not clean or have been improperly cleaned.
- Lines have not been flushed, or water has not been left in them overnight.
- Glasses are not clean.
- Storage area is too warm (if beer temperature is allowed to rise above 50° F (10° C), it can start fermenting again in the keg and turn sour).

Beer Too Warm or Cold

- Temperatures have been allowed to vary from normal either in storage or in the lines.
- Refrigeration equipment is malfunctioning.

Glass Head Unstable

- Beer tap or glass is not handled properly during dispensing.
- Glasses are not completely clean.

(Note that many of the causes of flat beer can also cause an unstable head.)

BEER SERVICE

The glasses in which beer is served must be clean and free of any film or towel lint. For this reason it is best to drain glasses dry rather than use a towel. Grease is a particular enemy, and so glasses must be absolutely grease free in order to maintain the beer's carbonation and froth head, as well as its taste.

Serving Draft Beer

To the customer, receiving a "good" glass of draft beer will depend on the way it is poured or dispensed. The term *good* refers to the amount of beer in the glass and the size of the beer's "head" or collar of foam that appears at the top of the glass. Two factors dictate the size of the head.

The first is the angle at which the glass is held while the beer is poured. The glass should be held about an inch below the dispensing tap at an angle of about 45° while the tap is fully opened.

The second factor is the length of time to hold this angle. When the glass is about half-full, it should be straightened upright and the beer allowed to run into the middle of the glass until the head rises slightly above the rim of the glass, at which point the tap should be closed. While dispensing draft beer from a tap, a constant and smooth dispensing pressure should be maintained.

The head on a glass of draft beer usually varies from one-half to one inch. For example, a small glass of beer with a one-inch head might be inappropriate, for to the customer, the amount of beer in the glass will look relatively small. Indeed, some operators manipulate their profits by altering the size of the head. Consider, for example, a half-barrel or keg of beer that is being dispensed in a ten-ounce footed pilsner glass. If a half-inch head were allowed, then approximately 215 glasses of beer could be drawn from that keg. At $2 a glass, that would amount to total sales of $430. But if the head size were adjusted to one inch, the number of glasses dispensed would increase to 250, or a total revenue of $500 and an additional profit of $70 per keg! In the short run that might seem to be a good way to run a profitable operation. However, beer-drinking customers generally know their "heads"—and if they think they are being cheated, they may take their business elsewhere. Therefore, the size of head must be evaluated not only against size of glass but also against customer repeat business.

Serving Canned or Bottled Beer

A proper head also looks good when a glass of canned or bottled beer is served. To get a good head in this case, the glass should be left upright when the pouring is started. The can or bottle should first be held at a steep, almost 45-degree angle and the beer poured into the center of the glass. As the glass fills and a foam is formed the pouring angle of the bottle or can is lowered into a virtual horizontal position so that the remaining beer is poured more slowly until the glass is filled.

Serving Temperatures

Storage temperature is important to beer, but so also is its serving temperature. Obviously, when beer is taken out of storage and served, its temperature will rise. In North America, the normal temperature for serving a lager beer is 38° to 40° F (3° to 4° C), whereas for ale or a dark beer (such as Guinness) it is about 45° F (7° C). Note also that the thickness of the glass used can alter the beer's serving temperature. The temperature naturally will rise more quickly if a thick glass is used, and more slowly in a thin glass. Indeed, the temperature in a thick glass may increase as much as 5° F (2° C) as the beer is served.

IMPORTED BEER

Many brands of beer sold in North America are imported from other countries. The names of some of them, along with their country of origin, are as follows:

Country	Beer Name
Australia	Foster
	Swan
Austria	Stefflebrau
Canada	Molson
China	Tsingtao
Czechoslovakia	Pilsen-Urquell
Denmark	Carlsberg
	Tuborg
England	Bass
	Watney
	Whitbread
France	Kronenbourg Alsatian
Holland	Heineken
Japan	Kirin
Mexico	Carta Blanca
	Corona
	Dos Equis XX
New Zealand	Steinlager
Norway	Frydenlunds
Scotland	McEwan
Sweden	Three Crowns

West Germany   Beck
                      Dortmunder
                      St. Pauli Girl

DISCUSSION QUESTIONS

1. What is the derivation of the English word pub, and why do pubs generally have pictures hanging outside to identify them?
2. Compare the average percentage of alcohol by volume in beer with that of wine and distilled spirits.
3. How can alcohol by weight of beer be converted quickly into alcohol by volume?
4. What are the four basic ingredients used to make beer?
5. Explain how grain is converted into malt to make beer. What effect does malting have on the starch in the grain?
6. In beer manufacture, what are adjuncts?
7. What are hops, and how are they used as an ingredient in beer?
8. What role does yeast play in beer manufacture?
9. Discuss the role of additives in beer.
10. How does the manufacture of ale differ from the manufacture of lager beer?
11. What is a pilsner beer, and where did it originate?
12. Name three well-known European lager beers and their country of origin.
13. What are stout and porter?
14. In beer manufacturing, what is the wort?
15. In beer manufacturing, what is lagering?
16. In beer manufacturing, what is krausening?
17. How is beer pasteurized, and if beer is not pasteurized, what must be done with it before it is consumed?
18. Discuss the storage requirements for canned or bottled beer.
19. Discuss the storage requirements for keg beer.
20. What does tapping mean with reference to draft beer?
21. Describe how a glass of draft beer should be properly dispensed.

12

Distilled Spirits—Gin, Rum, Whiskey, Vodka, and Others

CHAPTER OBJECTIVES

After studying this chapter the reader should be able to

- Discuss the origin and meaning of the term *aqua vitae*.
- Describe how distilled spirits are made.
- Define the term *proof* in relation to distilled spirits.
- Describe the characteristics of pure alcohol.
- Discuss the role of congeners and temperature in the production of distilled spirits.
- Differentiate between a pot still and a column still.
- Discuss the aging of distilled spirits both before and after bottling.
- Explain the origin of gin; differentiate among Dutch, English, and U.S. gin; explain what Genever, Hollands, and Schiedam are; and define the term *dry gin*.
- Identify the product from which rum is made, explain rum's history in the United States, and describe the two main types of rum and how they are used.
- Explain the origin of the word *whiskey*, differentiate between Scotch malt and blended whisky, name two malt whiskies, and explain how Irish and Scotch differ.
- Describe the origin of bourbon, define a sour mash, and explain the legal requirement in the United States for the use of the term *straight rye*.
- Describe vodka, akvavit, schnapps, and tequila and name their countries of origin.

DISTILLATION PROCESS

To manufacture a distilled spirit, a product—usually a grain—is first fermented through the action of yeast on the sugar in the product, which turns into alcohol and carbon dioxide. The carbon dioxide is allowed to escape, as is the case with still wine. (For beer and sparkling wines, the carbon dioxide is retained to give them their fizz or effervescence.)

Distillation was discovered by the alchemists of medieval Europe, who were looking for a medicine or potion that would cure all diseases. They believed that a distilled spirit would do just that and so named it *aqua vitae* (water of life). And they liked it, even though it failed to cure anything.

To obtain spirits, a fermented product (without carbon dioxide) is distilled, thereby separating the alcohol from the fermented beverage, by heating it to 173° F (78.5° C) in a container known as a *still*. At this temperature, the alcohol is converted into steam, rises, and is collected in a separate container and then is cooled to a liquid that is pure alcohol or distilled spirit. The water (along with most other ingredients) is left behind, as the temperature has to be raised to 212° F (100° C) before it will evaporate. This process is illustrated in Figure 12-1.

When a product is fermented naturally, its alcohol content cannot be higher than about 14 percent. At this percentage, any alcohol present will halt the fermentation process and prevent the production of any more alcohol, which is why most wines have less than 14 percent alcohol by volume. Fortified wines have as much as 24 percent alcohol by volume simply because they have had some sort of distilled spirit added to them to raise that

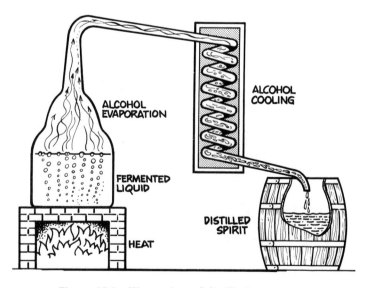

Figure 12-1   Illustration of distillation process.

percentage. Beers generally have from 4 percent to 8 percent alcohol by volume. However, a distilled spirit can have as much as 95 percent alcohol by volume, but when it is sold as a product such as whiskey, water is added, thereby reducing this to between 35 percent and 50 percent alcohol by volume.

Proof

Spirit alcohol levels are often quoted in *proof.* The proof scale in the United States runs from 0 to 200 (200 on the scale equals 100 percent alcohol by volume). In other words, proof in the United States is simply twice the alcohol by volume, or alternatively, alcohol by volume equals 50 percent of proof. For example, an 80 proof bourbon is half that in alcohol by volume, or 40 percent.

In Canada and Britain the proof scale runs from 0 to 175.2. This means that 175.2 (rather than 200 in the United States) represents 100 percent alcohol by volume. To convert from proof to alcohol by volume, proof must be multiplied by 57.1 percent (because 100 is 57.1 percent of 175.2). Thus, in Canada or Britain, 80 proof is 57.1 percent × 80 = 45.7 percent alcohol by volume.

Why is the word proof used? In early days, distillers tested, or proofed, the alcohol content of their products by mixing them in equal proportions with gunpowder and then lighting the mixture. If there was no flame, it meant that the product was under proof, or too weak. If it exploded, or burned with too strong a flame, it meant that it was too strong, or over proof. If it burned with a steady flame, it was just right, or 100 proof (50 percent alcohol by volume in the United States).

Proof and Alcohol Awareness

Many people do not realize that the amount of an alcoholic liquid in a drink is not a good indication of its alcohol impact. Consider the following:

Drink	Alcohol Content
12 oz. bottle of 4% beer	12 oz. × 4% = 0.48 oz.
5 oz. glass of 11% wine	5 oz. × 11% = 0.55 oz.
1.5 oz. of 80 proof bourbon	1.5 oz. × 40% = 0.60 oz.

In other words, a standard-sized glass of wine is almost 15 percent (0.07/ 0.48) stronger than a bottle of 4 percent beer, and a shot of bourbon is 25 percent (0.12/0.48) stronger than the beer. To consume the same amount of alcohol as in a bottle of 4 percent beer, one needs to consume only 4.4 ounces of 11 percent wine (4.4 × 11 percent = 0.48) and only 1.2 ounces of 80 proof spirits (1.2 × 40 percent = 0.48).

Pure Alcohol

Pure alcohol is colorless, tasteless, and odorless. In commercial distilled products, the differences (for example, between gin and whiskey) are created by the original ingredients that are used, the proof level to which they are distilled, and how they are aged after distillation.

When pure alcohol is not wanted, the temperature is controlled in the distillation process so that some of the water that would normally be left behind is allowed to evaporate along with the alcohol. If this were not done, 200 proof, or 100 percent pure alcohol, would result, and the product would have absolutely no color, taste, or odor. Alcoholic beverage products thus are distilled at less than 200 proof, the actual proof achieved depending on the product desired. For example, commercial vodka frequently has no distinctive color, taste, or smell; that is, it is almost a neutral spirit (a neutral spirit is any spirit distilled at 190 proof or higher—or 95 percent alcohol by volume or higher). It is proofed (distilled) at about 190 to make it this way. On the other hand, whiskies are proofed at as low as 110 and thus have more flavor and body.

Congeners

Along with the evaporated water, some minute elements known as *congeners* are also transferred to the resulting alcohol. These congeners are natural chemicals (such as acids, esters, and minerals) that are part of the original ingredients.

Distillers can vary the distillation time, temperature, and type of still used in order to control the amount of water and congeners in the end product. For example, at a lower distillation temperature, a higher-proof (less water is evaporated along with the congeners) and a lighter-bodied and less flavorful product will result. At a higher distillation temperature, more water and congeners are transferred along with the alcohol, and a heavier-bodied product will result.

Column Stills Versus Pot Stills

A *column still* (also known as a continuous or patent still) is a still inside which a fermented liquid is heated by steam. It is a continuous process that allows redistilling in order to achieve higher proofs. It can produce proofs as high as 196 and is used for items such as gin and vodka.

A *pot still,* on the other hand, is a batch process in which the fermented liquid is heated from below. High proofs cannot be achieved in a pot still, and it is therefore used for spirits characterized by more aroma, body and flavor, such as Scotch whisky, brandy, heavy rums, and many liqueurs.

Aging

Spirits distilled in a column still at high proofs are usually not aged, whereas spirits distilled in a pot still at less than 190 proof are aged. This aging can be for one year, or even as long as twenty years, as is the case with some select Cognac (brandy). Frequently this aging is done in wooden barrels that may be new or used and may or may not have also been charred on the inside—for different flavoring results.

Aging is an extremely complex process that scientists cannot completely explain. However, the congeners present in the distilled products interact with one another and with the inside of the barrels. New congeners are also absorbed from outside through the porous wood, and the spirit takes on a color. Over time, these processes mellow the product.

Products that are not aged—and would not change even if they were—such as gin and vodka, may have flavors added to them before being bottled. In other cases, any trace tastes in the product are removed. For example, vodka is often finely filtered to remove any possibility of congener flavoring, and so it ends up being absolutely tasteless.

Bottling

Before bottling, all spirits are diluted with distilled water in order to reduce their alcohol content to the desired proof. This dilution also tones down the product flavor. Once a distilled product is bottled and has no more contact with wood or air, no further changes in it can occur. Even when the bottles are opened, there is also no change other than that caused by some minor evaporation if the bottle is left unopened and unused for any length of time.

Types of Distilled Products

Early spirit makers tended to use whatever products were readily and abundantly available to distill. For example, barley, abundant in Scotland, was used by the Scots to produce what is today called Scotch whisky; wine was used in continental Europe to produce brandy; and sugarcane molasses was used in countries where it was grown to produce rum.

GIN

One of the earliest distilled spirits was first produced in Holland in the seventeenth century. It was a neutral spirit flavored with juniper berries and was named *jeneva* or *jenever* (a distortion of the French word for juniper: *genièvre*). In those early days it was considered to have medicinal value and was sold only in chemists' shops. But it proved to be so popular that many chemists set up their own distilleries. English soldiers in Holland liked it and brought it back to England where it was dubbed "Dutch courage." When the English decided to manufacture their own variation of gin, without the strong juniper flavor, they abbreviated its name to *gin*.

In the eighteenth century, gin was a cheap solace for England's poor, but there was no control over its production, and so gin concoctions would sometimes contain other ingredients, such as turpentine. It was during this time that gin became known as Mother's Ruin! And it was Rudyard Kipling who penned the line: "When the clergyman's daughter drinks nothing but water, she's certain to finish one gin."

Normally gin needs no aging: It can be consumed as soon as it is distilled. Usually it is stored after distillation in stainless steel or glass-lined tanks until it is bottled and, for that reason, remains a colorless product. However, one gin in North America is aged and has a golden color, Seagram's Golden.

Gin can be consumed as a straight drink, be mixed with a soft drink (for example, gin and tonic), or be mixed in cocktails (the most fashionable and famous being the Martini—gin mixed with vermouth and ice). The British have a cocktail named Pink Gin that is simply straight gin mixed with a dash of Angostura bitters, which gives it its pink color.

Today, three types of gin are manufactured: (1) Dutch gin, (2) English gin, and (3) U.S. gin.

Dutch Gin

Dutch gin is distilled at low proof from a variety of grains. It may undergo two or more distillations, the last one with juniper to give it its unique flavor. It is still sometimes named Genever but may also be referred to as Hollands or Schiedam. It has a very strong juniper flavor and is thus not suitable to be used as part of a mixed drink or cocktail. It is best drunk by itself either cold or over ice.

English Gin

The only thing that English gin has in common with Dutch gin is the word gin. *English gin* is not strongly flavored with juniper but is flavored during its last distillation with more mellow botanicals such as fruits, herbs, or spices. It is usually referred to as *dry gin* (dry referring to lack of sweetness, as no sugar products are added to it) or *London dry,* even when manufactured in North America. English gin is not often drunk by itself but is usually mixed with some other product and, of course, is the perfect base for a dry Martini.

U.S. Gin

U.S. gin is also made of high-proof neutral spirits redistilled with juniper and/or other flavors. Another type of U.S. "gin" is actually a compound of high-proof neutral spirits *mixed* (not redistilled) with a juniper flavor. However, this latter product is not allowed, by law, to use the word gin on the label.

RUM

Another early distilled product was rum, which was made fashionable in England because it could be made from sugar, and the sugarcane fields of what was earlier known as the West Indies (today the Caribbean) were controlled by the British. The first record of rum is from the seventeenth century in Barbados. To make rum, sugarcane juice is boiled into a concentrated syrup; the sugar is removed; and what is left is molasses (about 5 percent sugar). This molasses is then fermented and finally distilled.

Rum was made famous by pirates (who were reputed to consume it in large quantities) and also by the British Royal Navy. Indeed, one admiral insisted that his ship's crew take a daily tot of rum and water with fresh lime (their eating limes led to the British sailors' being called *limeys*) as a protection against scurvy. This particular admiral traditionally wore a coat made out of a coarse fabric—grogram—and rum was thus named *grog* by navy personnel. Today we use that same word in *grog shop* and *groggy.*

Rum is particularly palatable in cold climates, which is why it was quickly adopted as the drink of England and other European countries. Indeed, in the eighteenth century the early U.S. settlers also adopted it as their drink. Rum manufactured in New England was exchanged for African slaves, and the slaves, in turn, for West Indies molasses. The molasses was again turned into rum, and the next cycle began. Eventually the British taxes on New England rum were as much a cause for the American Revolution as were the tea taxes. Later, when the temperance movement began its drive to introduce prohibition into the United States, it was Demon Rum that became synonymous with the evils of all alcohol.

Today, rum is made in many hot countries around the world where sugarcane is grown. It can also be made from sugar beets grown in colder climates (such as Europe), but the end result is not as good.

There are two main types of rum: light bodied and heavy bodied. Light-bodied rums are generally made in countries with a Spanish heritage, such as Cuba and Puerto Rico. Light-bodied rums are most often used in North America (although not exclusively), as they are suitable for mixing in cocktails, because of their lightness and dryness. The heavier-bodied rums are made in countries such as Barbados, Jamaica, Trinidad, and Haiti. These rums are more pungent and are more favored in cold climates and go well in hot drinks (such as a hot toddy), but they also can be used in certain cocktails, such as the Cuba Libre (rum and cola).

The world's largest-selling alcohol product is Bacardi rum, which originated in Cuba where the Bacardi distillery used water from the Dacquiri River in its production. Today, a well-known cocktail that uses Bacardi rum as one of its ingredients is known as a Daiquiri (note the different spelling).

WHISKY/WHISKEY

How did whisky (whiskey) get its name? Remember that the early chemists who discovered the distillation process gave it the name *aqua vitae*, meaning "water of life." The first producers of whisky, the Highlanders of Scotland and their peers in Ireland, translated this into Celtic to *uisgebeatha* (in Scotland) and *uisgebaugh* (in Ireland). These words were eventually abbreviated to whisky (in Scotland) and whiskey (in Ireland). In North America, Canada adopted the Scottish spelling (whisky), and the United States, the Irish (whiskey with an "e").

Scotch Whisky

The early Scottish Highlanders used only barley as their grain to make whisky. From this barley they produced malt, by heating the grain and allowing it to sprout. This sprouting creates an enzyme (diastase) that turns the rest of the grain's starch into sugar. (The grain by itself cannot be fermented—it needs the sugar to start the fermentation.) The sprouted grain is then dried over peat fires, which is what gives Scotch whisky its smoky flavor.

The malt is mixed with hot water to create a mash, to which yeast is added. Fermentation begins to turn the remaining starch into sugar and the sugar into alcohol and carbon dioxide. The resulting product (with about 6 to 8 percent alcohol) is sometimes referred to as *distiller's beer,* because the production of whisky and beer is virtually the same up to this point. The distiller's beer is then distilled in a pot still to produce Scotch whisky. This is the process—using only barley—that is used even today for what is known as *single-grain malt whisky.* The pot stills allow each batch of malt whisky to develop its own character. The two best-known malt whiskies in North America are Glenfiddich and Glenlivet. Another quality malt is The Macallan. But today, not much single-grain malt whisky is produced, because the process (and the cost of barley) do not allow mass production.

Scotch whisky was not well known south of the English/Scottish border until about the middle of the nineteenth century when the invention of the *patent still* allowed the mass production of lighter-flavored whiskies that simplified the blending and standardization of the end product. The patent still was cheap to construct and could be installed close to the market. A patent still distillery can produce as much whisky in a week as a pot still distillery can in a year. Before scotch is bottled, it is aged for at least two or three years in oak casks. This aging mellows the whisky, and some is aged for up to twelve years.

Most of the Scotch (and other) whiskies available today are produced from neutral spirits made from a variety of cheaper grains, which may or may not contain malted barley. These whiskies are then blended to make them lighter and more palatable, particularly for the North American market. Scotch became popular in the United States during the days of Prohibition (1919 to 1933) when it was smuggled into the country from Canada.

Today's mass-produced, blended whiskies are frequently referred to as *grain whiskies,* in contrast with their early predecessors, the malt whiskies. The distillers of malt whisky look at the grain whiskies with disfavor, and many of them even deny that the blended products are scotch at all!

There is also one other difference between a blended grain whisky and a malt whisky. A blended whisky will not deteriorate when the bottle is opened, as long as it is properly reclosed. But malt whisky will lose its flavor if it is not all consumed fairly quickly.

Most scotch sold in North America is between 80 and 86 proof (40 to 43 percent alcohol by volume in the United States). Some scotch is labeled as light bodied, which does not necessarily mean light colored (some of its color can be from caramel coloring) or low in alcohol. Rather, light-bodied whiskies usually have been distilled at higher proofs to reduce the amount of congeners present and to make them lighter in flavor. Some of the better-known quality-blended Scotch whiskies are Chivas Regal, Johnnie Walker Black Label, and Haig and Haig Pinch.

Irish Whiskey

Irish whiskey is made in a similar manner to scotch, but the malt is not dried over peat fires, and so it does not have the smoky flavor characteristic of scotch. Irish whiskey is also triple distilled, whereas most scotch is only double distilled. Generally, Irish is aged for a minimum of five years and, like most scotch, is blended to create a lighter drink. The word *poteen* is sometimes heard in reference to Irish whiskey, referring to illegally made Irish. Two well-known Irish whiskies are Old Bushmill's Black Bush and Jameson's 1780.

Bourbon Whiskey

Bourbon has an interesting history. In colonial times in New England and in the Northeast, rum was the most popular distilled spirit drink. But the break with Britain and the end of the slave trade brought changes. Settlers of Scottish and Irish background predominated, and they were grain—primarily rye—farmers and grain (rather than molasses) distillers, and they produced whiskey for barter.

In 1791 George Washington levied a tax on this whiskey, and so many of the grain farmers moved south into Kentucky to escape the tax collectors. They continued to produce rye whiskey there until one year the rye crop failed, and so they decided to mix corn, which grew in abundance in Kentucky, with the remaining rye and found the result delightful. Because this first experiment with corn whiskey occurred in Bourbon County, the farmers decided to name their product Bourbon County whiskey, eventually shortened to bourbon.

Today U.S. law requires that bourbon be made from at least 51 percent corn. To confuse the issue somewhat, there is also corn whiskey, which must contain at least 80 percent corn.

Bourbon is sometimes described as being either sweet mash or sour mash (the mash being the mixture of hot water, grain, and malt to which yeast is added for fermentation before distillation). What differentiates a sour mash from a sweet mash is that a sour mash (sour because it has a slightly acid flavor) is a combination of mash from an old batch and that from the new batch. This is supposed to encourage yeast growth, reduce the possibility of bacterial contamination, and provide for flavor continuity from one batch to the next. But a sour mash does not add a sour flavor to the finished product. Tennessee distillers make their sour-mash whiskey with the added step of leaching it slowly through maple charcoal to give it its unique flavor and bouquet.

Bourbon must be aged at least two years in charred new oak barrels (good business for the barrel manufacturers). The charring of the inside of the barrels adds a special flavor. Bourbon may be aged up to six years to improve its mellowness.

Rye Whiskey

In the early days of whiskey production in the United States, rye was the farmers' prime crop, and so they used it to make most of their whiskey. But not much rye is used anymore. For a whiskey to be labeled rye whiskey in the United States, it must contain at least 51 percent rye grain. Note that this is not the case in Canada. Rye whisky (without the "e") is the most popular whisky there, but Canadian rye whisky may contain little or no rye.

U.S. Whiskey Labeling

The labels of U.S.-produced whiskeys can be confusing. Whiskey can be classified as straight, blended straight, and blended American.

A *straight whiskey* may be a mixture of various grains but must contain at least 51 percent of one grain. For example, a bourbon whiskey must contain at least 51 percent corn, and a rye at least 51 percent rye, in order to be called a straight bourbon or a straight rye. A straight whiskey is not a blended whiskey.

A *blended straight whiskey* is a blend of several straight whiskies of the same type.

A *blended American whiskey* is a combination of straight whiskies generally with a neutral spirit (distilled at a higher proof) to produce a lighter-bodied product. No aging is required.

In addition, in the United States, there are two other products: Canadian whisky and light whiskey. *Canadian whisky* (called rye in Canada, even though it may not contain any rye grain) is a blended, light-bodied, and mellow-flavored whisky generally aged for three years, although some of the better ones will have been aged a lot longer. *Light whiskey* is a U.S. product distilled at a higher proof than are other U.S. whiskies, to produce a lighter-bodied product that can compete more effectively with the imported light-bodied Scotch and Canadian whiskies.

VODKA

Vodka is basically a diluted pure alcohol or neutral spirit. It can be made from any fermented product, such as grain, rice, or potatoes, although the best vodkas are made from a grain. It is distilled at a very high proof and then finely filtered to remove any trace of congeners and to smooth the flavor, with the result that it has no smell and virtually no taste—perhaps the reason that it has become so popular and now has the largest share of the North American distilled spirit market.

Vodka can be drunk neat and is generally so consumed by northern Europeans. When chilled, it goes well with spicy foods such as smoked salmon and caviar. It also has the advantage of mixing well with almost anything, from a soft drink to tomato juice (in a Bloody Mary cocktail).

Although most vodka consumed today in North America is made there, two well-known imported (and some say "authentic") vodkas are Stolichnaya (from Russia) and Zubrowka (from Poland). No doubt these authentic vodkas, just like authentic scotch, are manufactured specially for the North American palate, as vodka traditionally made in Russia is often flavored with strong herbs or spices!

AKVAVIT (AQUAVIT)

Akvavit (or aquavit) is the Scandinavian version of vodka, and it is also the Scandinavian word for *aqua vitae*. Akvavit is distinguished by its slight caraway flavor. Like vodka, it is often colorless and drunk straight, often followed by a beer "chaser."

SCHNAPPS

Schnapps is a type of vodka produced in Germany. It may or may not be flavored, and like vodka and akvavit, it is colorless.

TEQUILA

Tequila is a product of Mexico, from a district surrounding the town of Tequila. True tequila is made from an agave plant (a type of cactus) known as *mezcal,* whose sweet sap is fermented and then distilled.

Tequila may be colorless. If so, it has not been aged. If it is silver colored, it has been aged for up to three years, and if gold colored, it has been aged in oak for up to four years. In Mexico, tequila is drunk straight, after a lick of salt from the back of the hand, and is followed by a slice of lime to suck on. In the rest of North America it is used mostly in cocktails (for example, the Margarita).

ARRACK (ARAK, RACK, RAKI)

Arrack—or arak, rack, or raki—is a strong spirit distilled chiefly in the Middle East from fermented juices or grains. For example, in the nineteenth century, Ceylon (now Sri Lanka) was well known for its palm arrack. Unfortunately, because of the primitive production methods in many countries, raw arrack was often harmful. But today, the production of arrack has declined because of the introduction of European spirits into the countries that used to produce it.

DISCUSSION QUESTIONS

1. What is the meaning and origin of the term *aqua vitae?*
2. Describe how a distilled spirit is made from a fermented product.
3. What are proof levels, and what is the origin of the word *proof?*
4. What are the characteristics of pure alcohol (neutral spirits)?
5. What are congeners, and how do they affect the taste of distilled spirits?
6. How does the temperature during distillation change the quality of the spirit?
7. How does a column still differ from a pot still?
8. Discuss the role of aging for distilled spirits, and explain why some distilled spirits are not aged.
9. What is the origin of the word *gin?*
10. Differentiate among Dutch gin, English gin, and U.S. gin.
11. What are Genever, Hollands, and Schiedam?
12. What is dry gin?
13. From what is rum made? Explain the history of rum in the United States.
14. What are the two main types of rum, how do they differ, and how is each type used?
15. How did whiskey get its name?
16. What is the main difference between Scotch malt whisky and blended Scotch whisky?
17. What are Glenfiddich and Glenlivet?
18. What are the two main production differences between Scotch whisky and Irish whiskey?
19. How was bourbon named? What is a sour-mash bourbon?
20. What is the legal requirement for a whiskey to be called a straight rye in the United States?
21. From what ingredient(s) is vodka made?
22. What are Stolichnaya and Zubrowka, and where are they from?

23. What is akvavit (aquavit), how did it get its name, and where is it generally manufactured?
24. What is schnapps, and where is it generally made?
25. What is tequila, what is its basic ingredient, and where is it generally made?

13

Distilled Spirits—Cognac, Brandy, and Liqueurs

CHAPTER OBJECTIVES

After studying this chapter the reader should be able to

- Differentiate between Cognac and brandy, explain how brandy derived its name, and identify where the Cognac region is located in France.
- Explain why no vintage date appears on Cognac bottles and spell out the acronyms that appear on their labels.
- Differentiate Grande Champagne, Petite Champagne, Fine Champagne and a *fine* and discuss how Cognac or brandy is usually consumed.
- List five well-known Cognac shippers.
- Describe Armagnac, Marc, and Grappa and where each of them is made.
- Briefly discuss Calvados, Kirsch, Slivovitz, Quetsch, Mirabelle, Pernod, and Ouzo, and state where each of them is made.
- Define the term *bitters,* and name two examples.
- Explain how liqueurs or cordials are made.

INTRODUCTION

The reader might wonder why this chapter title includes Cognac and brandy as separate topics. Isn't Cognac the same thing as brandy? No. Cognac is a type of brandy allowed to bear the name Cognac, whereas brandy that is not made in the Cognac region of France is not Cognac. This is similar to saying that although Champagne is a sparkling wine, not all sparkling wine is Champagne.

Brandy was first produced when a tariff was imposed on the table wine shipped from France to other countries. To reduce this tax, the Dutch came up with the idea of decreasing the volume of taxable liquid by distilling the wine into what was then known as *eau de vie* (French for water of life, or *aqua vitae*). The Dutch called this distilled wine *brandewijn* (or burned wine), which was later abbreviated to brandy.

Brandy can be made wherever wine is available, but the best brandy is considered to be made in France in the region of Cognac.

COGNAC

Cognac, the most prestigious of all brandies, is made from a white wine produced from a certain type of grape grown in the region around the town of Cognac, located north of Bordeaux in France. The wine from these grapes is of poor quality but produces excellent Cognac. Much of the grape crop is sold by the growers directly to the big Cognac-distilling firms owned by or under contract to the well-known Cognac shippers.

Although all brandy is distilled, only Cognac is distilled twice, in the traditional old pot stills. The alcohol resulting from this second distillation used to be matured in barrels made entirely of oak from the nearby Limousin forests. This oak is durable and not too porous, and no other wood has quite the same mellowing effect on the Cognac. But because now this particular oak is in short supply, it is not always used today.

It takes about ten barrels of wine to make one barrel of Cognac, and the flavoring congeners retained during both the distillation and the oxidation that take place through the porous oak wood produce Cognac's unique personality. Cognac, like all distilled spirits, is colorless when first distilled. It acquires its color during barrel aging, the color varying according to age and the kind of barrel used, from pale brown to dark brown. In order to ensure a consistent color, some shippers use caramel coloring at the time of bottling. This coloring does no harm to the product. Also, like all distilled products, Cognac ages only while in the barrel, and it is the time spent in wood that dictates a Cognac's quality.

Aging is expensive, not only because the product is held in inventory during this period, but also because of its evaporation while in casks. For example, if a barrel were kept for twenty years without being continually topped up, it would end up filling only half the barrel. Some Cognacs age for as long as thirty to forty years in their barrels.

Bottle Labels

There is no vintage Cognac because it is always blended, and for this reason the year does not appear on the label. Instead, Cognac is labeled by means of symbols. This labeling is governed by the strict French appellation laws and is determined by the age of the youngest brandy in each blend. Note that the minimum age at which Cognac may be marketed varies from one country to another. For example, in France it is three years, whereas in the United States it is two years.

Cognac bottle labels often list acronyms of the following letters and meanings:

V—very
S—superior or special
O—old
P—pale
E—especial
F—fine
X—extra

For example, the acronym VSOP stands for Very Superior (or Special) Old Pale. Note that the use of these acronyms may depend on the manufacturer and do not always indicate age. Why are these symbols equivalent to English words? When Cognac was first produced, the British market was extremely important to the French producers, and therefore they used symbols that would be meaningful in English.

Cognacs marketed in the United States fall into two basic categories, Three Star (or Five Star) and VSOP (Very Superior Old Pale). The stars on a label have no meaning except to place the Cognac in the youngest age bracket. Shippers are now replacing the stars with their proprietary brand names and the initials VS or VSP, but neither of these has any age significance. VSOP does, however, have a special meaning, because that Cognac must be at least four years old.

There is one other age designation: The word *Napoleon* can be used only for Cognac at least five years old, even though no Cognac can legally be described as older than five years (because the French government no longer issues age certificates to this effect, even though the Cognac may be much older). Some Cognac labels, however, state Extra, XO (extra old), Grande Reserve, or Vieille Reserve. These bottles contain brandies that can be much older than five years and even as much as fifty or more years old.

Bottle Labels in France

To guide the French in their own country, Cognac labels may bear the words Grande Champagne (sometimes Grande Fine Champagne) or Petite Champagne for the very best Cognac from the heart of the Cognac district. These two types of Cognac carry the *appellation contrôlée* designation Fine Champagne. Fine Champagne must be made from at least 50 percent grapes from the Grande Champagne district. (Note that the use of the word *champagne* in this context means field and has nothing to do with Champagne wine.) One may also order a *fine,* meaning an *appellation contrôlée* Cognac.

Besides Grande Champagne and Petite Champagne, there are five other districts, listed in descending order of the quality of Cognac produced:

Borderies
Fins Bois
Bons Bois
Bois Ordinaires
Bois communs

None of the Cognac produced from these five districts is allowed to bear the words *appellation contrôlée.*

Serving Cognac

Cognac is usually served in a special stemmed brandy glass big enough to allow the bowl to be cradled in the palm of the hand so that its warmth will release the Cognac's bouquet. Brandy glasses are often large enough to permit the nose to be lowered inside the rim to catch this bouquet. In fact, Cognac glasses are sometimes referred to as snifters.

Cognac should not be chilled or served on ice but should be consumed at room temperature. At least, that is how the French drink it at the end of a meal. However, many people in other parts of the world drink it on the rocks; diluted with water, soda water, ginger ale, or tonic water; or in long drinks such as a Cognac and cola. It is also served in French Coffee, which is similar to Irish Coffee but made with Cognac instead of Irish whiskey.

Cognac Shippers

Four shippers of Cognac produce about 75 percent of all the Cognac exported:

Courvoisier
Hennessy
Martell
Rémy Martin

Some of the other better-known Cognac shippers are

Bisquit
Camus
Delamain
Denis-Mounie
Gaston de Lagrange
Hine
Monnet
Otard
Polignac
Salignac

Today, many of the major brand-name Cognacs are shipped from France in bulk and bottled in North America for sale there. If a bottle is simply labeled French Brandy, it will be a lesser-quality product and not a Cognac.

ARMAGNAC

Armagnac is another well-known French brandy (not entitled to use the word Cognac) that is made from grapes grown just south of the Bordeaux region. Some people prefer a good Armagnac to Cognac, as it is distilled only once and has more body and flavor and ages more quickly than Cognac. It is generally drier than Cognac, with a less distinct aroma and also a less expensive price.

MARC AND GRAPPA

Marc is a distinctive and pungent type of brandy also distilled in France. It is distilled from the *marc* or pulp (skins and other residue from grapes) that is left over after the grapes have been pressed and their juice used for making wine. Water is then added to the *marc;* it is refermented; and then it is distilled. The best Marc produced in France comes from Burgundy.

In Italy a similar type of distilled brandy is known as Grappa and is a little bit rougher (less mellow) and richer than the French Marc. Grappa is not usually aged in wood and so is colorless. In Spain, Marc is known as Aguardiente, and in Portugal, Bagaceira.

OTHER BRANDIES

Spanish brandy is noted for its heavy and sweet flavor, compared with that of the finer brandies of France. Spanish brandies, unlike Cognac and Armagnac, are usually distilled from a blend of wines. German brandy is more dry and delicate than either Spanish or French brandy. Another brandy is Pisco (from Peru) used in the Pisco Sour cocktail.

Most of the brandy consumed in the United States is American and is made from raisin and table, rather than wine, grapes. It is produced primarily in California. It is rarely consumed on its own and is more commonly used as a distilled spirit in cocktails that call for brandy.

FRUIT BRANDIES

Although the term brandy is generally used to denote a distilled product made from grape wine, brandy can be distilled from many other fruits as well. One fruit that is particularly suitable is apples, and one of the best-known French apple brandies is Calvados, distilled from apple cider. Apple brandies retain the flavor and fragrance of the apples from which they are distilled. In Germany apple brandy goes by the name Apfelschnapps.

In the United States, apple brandy is usually referred to as applejack and is a traditional New England brandy made from a blend of cider brandy and neutral grain spirits. It is lighter than Calvados and has less of an apple taste.

Another well-known fruit brandy is Kirsch or Kirschwasser, which is made from black cherries and is produced and is popular in France (Alsace), Germany, and Switzerland. Kirsch is colorless.

Plum brandies are popular in countries in Central Europe such as Yugoslavia and Czechoslovakia, where it is known as Slivovitz. Plum brandies are also known as Quetsch or Mirabelle in France. Plum brandies are usually gold colored.

Another popular fruit brandy in France and Switzerland is pear brandy, which is usually labeled as Poire Williams or Pear William. It too is colorless. Finally, Framboise is made from raspberries.

One of the reasons that fruit brandies are so expensive is that as much as thirty to forty pounds of fruit is required to produce a single bottle. Also, do not confuse these fruit brandies with fruit products such as apricot brandy, which are much sweeter and made quite differently. These products are commonly referred to as liqueurs or cordials and will be discussed at the end of this chapter.

ABSINTHE (AND SIMILAR PRODUCTS)

In the early part of this century an emerald green, toxic spirit, distilled from wormwood and other aromatics and known as absinthe, was commonly consumed in Europe. Genuine absinthe was as high as 70 to 80 percent alcohol and had a licorice flavor. But later it was discovered that the excessive consumption of absinthe affected not only the digestive organs but also the nerve centers and could produce delirium and idiocy. Thus, by the early 1900s the manufacture and sale of absinthe were prohibited in most European countries.

Some derivatives of absinthe have survived in a less toxic form and are sold today under such names as Pernod (in France, where it is sometimes referred to as *pastis*) and Ouzo (in Greece). These colorless, licorice-flavored spirits become cloudy if water is added.

BITTERS

One family of distilled spirits is known as *bitters,* which are distillations flavored with bark, fruit, herbs, and/or roots of various kinds. One of the most common bitters is Angostura, which is used in several cocktails (for example, the Champagne Cocktail and Pink Gin). Orange bitters is a similar product also used in certain cocktails.

Campari is a low-proof, red-colored bitters made in Italy. It can be consumed straight but is more often mixed with soda or tonic. It is also used in Europe in the popular cocktail Americano, for which it is mixed with Italian vermouth and soda and garnished with a lemon slice. Other bitters are Amer Picon and Fernet Branca, both products of France. Peychaud's bitters is made in New Orleans.

LIQUEURS (CORDIALS)

Liqueurs, sometimes referred to as cordials, come in many varieties. They were popularized by monks (primarily in French monasteries) who created liqueurs that—even though today they may no longer be produced in the monasteries—are among the greatest in the world.

A liqueur is basically a distilled spirit that is steeped in, has macerated in it, or is percolated or redistilled with any number of fruits, flowers, juices, extracts, barks, herbs, seeds, spices, plants, or other natural flavorings. The basic distilled spirit may be brandy, whiskey, rum, vodka, or a neutral spirit. Only the manufacturer's imagination limits what may go into a liqueur.

Most liqueurs are sweetened with a little or a lot of sugar, honey, or maple or corn syrup. Any color present is usually added for effect (for example, yellow or green Chartreuse, green crème de menthe, blue Curaçao). Some liqueurs are aged before bottling; others are not.

One of the first liqueurs was produced in 1510 at a monastery in Europe. It was named Benedictine and was made from a Cognac base. On Benedictine bottles today appear the letters DOM, for *Deo Optimo Maximo* (to God most good, most great). Another long-lived liqueur is Chartreuse, which comes in both a yellow and a green color (the yellow has a higher alcohol content).

Traditionally, liqueurs are served at the end of a meal, by themselves at room temperature, or chilled, on ice. They may also be served in long drinks, over ice, and with a soft drink or other mixer.

Some of the more popular liqueurs, with their spirit base and basic flavoring, are the following:

Name	Spirit Base	Basic Flavor
Advocaat	Brandy	Eggnog
Amaretto	Neutral spirit	Almond/apricot
Anisette	Neutral spirit	Licorice
Apricot brandy	Neutral spirit	Apricot
Benedictine	Cognac	Herbs/spices
B&B	Neutral spirit/Cognac	Herbs/spices
Blackberry brandy	Neutral spirit/brandy	Blackberry
Chartreuse	Neutral spirit/brandy	Herbs/spices
Cherry brandy	Neutral spirit/brandy	Cherry
Cherry whisky	Whisky	Cherry
Cointreau	Neutral spirit	Orange
Crème de bananes	Neutral spirit	Banana
Crème de cacao	Neutral spirit	Chocolate/vanilla
Crème de cassis	Neutral spirit	Black currant
Crème de menthe	Neutral spirit	Mint
Curaçao	Neutral spirit	Orange
Drambuie	Scotch whisky	Scotch/honey
Galliano	Neutral spirit	Licorice/vanilla
Glayva	Scotch whisky	Scotch/honey
Grand Marnier	Cognac	Orange
Irish Cream	Irish whiskey	Irish/chocolate
Irish Mist	Irish whiskey	Irish/honey
Kahlua	Neutral spirit	Coffee
Kirsch liqueur	Kirsch	Cherry
Kummel	Neutral spirit	Caraway
Maraschino brandy	Neutral spirit	Cherry/almond
Peach brandy	Neutral spirit	Peach
Peppermint	Neutral spirit	Mint
Peter Heering	Neutral spirit/brandy	Cherry
Raspberry brandy	Neutral spirit	Raspberry
Sloe gin	Neutral spirit	Plum

Name	Spirit Base	Basic Flavor
Southern Comfort	Bourbon	Bourbon/peach
Strawberry brandy	Neutral spirit	Strawberry
Strega	Neutral spirit	Herbs/spices
Tia Maria	Rum	Coffee
Triple Sec	Neutral spirit	Orange
Vandermint	Neutral spirit	Chocolate/mint

DISCUSSION QUESTIONS

1. How do Cognac and brandy differ?
2. How did brandy derive its name?
3. Where is the Cognac region in France?
4. Why is Cognac never labeled with the vintage year?
5. What do the letters V, S, O, P, E, F, and X stand for on Cognac bottle labels?
6. How do Grande Champagne, Petite Champagne, and Fine Champagne differ?
7. What is a *fine?*
8. How and when is Cognac or brandy usually consumed?
9. List five of the main Cognac shippers.
10. What is Armagnac, and where is it made?
11. What are Marc and Grappa, and where are they made?
12. What is Calvados, and where is it made? What is the U.S. equivalent of Calvados?
13. What is Kirsch? In which countries is it made?
14. What are Slivovitz, Quetsch, and Mirabelle, and where are they made?
15. What are Pernod and Ouzo, and where are they made?
16. What is bitters? Name two examples.
17. How are liqueurs or cordials made?

14

Cocktails

CHAPTER OBJECTIVES

After studying this chapter the reader should be able to

- Describe in general a cocktail and discuss the requirement and use of ice for mixed drinks.
- Discuss cocktail ingredients such as juices and garnishes.
- List the three basic types of glassware used in a bar, identify glassware requirements, and explain how glassware inventory needs can be calculated.
- Describe the three basic methods for mixing drinks.
- Recognize the various categories of cocktails (such as liquor on ice, fizzes, and cream drinks) and, for each major category, list the prime ingredients for the most common cocktails.
- Discuss how a bar's choice of drinks will affect its drink menu.
- Define *standard recipe* and explain the terms used with standard recipes, such as *neat* and *soda out*.

INTRODUCTION

Cocktails date from about the middle of the nineteenth century. They first were served, with a canapé or hors d'oeuvre, to diners seated at the table. Later, when the grand hotels and the fashionable railway resorts blossomed and ice became readily available, bartenders were encouraged to become more creative in the drinks they offered their customers. Today's bartender thus must be highly skilled and not only must know the names of drinks (as well as their ingredients, mixing methods, and best way of presentation) but also must be aware of market trends and be able to create new drinks (or variations of old drinks) as customers' habits change.

COCKTAIL INGREDIENTS

A cocktail (the origin of this curious word is not known) is basically a mixed drink in which a type of alcohol (usually a distilled spirit, but not always) is mixed with one or more liquids (alcohol or some other ingredient such as a soft drink or fruit juice), with other ingredients (such as ice or a garnish) added when necessary. In most cocktails the major alcoholic ingredient is intended to predominate and give the drink its body, flavor, and personality; any other items added are used only to complement that flavor. But the main alcohol ingredient may not form most of the liquid in a drink; in many drinks it may be only 50 percent or less.

Ice

Ice is a key ingredient in many cocktails. It may be used to chill the glass, chill the drink, dilute the drink, or fill up a glass with a drink in it—or all of the above. To save money, most bartenders are advised, when required, to fill the glass with ice before adding any soft drink (carbonated mix), because ice is cheaper than mixer. The type of ice is also important. For example, a drink in a glass with shaved ice leaves less room for mixer than does a glass filled with cubed ice.

Ice should always be clean and fresh and should be put first in the drink-mixing utensil or glass, to prevent the drink's splashing. Highballs (liquor with ice and either water or a carbonated beverage added) and drinks on the rocks usually call for cubed ice, whereas drinks to be stirred or shaken usually require crushed ice. Shaved ice is used in specialty drinks such as frozen cocktails or frappés.

For sanitary reasons ice should never be picked up by hand and should never be reused, even if it is washed, nor should the ice bin be used for cooling other cocktail ingredients. Finally, a metal ice scoop should be used to pick up the ice, and not the glass into which the ice is to be put, which can easily break or chip.

Soft (Carbonated) Drinks

Most bars carry the standard soft, or carbonated, drinks, such as soda water, ginger ale, cola, tonic, and 7-Up. Others such as Sprite and root beer may be carried, depending on local preferences and customer demand. It is important that these soft drinks be kept chilled before serving, for if they are warm when dispensed, they will fizz up in the glass, lose their carbonation, and go flat. Some bars also carry specialty waters such as Perrier or Evian.

Fruit Juices

Fresh fruit juices, such as orange and grapefruit, should be used for drinks whenever possible. Fresh juices do take time to prepare, but they make a better beverage, even though the flavor may vary with the origin of the fruit and the fruit can spoil if too much is carried in inventory. As an alternative, many bars use frozen concentrated juices, because they have a long shelf life, can be quickly prepared, and provide a consistent flavor. Others use fresh juice in cartons. Few bars use canned juices, because of their tinny taste.

Lemon and lime juice are also best if freshly squeezed, although the frozen, concentrated juices are also of good quality. Lemon and lime juices are also needed in the form of sweet and sour mixes (that is, with sugar added). These sweet/sour mixes can be mixed on the premises or be purchased premixed in bottle or frozen, concentrated form. For convenience, many bars use the powdered products available from suppliers. These powdered products may also include a foaming agent that simulates the use of egg white, forming a kind of head on the top of the cocktail.

Apart from orange, grapefruit, lemon, and lime juice, some bars need to carry juices and syrups such as tomato, pineapple, cranberry, V-8, grenadine (pomegranate base), passion fruit (mixed tropical juices), orgeat (almond-flavored syrup), cream of coconut, and falernum (almond, ginger, and lime flavored), and even beef bouillon for some cocktails. The variety carried depends on the drinks served, geographic location, and customer demand.

When not in use, opened containers of juices and liquid mixes should be refrigerated in plastic or glass containers. If purchased in metal containers, they should be transferred into plastic or glass before refrigeration. Refrigeration is necessary because it reduces the possibility of bacteria growth and flavor loss. Also, if room-temperature liquids were used in drinks, they would melt the ice quickly, thus diluting the drink. Most opened juices should be used within forty-eight hours, although some, such as tomato and pineapple, will keep for a few days.

Dairy Products

Many bars carry milk, cream, and fresh eggs, the items most susceptible to bacterial spoilage. They thus should always be refrigerated at a temperature below 40° F (4° C).

Any egg ingredients should be put into the mixing glass or shaker before the liquor is added, and drinks containing eggs will be smoother if blended rather than shaken.

Fruit and Other Garnishes

Most bars carry a supply of fresh fruit and other items for garnishes, including fresh fruits cut up into wheels, half-wheels, quarter-wheels, or wedges. Lemon, lime, and orange wheel garnishes should not be cut too thinly, as otherwise they will go limp and curl on the glass rim. When cutting lemon or lime peel to make a zest for twists, use only the colored part of the peel and not the white rind. Fruit should be kept refrigerated, both before and after being cut up. Cut-up lemons and limes can be kept for up to twenty-four hours if placed in a lidded jar and covered with Sprite or a collins mix. Cut-up oranges do not keep well overnight.

Other common garnishes are maraschino cherries (both with and without stems), olives (sometimes stuffed with pimientos or anchovies), cocktail onions, pineapple chunks or spears, and cucumber or celery sticks. Again, such items should be refrigerated. To be stored overnight, any unused olives, onions, and cherries should be put back into the liquid in their jars and be tightly lidded.

Sugar Syrup

Granulated sugar does not combine readily with alcohol, but a simple syrup will. A simple syrup is made by combining powdered sugar (preferable to granulated) with water in the ratio of 4.5 pounds of sugar to 160 ounces of boiling water. It then should be mixed completely and refrigerated as soon as possible. Sweet and sour juice or mix is made by dissolving one part sugar in three parts lemon juice. Some bars also carry sugar cubes, which may be needed for some flambéed drinks and in the Old Fashioned cocktail.

Other Ingredients

Other ingredients used in some bars are mixes for such cocktails as the Bloody Mary, Daiquiri, and Margarita. These come in both powdered and frozen concentrated form. Condiments such as Tabasco and Worcestershire sauce, salt, and spices (for example, cinammon, nutmeg, and pepper) are often used. Finally, bitters, such as Angostura, Peychaud, and orange are needed for some cocktails. Only a dash of these is used when called for in a drink recipe.

GLASSWARE

The three basic types of glassware needed in a bar are tumblers (straight or slope-sided glasses without a stem, including beer mugs, or tumblers with handles), footed glasses (with a bowl, short stem, and base or foot), and stemmed glasses (bowl, longer stem, and base or foot). These three types are shown in Figure 14-1. The names of glassware are often directly related to the type of drink served in them, although the name is not necessarily as important as the glass size, as a highball glass, for example, can vary in size from seven ounces to ten ounces. The quality of glassware (for example, weight, durability, heat-resistance) is often determined by the type of customer being served.

The variety of glasses a bar actually carries depends on such factors as the variety of drinks served, the size of drinks, and the type and amount of ice to be used. It is preferable, for cost and other reasons, to minimize the variety of glasses used and to use a particular type and size of glass for more than one purpose. A rule of thumb is to carry in inventory between two and four times the number of glasses that are needed during a peak period.

Figure 14-1   Types of glassware: (a) tumbler, (b) footed, and (c) stemmed.

Stem glassware can be conveniently and hygienically stored in racks over the front bar, with the stem of the inverted glass pushed into slots in the racks with the glasses suspended upside down from their base.

It is a good idea to chill cocktail glasses before use (in the refrigerator for half an hour or in the freezer for ten minutes) or, alternatively, to fill glasses with ice while the drink is being prepared and then to discard the ice before the drink is poured into the glass. This keeps the drink cold longer.

Serving Accessories

Drink-serving accessories used by most bars include picks (either wood or plastic) for spearing garnishes, straws of various lengths, plastic stir sticks, sip sticks (a cross between a stir stick and a straw), cocktail napkins, and drink coasters.

Mixing Cocktails

Appendix A contains sixty-six standard cocktail recipes, some of which are discussed in the following sections. There are three basic methods for making (mixing) cocktails: building, stirring, and shaking/blending.

BUILD DRINKS

To build a drink, it is mixed step by step in the glass in which it is to be served. The glass is filled about three-fourths full with ice; the ingredients are added, with spirits first; and then juice, soda, or other mixer as required. Finally, any garnish is added, along with picks, straws, or other items. Any stirring necessary is left to the customer. This method is used for the following types of drinks.

Liquor on Ice

Liquor on ice, such as scotch or bourbon on the rocks, is usually served on ice in a five-ounce old fashioned, footed, or rocks glass, depending on the type of ice used. If it is served on crushed ice, it is sometimes referred to as a frappé. Sometimes the liquor is complemented with a liqueur added after the liquor (the liqueur, being denser, will filter down). Typical examples are the Rusty Nail (scotch and Drambuie), Stinger (brandy and white crème de menthe), and Black Russian (vodka and Kahlua).

Highballs

Highballs are a mixture of liquor on ice and either water or mixer (carbonated beverage). Highballs are usually served in a six- to ten-ounce highball glass, with ice first, then liquor, and finally mixer. The mixer is heavier, filters down, and destroys a minimal amount of bubbles. Again, any stirring is left to the customer, as it reduces the mixer's effervescence and dilutes the drink. Examples of highballs are scotch and soda, rye and ginger, and rum and cola.

Fruit Juice Drinks

Fruit juice drinks are similar to highballs, with the water or mixer replaced with a juice. Examples are the Screwdriver (vodka and orange juice), Bloody Mary (vodka and tomato juice), Harvey Wallbanger (vodka, orange juice, and Galliano), Freddy Fudpucker (tequila, orange juice, and Galliano), and Tequila Sunrise (tequila, orange juice, and grenadine).

Fruit juice drinks may contain less ice so as not to reduce the juice flavor and so may require some stirring to mix the liquor with the juice. Garnishes may be added, depending on the drink. If fruit juice cocktails are built in a collins or zombie glass requiring more ice (and a more diluted drink), they are sometimes referred to as tall drinks.

Collinses, Rickeys, and Bucks

The main ingredients of a collins are liquor, lemon juice, sugar, soda, cubed ice, and fruit garnish. The lemon juice and sugar are sometimes replaced with a prepared mix known as a collins mix. The collins is named after the basic liquor used. For example, a Tom collins has a gin base, and a John collins has a whiskey base.

A rickey is similar to a collins, but with fresh lime juice instead of lemon juice and little or no sugar.

A buck is like a collins, but with ginger ale instead of soda. Again, little or no sugar is used, as the ginger ale is already sweet.

Coolers, Spritzers, and Sangria

Although coolers and spritzers can be made with liquor, coolers are today more commonly made with red wine mixed half and half with 7-Up over cubed or crushed ice in a tall, eight- to ten-ounce glass. A spritzer is like a cooler but made with white instead of red wine. Packaged bottled or canned coolers, made and premixed by wineries, are also available. They include fruit juice and mineral water (either still or carbonated) plus a wine base.

Sangria is a sweetened wine cooler made with brandy, sugar, fruit, club soda, plus any good dry red wine such as a Spanish Rioja.

Other Special Drinks

Other drinks that fit into the build category are the Old Fashioned, the Mint Julep, and the Swizzle. Recipes for these are included in Appendix A.

One rather special drink that has to be carefully built is the Pousse Café (meaning Coffee Pusher). It is usually consumed with coffee as an after-meal drink. The Pousse Café uses as many as half a dozen different liquors, liqueurs, and other liquids with different specific gravities (or densities) that are floated on top of one another, with the densest at the bottom, in a narrow liqueur glass or long-stemmed pony glass. The various bands or layers stay separate and present a colorful contrast. Sometimes cream is floated on top.

Coffee Drinks

Coffee drinks are popular and also represent high-profit items to the operator. These drinks are basically coffee mixed with a liquor or liqueur and usually topped with whipped cream and sprinkled with flavorings such as nutmeg or chocolate. One of the most popular is Irish Coffee, made with Irish whiskey. Other well-known coffee drinks are Coffee Calypso, also known as Jamaican Coffee (rum and Tia Maria), Diablo Coffee (Cognac and Grand Marnier or Cointreau), Royal Coffee (bourbon or brandy), Greek Coffee (Metaxa and Ouzo), Mexican Coffee (tequila and Kahlua), and Roman Coffee (Galliano).

Toddies

Finally, we come to the category of build drinks known as hot toddies. A hot toddy is a measure of liquor plus sugar and hot water, and if the water is replaced with egg and hot milk, it becomes a Hot Flip, Eggnog, or Hot Milk Punch. If lemon juice is added to a Hot Toddy, it becomes a Hot Sling. If rum is the basic liquor, it may be called a Grog or Hot Grog. And if butter and spices are added to a Hot Grog, it becomes a Hot Buttered Rum.

STIR DRINKS

Stir drink ingredients are first stirred together in a mixing glass and then poured through a strainer into a serving glass (sometimes prechilled). The purpose of stirring is to mix, cool, and dilute the ingredients (with water from the ice) and then to pour them into a drinking glass, without any ice, to prevent any further dilution of the alcohol. It is important to stir the drink properly. Too little stirring and the drink will not chill enough; too much stirring and the drink will be too diluted. The stir method is used for drinks such as the Martini and Manhattan.

Martini

The basic Martini is a mixture of gin and dry vermouth in a ratio varying from four parts gin to one part vermouth to as much as eight parts gin to one part vermouth, stirred over cubed ice in a mixing glass, strained into a cold four-ounce cocktail glass, and garnished with an olive and a lemon twist. A dry Martini uses less vermouth. A Gibson is a Martini garnished with a small pickled onion instead of a stuffed olive. A Vodkatini uses vodka instead of gin. A Martini can also be made with rum or tequila instead of gin. A Perfect Martini uses equal parts dry and sweet vermouth.

Manhattan

The Manhattan is a mixture of whiskey and sweet vermouth, again in a ratio varying from four parts whiskey to one part vermouth to as much as eight parts whiskey to one part vermouth, stirred over cubed ice in a mixing glass, strained into a cold four-ounce cocktail glass, and garnished with a cherry. If a dry Manhattan is called for, then dry instead of sweet vermouth is used. The whiskey used depends on where the Manhattan is made or what the customer requests: It can be scotch, bourbon, or rye. A Paddy Manhattan uses Irish whiskey. Brandy or rum may also be used; a Perfect Manhattan uses equal parts dry and sweet vermouth, and a Rob Roy is a Perfect Manhattan made with scotch.

If requested, a Martini or Manhattan can be served on the rocks. Bars that sell a heavy volume of these drinks often premix them in bulk and keep them refrigerated in pouring bottles for speedy service.

SHAKE/MIX/BLEND DRINKS

With the shake method all the ingredients are put into a hand shaker and then are vigorously shaken by the bartender before being strained into a drinking glass. This method is used when certain ingredients—such as sugar, fruit juices, cream, and eggs—might not mix well if the drink were simply stirred before serving. Traditionally, shaking was done by hand in a stainless steel shaker and mixing glass, and some bartenders still use this method. However, today, in the interest of speed, the shaking is often done in a mechanical mixer.

Any drink that can be shaken may instead be blended. This is done in a mixer that has cutting blades on the bottom. This method is also required for any drink that contains solid items (ice, fruit) that need to be cut up and incorporated into the drink.

For drinks that need to be shaken or blended, some bars—again in the interests of speed and cost—use premixed products instead of certain fresh or raw ingredients.

Sours

One group of shaken/blended drinks is the sour family. The basic sour is made with a liquor, lemon or lime juice, and a sweetener (such as simple syrup or grenadine), which are shaken/blended and then strained into a chilled five-ounce sour or cocktail glass, or poured over cubed ice in a rocks glass. Sometimes egg white (or a prepackaged frothing product) is included to give the sour a fizzy topping. The sour can be made with gin to produce a Gimlet, with brandy to produce a Side Car, with rum to produce a Daiquiri, with tequila to produce a Margarita, or with vodka or scotch. Frozen drinks are usually sours that are blended with crushed ice until they have the consistency of slush and then are poured and a fresh fruit garnish is added.

Collins Sours

A collins sour is a basic sour poured into a collins glass, with soda water added to create a tall drink. This type of drink uses the shake/blend method and then the build method, by adding soda: The soda is not shaken because it would lose its bubbles. A French 75 is a gin sour with champagne replacing the soda.

Fizzes

A fizz is like a short collins sour served in a highball or eight-ounce stem glass but, because of the smaller glass, with only a small amount of soda added. A Silver Fizz is a gin fizz with egg white added; a Golden Fizz uses egg yolk; and a Royal Fizz uses the whole egg and sometimes cream.

Slings

A sling is basically a collins sour with added liqueur and other special flavoring ingredients. The Singapore Sling (see recipe) is well known.

Tropical Drinks

Tropical drinks are made by the shake/blend method. They contain some
type of liquor base, to which fruit juices, syrups, coconut milk or flavor, and
fruit garnishes may be added. They are often served in special decorative
glasses. Tropical drinks often have rum as their base (such as the Mai Tai,
Piña Colada, Planter's Punch, and Zombie) but can use vodka (Chi Chi) or
rum with some other liquor, such as the Scorpion which uses rum and
brandy.

Cream Drinks

Cream drinks are usually quite sweet, use one or more liquor–liqueur combinations along with cream, and are served in a chilled cocktail or champagne glass. For example, the Brandy Alexander uses half brandy and half
dark crème de cacao plus cream. Variations are the gin, rum, and vodka
Alexander (also known as a Russian Bear). The Grasshopper is made with
half green crème de menthe and half white crème de cacao plus cream.
Other common cream drinks are the White Cadillac, Golden Cadillac, Pink
Lady, and White Russian (see recipes).

Milk Drinks

Sometimes cream drinks replace the cream with milk to produce a tall drink
that is poured into a collins glass. Or a basic cream drink can be converted
into a tall one by shaking/blending the cream drink, pouring it over ice
cubes in a tall glass, and then adding a carbonated beverage.

Ice-Cream Drinks

Another variation of cream drinks is to substitute ice cream for the cream.
These drinks generally call for soft ice cream, which means that the bar will
need a soft-ice cream freezer. Because of the health hazard that ice cream
can create in warm climates, there may be strict health regulations governing these drinks.

DRINK LIST CONSIDERATIONS

The choice of drinks that a bar or restaurant decides to serve will depend on a number of factors, such as the types and sizes of glasses needed; the number and type of ice-making machines required; the refrigerator and/or freezer equipment and space needed; the utensils and tools required; the kinds of liquor, liqueur, and other alcoholic beverages and supplies required; the amount of inventory to be carried; and the skills needed by the bartenders and servers.

STANDARD RECIPES

Today in most bars, bartenders are required to follow standard recipes established by management. These recipes specify the amount of the main ingredient, the amount of other ingredients, the type of garnish required, and the amount and type of ice to be used. Because there is a relationship between all of these and the glass type and size to be used, the standard recipe generally states the kind of glass required. The drink's taste can be affected by a number of variables, such as the amount of ice and the size of the glass: More ice equals less mixer equals a stronger liquor taste. A larger glass equals more mixer equals a less pronounced liquor taste.

Most bars also require bartenders to use measuring devices in order to control the amount of alcohol used. Standard recipes and measuring devices are discussed in more detail in Chapter 18.

Standard recipes frequently use certain terms whose meanings are summarized here:

Dash—About three drops.
Lemon twist—A zest of lemon peel twisted over a cocktail so that its oil sprays the surface of the drink.
Neat—A drink without ice.
On the rocks—A drink poured over ice.
Shell out—Discarding a lemon or lime shell after its juice has been squeezed into a drink.
Simple syrup—A sugar/water mixture added to cocktails to sweeten them.
Soda out—A drink topped up with soda.
Straight up—A stirred cocktail that is then strained into a drinking glass without ice.
Virgin—Without alcohol.
Water (soda) back—A drink served with a separate glass of water (soda) so that the customer may mix his or her own drink.

Many of the other words and terms used to describe how a drink is to be made are regional or local terms.

HOT SNACKS

For sanitary reasons, particular attention should be paid to any hot snacks (such as hors d'oeuvres) carried in bars. There is a high risk of bacteria growth if these items contain any meat, fish, poultry, sauce, or dairy ingredients. The danger zone is from 45° to 140° F (7° to 60° C). If these items are to be kept hot until served, they should be kept at above 165° F (74° C) to avoid any risk of food-borne illness. If they are cooked and then to be refrigerated until served, they should be refrigerated at below 40° F (4° C). Needless to say, serving trays or utensils, plates, counters, and tabletops must also be kept scrupulously clean.

DISCUSSION QUESTIONS

1. What is a cocktail?
2. Briefly discuss the requirement for ice in a cocktail.
3. Discuss fruit juices and their storage requirements.
4. Discuss fruit garnishes and their storage requirements.
5. What three types of glassware are used in a bar?
6. How does a bar decide on the types of glasses it will carry? How is glassware inventory requirement calculated?
7. Why is it a good idea to chill cocktail glasses before they are used?
8. Briefly describe the three basic methods for making cocktails.
9. What are the ingredients of a Rusty Nail and a Stinger?
10. What are the ingredients of a Bloody Mary, Harvey Wallbanger, and Freddy Fudpucker?
11. What are the ingredients of a collins? How do a rickey and a buck differ from a collins?
12. How do a cooler and a spritzer differ?
13. Describe a Pousse Café and how it is made.
14. What are the ingredients of a Martini and a Manhattan?
15. What is a Perfect Martini or Manhattan? What is a Rob Roy?
16. What are the ingredients of a sour? What is the principal liquor used for a Gimlet, Side Car, Daiquiri, and Margarita?
17. What is a French 75?
18. How do a Silver Fizz, a Golden Fizz, and a Royal Fizz differ?
19. The Mai Tai, Piña Colada, and Planter's Punch are often referred to as tropical drinks. What is the main liquor used in them?
20. What are the principal ingredients of a Brandy Alexander and a Grasshopper?
21. How will a bar's choice of drinks affect its operation?
22. What is a standard recipe?
23. Define the terms neat, soda out, shell out, water back, and dash.

15

Bar Equipment, Tools, and Glassware

CHAPTER OBJECTIVES

After studying this chapter the reader should be able to

- List and briefly discuss the three major items of underbar equipment and explain what a handgun is and how it operates.
- Differentiate between pre- and postmix carbonated beverage systems. Discuss the pros and cons of each as well as the use of bottled soft drinks instead of pre- or postmixes.
- Discuss the glass-washing requirements for a typical bar, including the use of machines.
- Explain what the back bar is used for and describe the use of some of the equipment (such as a frozen-drink dispenser) sometimes placed there.
- Describe and explain the use of equipment and hand tools such as a hand shaker, mixer, blender, bar strainer, bar spoon, and fruit squeezer.
- Discuss a bar's requirements for ice and for an ice-making machine.

INTRODUCTION

The critical factors in beverage cost control are bar design, work area layout, equipment, and the proper and efficient use of that equipment.

Although from the customers' perspective, all bars look different (and they may well be from a decorative point of view), in regard to bar equipment, dimensions, and functional layout, most bars are fairly standardized. Some bars may have more equipment and more working stations than others, and local health and fire regulations and plumbing and electrical requirements may differentiate some. Again, the type of drinks served can determine many aspects of bar design. For example, a bar that decides to serve virtually any drink that a customer orders will need a lot of space, which may be all right if it serves little or no food or is a service bar for an exclusive restaurant. However, many bars limit the variety of drinks that they serve (just as many restaurants do with the food items they offer). This reduces equipment space and investment requirements as well as inventory and operating costs (for example, the need to train highly skilled bartenders). In such a bar, drink lists will offer only the most often demanded drinks. Any specialty drinks offered will only be those that do not require special liquors or liqueurs.

Most bars have a front part (the front bar) and a back part (the back bar), as illustrated in Figure 15-1.

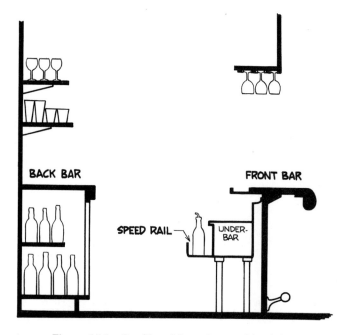

Figure 15-1   Profile of front bar and back bar.

THE FRONT BAR

The front bar contains a counter, which generally has stools for customers to sit at and provision for one or more pickup stations where waiters/waitresses order and pick up drinks to be served to customers seated at tables.

The front bar also contains the bartender's working station. Most of the frequently used work equipment is located in what is known as the under-bar. The underbar is usually made of stainless steel, which is easy to keep clean and thus more sanitary and pleasing to the eye.

The Underbar

Ice Bin

A major part of the underbar is the ice bin or ice chest. The ice bin usually contains separate sections for different types of ice, such as cubed and crushed. In today's bar, ice is extremely important. In the early "wild west" days, customers poured their own whiskey straight from the bottle into a drinking glass and consumed it that way. But with the advent of ice in the mid-nineteenth century, bars began to look as they do today. The availability of ice also ushered in the cocktail and the thousands of its variations (most of which require the use of ice). Ice also requires the use of equipment and tools not needed in earlier times.

Bottle Wells

The underbar also contains bottle wells, heavy-duty plastic containers surrounding the ice bin (as illustrated in Figure 15-2) or else surrounded by ice to chill them. They contain bottles of juices, prepared mixes, milk, cream, and other liquids that need refrigeration.

Speed Rail

Also part of the underbar is a section known as the speed rail, an un-chilled, long stainless steel compartment that contains the bottles of distilled spirits (liquor) that are most often used at the bar. These include whiskeys of various types (scotch, bourbon, and rye), gin, vodka, rum, brandy, and possibly tequila. The location of the speed rail on the underbar is indicated in Figure 15-1. The speed rail is also known as a *well*, which is why the fast-moving liquors held in it are often referred to as *well brands*. Well

Figure 15-2   Ice bin and surrounding bottle wells.

brands are also sometimes known as pour, house, or nonpremium brands. If space permits, the speed rail may also contain other types of commonly used drinks (such as vermouth).

These three major underbar components (the ice bin, bottle wells, and speed rail) together are referred to as a bartender work station, cocktail station, cocktail unit, or beverage center. Depending on its volume of business, a bar may have one or more of these cocktail stations.

Handgun

In many bars today an important item of equipment at each bartender's work station is the *handgun,* a flexible hose connected to half a dozen different tanks of soft drinks (carbonated beverages) housed under the bar or nearby. These soft drinks are automatically dispensed at the push of a button at the head of the handgun. Normally six buttons are available for six different carbonated beverages, and a seventh button is sometimes added for dispensing water. This soft drink–dispensing handgun is sometimes referred to as a sixshooter or a cobra and is shown in Figure 15-3.

Carbonated mixes used with the handgun are either premixes or postmixes. Premix tanks have the syrup and water already mixed in the five-gallon tank. The mix runs from the tank through plastic tubes that are chilled before reaching the dispensing head, where carbon dioxide is added.

Figure 15-3   Handgun for carbonated beverage system.

Premix is not often used today because the tanks are large and take up a lot of space.

Postmix is simply a syrup container. The syrup runs through plastic tubes from the tank and is mixed with five parts of chilled water at the handgun head at the time the carbon dioxide is also added. Postmix is most often used because it is much cheaper than premix and requires far less space. One possible problem is that if the syrup is mixed when it is dispensed with regular tap water, rather than with purified water, the result may not be as good.

Some bars use neither premix nor postmix but, rather, carbonated beverages in small bottles. These bottles are more expensive than either of the other two systems, take up a lot of space, and often mean wasted soft drinks from bottles not fully emptied. But bars use them because the bottles hold the carbonation better; the soft drinks often are made of high-quality water; and they are demanded by a certain clientele.

Liquor-dispensing Heads

Some bars use automatic liquor dispensers (similar to the handgun for mixers) for their major brands of spirits. The pros and cons of this type of equipment are discussed in Chapter 19.

Glass Washing

Another important part of the front bar is the glass-washing area. The actual washing equipment is often dictated by local health codes. Three sinks are usually required—one for washing, one for rinsing, and one for sanitizing glasses with a chemical solution to kill any remaining bacteria. Sometimes the wash sink is equipped with an upright wash brush in the soapy water. The inverted glass is pushed over the brush and manually rotated, or else the brush is turned on automatically by pressing down on it with an inverted glass or by a push of a button.

The water temperature in the wash sink and rinse (or middle) sink should be maintained at a minimum 110° F (43° C). Detergent package instructions should be carefully followed with reference to water/detergent ratios in the wash sink. It is a good idea to use a nonfat detergent, as it allows the same wash water to be used for beer glasses, which must be kept completely free of grease or fat. The rinse water in the middle sink should be frequently changed. The sanitizing solution instructions concerning the water/sanitizer ratio must also be carefully followed, as too little solution will not do the proper sanitizing job, and too much may create a film on the glasses.

Also available today for busier bars are glass-washing machines that use very hot water for sanitizing. Some health departments require their use, even though they can be noisy. Some are under-the-counter machines operated by the bartender. Others are through-the-counter models into which the servers put the dirty glasses, which are then removed by the bartender after they have been washed.

If glasses need to be dried, they should be drip dried on a drainboard or some sort of perforated or corrugated mat. If they are dried on a smooth surface or a towel, there will be no air circulation and bacteria can multiply.

For sanitary reasons all beverage employees must be trained in proper glassware handling. Their fingers should never touch the rim or the inside of the glass and should be used only to grasp the outside of glasses well below the lip.

THE BACK BAR

The back bar is the part of the bar that is behind the bartenders and in full view of the customers seated at the front bar. The bottom part of the back bar contains refrigerated cabinets (for example, for beer and other bottled or containerized items such as white wine, juices, and mixes). These cabinets may also contain fruits, cream, eggs, condiments, and other perishables that need to be refrigerated. Shelves above these cabinets display the premium brands of liquor and other less frequently used liquors and liqueurs. The top of the cabinet section and the shelves above it may also be used for storing glassware. Other glassware (and bottles) may be stored on shelves above the front bar's serving counter.

The back bar is also normally used for storing items such as bar towels, napkins, straws, stir sticks, picks, matches, and any other similar items. Equipment that cannot be stored on the front bar will also be on the back bar; examples are a frozen-drink dispenser and a glass chiller/froster.

Frozen-Drink Dispenser

Some bars need a frozen-drink dispenser, which is similar to a soft-ice cream machine. It freezes large quantities of premixed frozen drinks (such as Margaritas) to a slush in a few minutes and then dispenses them one by one as required.

Glass Chiller/Froster

Cocktail glasses or beer mugs that need to be chilled and be given a frosted surface are placed in a special machine known as a glass chiller or froster. The glasses are rapidly chilled and take on a frosty appearance. The same effect can be achieved by putting wet glasses for a time in the freezer.

OTHER EQUIPMENT

Some of the other equipment and tools that most bars need to have are illustrated in Figure 15-4 and are discussed in the following sections.

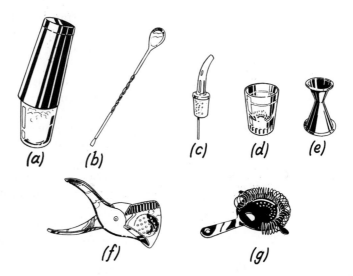

Figure 15-4 Small bartending tools: (a) hand shaker (mixing cup and mixing glass), (b) spoon, (c) pourer, (d) shot glass, (e) jigger, (f) fruit squeezer, and (g) strainer.

Hand Shaker

The hand shaker has two parts: a stainless steel shaker (also known as a mixing cup or mixing steel) and a mixing glass—a heavy, sixteen-ounce glass container that fits on top of the stainless steel shaker, which is used to shake drinks mixed with ice, fruit juice, sugar, cream, eggs, or other ingredients. The mixing glass is also used for stirring liquors with ice and other ingredients, as required for drinks such as the Martini or Manhattan.

Mixer/Blender

Bars usually need a mixer, which is similar to a milk shake machine. Indeed, it is sometimes known as a shake mixer. It serves as a mechanical substitute for hand shaking cocktails and is used primarily for drinks containing fruit juices, sugar, cream, eggs, and similar items that do not blend easily (even with hand shaking) with distilled spirits.

The blender is similar to the mixer except that it has blades for grinding ice and solid food items such as bananas for a Banana Daiquiri.

Small Equipment

Most bars need a number of small hand tools or equipment, such as the following:

Bar strainer—A round metal strainer with a wire spring around it and a handle on the end. The spring fits on top of the stainless steel shaker for straining hand-shaken drinks before they are poured into a drinking glass.

Bar spoon—A teaspoon-sized spoon with a long handle with a knob on the end used for stirring drinks in a mixing glass before pouring them into a drinking glass.

Pourers—Devices that fit into the neck of an opened bottle of liquor and allow drinks to be poured smoothly. Different types allow different pouring speeds. The "cork" may be made of cork or plastic. Sometimes the plastic corks are color coded for quick identification.

Jiggers/shot glasses—Glasses used for measuring a specific amount of a poured drink.

Fruit squeezer—A device used to squeeze oranges or lemons and to strain the desired liquid away from the unwanted pulp and seeds.

Other items used by most bars are ice scoops, ice tongs, bottle openers, corkscrews, funnels, cutting boards, bar (paring) knives, relish forks, zesters (for cutting the rind or zest of oranges and lemons), and serving trays.

ICE MACHINE

An ice-making machine is a necessity in most bars. Because it can be noisy and take up a lot of valuable space, it is sometimes located away from the bar in a nearby but easily accessible area. The type and size of machine used depends on the volume of business, the type of ice required (for example, cubed or flaked), and the types of drinks and glassware used. Sometimes two ice machines are required to produce two different types of ice. Even though the machines can be adjusted for ice size, they can produce only one type of ice at a time. Crushed or cracked ice is made by running cubed ice through an ice crusher. Shaved or flaked ice is not used in most cocktails because it melts too fast, but it is needed in frozen drinks and for white wine bottles chilled in wine buckets. The amount of ice required by a bar depends on its glass sizes, cube shapes and sizes, the amount of ice in the glass, and the number of drinks served per day.

Note that larger cubes melt more slowly but that smaller cubes stack better in the glass and therefore require less juice or mixer. Round cubes fit better in the glass, but rectangular cubes stack better than round ones do and also require less juice or mixer.

Ice machine sizes generally refer to the number of pounds of ice they can produce in twenty-four hours. For example, if a bar on average serves five hundred drinks per day in eight-ounce highball glasses , each of which contains three ice cubes and totals four ounces, then $500 \times 4 = 2,000$ ounces of ice per day that will be needed. This requires a *minimum* machine capacity of $2,000/16 = 125$ pounds. However, note that the surrounding air temperature can affect production capacity, and so it is always wise to buy a machine with a somewhat higher ice capacity than might be needed on the busiest day.

SALES REGISTERS

Rare is the beverage operation today that does not have a sales register. In some cases there will be one register on a pivot on the bar that can be used by both bartenders and table servers to record sales. In other cases the bartender will have a register just for sales at the bar counter, and one or more registers will be located elsewhere convenient to the table servers.

Most beverage operations today use precheck or preset–precheck registers for sales control. In some operations these registers are connected to automatic liquor-dispensing devices, for added sales control. The pros and cons of these items of equipment will be discussed in Chapter 19.

DRAFT BEER REQUIREMENTS

Most beverage operations today serve draft beer, which requires special storage and dispensing equipment, discussed in Chapter 11. In addition, note that some bars (usually those that sell little beer) store their beer in an underbar beer box (or tap box) that holds only one or two kegs.

WINE

Bars that serve wine need little more than wineglasses and proper wine storage areas, as well as a supply of ice buckets for serving full bottles of white or sparkling wine. As mentioned, ice buckets should be filled with shaved rather than cubed ice.

Today some beverage operations do a large volume of sales of wine by the glass, half-carafe, or carafe. To dispense such volumes they buy wine in large containers, and to prevent the unused wine's spoiling, they use machines that force out the wine under pressure. That is, nitrogen replaces the air that would otherwise remain in the bottle. Unlike oxygen, nitrogen does not react with the wine, and thus the wine does not spoil. Some wine-dispensing equipment automatically measures out a glass, half-carafe, or carafe of wine and keeps a sales record of each measure sold.

SANITATION

Needless to say, in all areas of a beverage operation, sanitation is important—for food and beverage supplies, glassware, all small and large equipment, cupboards, counters, sinks, and tables. The need for cleanliness at all times cannot be stressed too much.

DISCUSSION QUESTIONS

1. List the three major items of equipment found in the underbar, and briefly describe each.
2. Explain what a handgun is and how it operates.
3. Differentiate between pre- and postmix soft drinks (carbonated beverages) and explain the pros and cons of each.
4. Discuss the pros and cons of using bottled soft drinks (carbonated beverages).
5. Discuss a typical bar's requirements for glass washing, with particular reference to sanitation, and describe the two types of glass-washing machines that are available.

6. Why should glasses that need to be dried be drip dried on a perforated mat?
7. Explain what a back bar is used for.
8. Explain what a frozen-drink dispenser is and what it is used for.
9. Explain what a glass chiller/froster is and what it is used for.
10. Describe a hand shaker.
11. How does a blender differ from a mixer?
12. Briefly describe a bar strainer, bar spoon, and fruit squeezer and what each is used for.
13. What must be considered when selecting an ice machine?
14. How does a bar determine how much ice it will need per day?
15. Why should shaved ice (rather than cubed ice) be used in wine ice buckets?

16

Beverage Purchasing, Ordering, and Receiving

CHAPTER OBJECTIVES

After studying this chapter the reader should be able to

- Differentiate and discuss control or monopoly situations and license or open situations.
- Discuss the problem of kickbacks in purchasing.
- Discuss the pros and cons of having only one or two suppliers versus having many suppliers and list some of the factors to consider, other than price, in selecting suppliers.
- Differentiate between well or house liquor and premium or call liquor.
- Calculate the cost per ounce of liquor and explain why this is necessary.
- Discuss the problem of determining which products to carry and how much to order of each and describe a purchase order form and its purposes.
- List the factors to consider in purchasing nonalcoholic bar supplies.
- Describe how alcoholic beverages are received, what a receiving stamp is, and how it is used in control.
- Explain why cases of liquor should be marked with their date of receipt.
- List the control steps necessary before invoices are paid.
- Explain how a bar operator can take advantage of a supplier's invoicing practices.
- Solve problems concerning purchase discounts.

For most bar operations, purchasing alcoholic beverages is not as big a problem as buying food items can be for a restaurant. Beverage purchasing is simpler because it is easy to find out the brands that customers like to drink. Furthermore, alcoholic beverage purchases can be relatively easy to control because these beverages are usually purchased in sealed cases or bottles that are easy to count. In addition, the product quality is consistent from one purchase to the next for a particular type or brand of beverage. Finally, because most beverages have a fairly long shelf life (except for keg beer), they can be bought periodically rather than daily.

CONTROL OF DISTRIBUTION

In most jurisdictions the government is the sole wholesaler/distributor of alcoholic beverages and thus controls the prices, with few opportunities (if any) for "sales." If the government is the sole supplier, it may also regulate the liquor-ordering and invoice-paying procedures. In the United States, those states that control the distribution of liquor are known as *control* or *monopoly states;* the others are known as *license* or *open states.* In most Canadian provinces, the government also has a monopoly (or control) on the distribution of alcoholic beverages.

Monopoly Situations

In control situations there is generally only one price for each product, and so the bar manager cannot shop around for lower prices, with the result that the product usually costs more than in license situations. There may also be a smaller selection of brands, as the government monopoly usually carries only products that sell well, and may be less responsive to purchasers' needs, although some monopoly governments will bring in specialty products for a purchaser if the purchaser is willing to buy them in a specified minimum number of case lots.

In control situations the government also normally requires purchasers to pay in cash, or by certified check, at the time of pickup, as well as to arrange and pay for their own pickup and delivery.

Competitive Situations

Even in competitive (license) situations, most distributors still have exclusive distributorships for their products. Most license states in the United States publish monthly a list of the names of their wholesalers, including the products they carry and the prices they charge. Many states impose wholesale and retail price controls. But local laws sometimes override state laws, and the regulations for beer and wine sometimes differ from those for distilled spirits. Some manufacturers—for example, breweries—have their own distribution networks and do not sell through other wholesalers or distributors. Some wholesalers and distributors handle the products of many manufacturers and vintners, and some importers handle products from many different countries.

In license situations, because of competition, prices may be lower, but not necessarily on all items. For example, some manufacturers grant exclusive distribution rights for some products to a particular seller, who then will have no competition. Also, in a competitive situation, the sellers may be reluctant to compete on the prices of products that a bar must stock. These "must stock" items are the heavily advertised brands; that is, the consumer dictates in most cases what a bar will carry, and so the suppliers can maintain prices even in a competitive situation. Suppliers thus compete only on the discretionary products that a bar may wish to carry, or through discounts or other inducements not allowed in government-controlled jurisdictions.

In license situations, reputable bar operators also have access to supplier credit and thus are allowed to pay the invoice by a certain date. In many jurisdictions, if the invoice is not paid by that date, the supplier is required to advise the licensing authorities, who can prevent the operator from making further purchases until the bill is paid.

Familiarity with Local Situation

The alcoholic beverage purchaser must be familiar with all the necessary legal requirements and distribution channels in the jurisdiction where the establishment is located. Even if the government is the sole supplier, importers, wholesalers, and dealers, or their agents or sales representatives, may try to influence purchasers to buy their products through their government supplier.

In addition, suppliers will be anxious to tell purchasers about any new products they have or (when allowed) any discounts or other purchase incentives they are offering. But purchasers must watch out for discounted wines and beers that may have reached the limit of their freshness. Suppliers may also advise about local or regional drinking trends.

The number of such people with whom a purchaser must deal depends in large part on the number of products the establishment wishes to carry. In any case, regardless of the number, it is a good idea to have suppliers visit only during fixed hours on a specified day each week. Otherwise, purchasers will have constant interruptions.

PURCHASING

When there is a choice of suppliers, the purchaser must determine the number of purchase sources to deal with. If orders are given to only a few suppliers, this will mean larger orders and thus may make the purchaser a more important customer. In recognition, the supplier may offer lower prices and/or better services. But if the purchaser decides to use several suppliers, this may force them to compete harder, although on some products, as mentioned earlier, they may be reluctant to do so. A purchaser may order each product from a different supplier simply because that supplier currently has the lowest price for that item and meets the quality standards desired. The alternative is to order all products from a single supplier who, even though the cost of one or two products may be higher, provides the lowest overall cost on all products. Because this approach simplifies purchasing, ordering, receiving, storing, and invoicing, it is recommended. But unfortunately, most bar operators and/or purchasers do not use it because they think about their purchasing only on a product-by-product basis.

Weekly Purchasing

Purchasers should also try to streamline their purchasing routine and make purchase orders only once a week, to reduce the demands on their time and the possibility of errors and to simplify paperwork and bookkeeping. In a small independent bar the owner should do the purchasing himself or herself, as it is a key element in cost control. If it is delegated, the owner/operator should be alert to any supplier/purchaser kickbacks or bribes.

Kickbacks

Kickbacks may be cash or merchandise given to a purchaser who favors a supplier or agent, even when liquor must be purchased from a government outlet. Or a supplier may sell to the purchaser directly but inflate the prices, include items on the invoice that were not actually delivered, or substitute low-quality products but charge for higher-quality products. The "savings" to the supplier are then split with the purchaser.

These kinds of kickbacks can be spotted through effective management supervision. The manager should watch for a supplier whose products seem to be favored by the purchaser. The best protection is to ensure that the purchasing and receiving functions are separated and that proper receiving controls are implemented and practiced. (Receiving will be discussed later in this chapter.)

Supplier Services

In some jurisdictions, liquor, wine, and beer producers may offer certain useful services such as supplying an operator with blank purchase orders, bin cards, and other control forms (the use of some of these forms will be discussed later). These "free" forms can save an operator money, as they help control the purchase, storage, and use of alcoholic beverages. In some cases a wine supplier may also help create wine menus or lists, train wine service employees, and provide sales and promotion suggestions.

A beverage operator should not, however, be unnecessarily influenced to favor a particular producer or supplier. Instead, the purchaser should buy the products that, at a reasonable price, will also satisfy the bar's customers. Local governments may also determine the suppliers' services and the distributors' credit terms.

Other Supplier Considerations

Other questions or considerations in purchasing are the following:

1. What is the frequency of delivery? A supplier who is prepared to deliver daily, even though orders are placed less frequently, is valuable, because an operator can carry less in inventory and obtain needed supplies in an emergency.
2. How large is the variety of products offered by that supplier? A supplier with a large and varied inventory is of more use to an operator than is one with a limited inventory.
3. For beer, does the supplier have a refrigerated warehouse and delivery vehicles? It may be wise to visit the supplier's warehouse to check how beer and wine are stored (for example, are corked wine bottles stored on their sides?).
4. Where is the supplier located? If the supplier is far from the beverage operation, how will this affect delivery times, travel time, and weather affecting the products' quality?
5. Does the supplier offer other bar supplies such as carbonated drinks and drink mixes?
6. What are the minimum quantities that must be ordered at any one time?
7. What are the supplier's credit terms?
8. Is the supplier's representative an order taker or a salesperson? An order taker simply processes the order, but a salesperson offers advice about the products.
9. Does the supplier deliver as promised? Undelivered products may mean lost profits.

Premium and Nonpremium Liquor

The principal decision when purchasing liquor concerns the premium and nonpremium liquor brands to be carried. Most bars serve a house brand (sometimes known as well liquor) that they use when a customer does not specify a particular brand but merely the type of drink desired (for example, a scotch). Premium, or call, liquor refers to specific brand names, such as Chivas Regal scotch.

Well Liquor

In most cases, well liquors are the largest-selling types of liquor (rye, gin, rum, scotch, vodka, and bourbon) in the typical beverage operation. They usually provide the best (lowest) cost to the operator and thus to the customer. Customers order well liquors because they are less expensive. Also, because they often are served with other ingredients such as a soft drink or other mixer, the consumer probably will not notice the difference. Nonetheless, some brands are just not acceptable, and a purchaser should not purchase Rotgut Rum just because it is ten cents a bottle less than better brands. When the government controls the purchase and distribution of liquor, such unacceptable brands are probably less likely to be available. For the bar that offers a slightly higher quality of liquor for a slightly higher price, the cost per drink will not be that much more. For example, consider two well liquors, one costing $10 and the other $9 a bottle, from which an operator can obtain thirty-five drinks. For the $10 bottle the cost per drink is $0.2857, and for the $9 bottle, $0.2571. The difference is less than three cents a drink!

Call Liquor

There is less control over cost in regard to premium or call liquor, as premium brands often are available only from one distributor, who can thus charge whatever the market will bear. And bar customers expect to pay more for premium brands.

A rule of thumb with call liquors—which also applies to liqueurs—is that if they sell, they should be carried in inventory, otherwise not. An inventory of unsold call liquors and liqueurs is money not earning any income. One good inventory-operating rule is never to add a new product without removing an old one. Call liquor that is not moving might be sold as house or well liquor. In this way, even if it costs a little more than the usual well liquor, money from dead inventory will be recovered.

It is impossible for most bars to offer every liquor available on the market, and so sometimes an operator will be asked for brands not carried.

The best that can be done is to suggest to the customer the closest alternative available. By offering an alternative—but not substituting it without first asking the customer—an operator will probably keep his or her patronage.

An operator should invest in liqueurs and some less-common distilled spirits only if he or she is sure that customers want them.

One bar marketing device is to limit the number of brands carried and to print a list of the brands offered. Which brands to carry depends on the type of bar, volume of business, type of clientele, cash available for investment in inventory, and changes in customer preferences over time.

Cost per Ounce

In some jurisdictions, quantity discounts (for example, for case lots) may be available, but in other jurisdictions such discounts may be illegal or be allowed only if the bill is paid within a certain number of days. Or a purchaser may have to pay a premium over the list price if ordering less than a full case.

Regardless of the situation (discount, list, or premium price), a good costing approach is to convert all prices to a per-ounce cost before making the final purchase decision. This allows easier comparison between brands and between different container sizes. Generally, the larger the container is, the lower the cost per ounce will be. Cost per ounce may not be the only factor. Consider also the volume of business and the value of having a container size that is convenient for pouring. Also, the quantity that an operator is required to buy to earn a discount may mean investing in inventory that may not be used up for several months or longer. The purchaser should therefore weigh the resulting loss of interest on this money.

Metric Equivalents

It may be necessary to convert metric containers to an equivalent ounce size. See Table 16-1 for a guide to distilled spirits and Table 16-2 for a guide to wine bottles.

ORDERING

The typical bar will probably order liquor, beer, and wine on a weekly basis. The biggest decision then is how much to order. For items used in quantity, about ten days' supply should be on hand after each order is received. In such cases, quantities are usually ordered in case lots. Slow-moving items may be ordered in multiples of bottles, unless the supplier refuses to sell

Table 16-1   Conversion table for distilled spirits.

Metric Size	Ounce Equivalent	
	United States	Canada
1.75 liters	59.2	61.6
1 liter	33.8	35.2
750 milliliters	25.4	26.4
500 milliliters	16.9	17.6
200 milliliters	6.8	7.0
50 milliliters	1.7	1.8

partial cases, in which situation an operator may have to order a case of an item that may take a year to sell.

The supplier may be willing to sell a split case, or a case of several different brands making up a full case of, say, twelve bottles. In such situations an operator may or may not be charged the case price.

How Much to Order?

One problem in beverage purchase control is knowing (without having to take a physical inventory) how much of each product to purchase to carry the bar through until the next order date. One of the easiest solutions is to use a system of perpetual inventory cards. From each card (one for each type and size of product carried in stock), one can quickly read what is on hand at any time. Because each card may also list the maximum quantity that is normally carried of that product, the order quantity will be the

Table 16-2   Conversion table for wine bottles.

Metric Size	Ounce Equivalent	
	United States	Canada
4 liters	134.8	140.8
3 liters	101.0	105.6
1.5 liters	50.7	52.8
1 liter	33.8	35.2
750 milliliters	25.4	26.4
375 milliliters	12.7	13.2
187 milliliters	6.3	6.6
100 milliliters	3.4	3.5

amount that increases the current stock to the maximum level, allowing, if necessary, a safety margin for any time delay between ordering and receiving the goods. (Perpetual inventory cards will be discussed in more detail in Chapter 17.)

When establishing stock and reorder levels, the consumption rate of the item and the time lag between ordering and delivery should be considered. For example, suppose a beverage operation that is open seven days a week normally uses twenty-one bottles of a certain liquor a week (three a day) and reorders once a week. Normally, therefore, twenty-one bottles would be ordered each time. However, a safety or minimum level of six bottles for that item has been established, and therefore, the maximum stock would be twenty-seven bottles. If on a particular order day nine bottles are in stock and two days are required for delivery, then twenty-four bottles should be ordered.

Who Orders?

In a small bar, the owner/manager will probably purchase and order the beverages. In a larger operation, particularly one associated with a restaurant or hotel, one person is usually assigned to purchase food and beverages. Regardless, the person who does the purchasing must be familiar with alcoholic brands and types.

For most bars, the greatest consumption will be of the lower-priced brands (the house brands). The quantity of each to be carried will depend on such factors as frequency of ordering, volume of business, and season of the year. Specifications (detailed descriptions of quality required) are generally not necessary for a particular beverage, as there may be only one vendor or agent. In fact, both the quality and the price of most beverages remain constant from one purchase to the next. However, the purchaser should be aware of any quantity discounts or sale items.

Order Form

When ordering a large variety of items, a purchase order form is useful, as it helps the person responsible for receiving to know what is to be delivered from each supplier, and at what prices (see Figure 16-1). An order form

1. Provides the receiver with data for checking deliveries.
2. Provides the accountant with data for checking invoices.
3. Minimizes uncertainty and/or misunderstanding between bar operator and supplier.

Order Date _Dec. 28_		Delivery Date _Dec. 30_				
Supplier	Item	Size	Ordered	Received	Price	Total
H & J	Old Kentucky	1.75 L	36	36	8.10	291.60
H & J	Chivas Regal	1.75 L	12	12	17.50	210.00
Vintage	Kressman red	750 ML	12	12	4.75	57.00

Figure 16-1   Order form.

NONALCOHOLIC BEVERAGES AND OTHER BAR ITEMS

The purchase of nonalcoholic beverages used in a bar usually is similar to that of alcoholic drinks. An additional decision in regard to soft drinks may be whether to purchase them by the can, bottle, or dispensing container. In general, canned and bottled soft drinks offer less profit but more convenience.

Brand Loyalty

Most alcoholic beverage drinkers who are loyal to a particular liquor brand are not as loyal to a soft drink that they might use as a mixer. Thus if various soft-drink brands offer equal quality and customer acceptance, it will pay to shop around for the best price. In some cases an operator may be able to promote certain brands of soft drink to be used in the bar and obtain as a result a discount from the supplier.

Generally, the quality and price of soft drinks, as is the case with liquor, go hand in hand—the higher the price is, the higher the quality will be. For example, a less expensive soft drink may mean that the flavoring is artificial and/or that it will not hold its carbon dioxide for as long once the container is opened.

Dispensing Equipment

In some cases the soft drink supplier may agree to install soft drink–dispensing equipment free as long as the operator uses the supplier's particular brands of soft drink. There is nothing wrong with this as long as the quality is what is desired and what customers expect and the price paid for the product is reasonable, considering that "free" equipment is being used.

In some cases, if the equipment is not offered free, an operator may be allowed to purchase the equipment on an installment basis, with the cost of the equipment added to the cost of the soft drink products.

Whenever such an arrangement for the use of equipment is made, one should determine how well the distributor will maintain the equipment, as well as his or her delivery schedule, ordering procedures, and minimum order requirements. Sometimes the choice of suppliers is determined by the services offered. Some suppliers also provide free straws, stirrers, coasters, and similar items, sometimes containing their advertising logo. It is a question of management policy whether to accept this form of supplier advertising.

Ordering

Ordering and delivering nonalcoholic beverages are sometimes easier than for alcoholic drinks, because one is not dealing with a government agency that dictates its policies and procedures. For the same reason an operator will probably have more freedom with regard to credit terms and methods of payment.

The main decision is how much to order. Generally, for soft drinks, three to five days' supply is adequate, although some perishable products, such as milk or cream, should be ordered daily.

Most establishments do not control too strictly the purchase and use of nonalcoholic beverages, as this may cost more than any savings gained. Also, employees are often permitted to drink these items for free (a good idea if it stops them from drinking the establishment's alcoholic beverages!). However, one important consideration is to ensure that any deposits paid on returnable empty containers are properly accounted for so that money is not lost from empty containers not returned to the supplier for credit.

Other Bar Supplies

Most bars must also buy other supplies such as napkins, stir sticks, limes, lemons, oranges, cocktail onions, olives, and maraschino cherries. These are commonly available from many suppliers and, if the law allows, may be offered by alcoholic beverage suppliers at a very reasonable price (because the supplier can obtain a quantity discount price that might not be available from the local grocery) or at little or no profit, in order to retain the establishment's business.

The important thing to consider when purchasing perishables (milk, cream, fresh fruit) is deterioration. Buy as frequently as is practical to avoid loss from spoilage. Even nonperishables such as unopened containers of olives, cherries, and cocktail onions will not remain fresh long once the container is opened. Thus, buying large containers may reduce the cost per item of these products, but the saving will disappear if half the contents have to be thrown away before the container is empty.

RECEIVING

Because alcoholic beverages are apt to "evaporate" or be removed if left unattended, it is important that the person responsible for receiving and storing them be present at the time of delivery. At the point of receiving, the responsibility for ownership moves from the supplier to the purchaser.

In a small operation, the manager should do the receiving, or this task should be delegated to a responsible individual. The receiver should not be the same person who does the ordering.

Suppliers should provide invoices with each shipment of items, as without an invoice it is difficult for the receiver to check all the details. If an invoice is not received, a "dummy" or memorandum invoice should be prepared, listing the quantities actually delivered and their prices. This dummy invoice can later be matched with the supplier's actual invoice.

Receiving Steps

Several routine steps should be followed when receiving goods:

1. Check that the brands, quantities, and sizes received agree with those listed on the order form (if one is being used) and with those on the delivery slip or invoice. This means counting bottles or containers. If items are delivered in cases, it may be advisable to open sealed cases to ensure that they are not missing any bottles or that the case weight agrees with that printed on it. A short weight may indicate that a bottle or more is missing or is broken and leaking. If bottles are supposed to be sealed, the receiver should spot check them to ensure that no seals are broken or missing.

2. Make sure that the invoice prices agree with the quoted prices or the prices recorded on the order form. Because goods are paid for according to what appears on the invoices, this is the time to ensure that the invoice is correct in regard to quantities received and prices charged.

3. Verify that the quality of the product is acceptable (proof of liquor, vintage of wines, freshness of keg beer). In the case of wines, if the establishment is large enough to have a wine steward, that person could be asked to verify wine quality.

4. If any containers are broken, items are missing, or items are received that were not ordered, are not of acceptable quality, or are the wrong sizes

or brands, a credit memorandum should be prepared, as shown in Figure 16-2. This memorandum should explain why it has been prepared and should be signed by the delivery driver so that there is proof that the items were returned. If it is prepared in duplicate, one copy can go back to the supplier, the other copy remaining with the establishment to ensure that proper credit is received from the supplier. Never accept a short shipment of goods without completing a credit memorandum. An alternative to using a credit memorandum form is to make a note on the invoice and have the delivery driver sign that.

5. Once all receiving checks have been completed, the receiver should sign the supplier's copy of the invoice, and the establishment's copy of each invoice (or dummy) should be stamped with the receiving stamp (see Figure 16-3), and the stamp initialed in the appropriate places. Finally, the beverages should be immediately moved to the locked beverage storeroom or, in the case of keg beer, to locked refrigerated areas. If there is a storekeeper separate from the receiver, he or she may need to go through the same checks for quantities before signing and accepting responsibility for the goods to be put into the storeroom.

6. It is a good idea to mark the date of receipt on each case, to help ensure proper stock rotation.

7. The order form, invoices, and credit memos should then be forwarded to the person who does the bookkeeping or accounting.

A problem may arise in receiving when a supplier offers a discount in the form of a full bottle. That is, instead of offering a $10 discount off the total case price, the supplier delivers an extra bottle worth $10 (although the cost to the supplier is probably less than $10). But this extra bottle may not be recorded on the invoice, and a dishonest receiver—or bartender who does the receiving—may remove that extra bottle for personal use or,

Supplier _Vintage Imports_ Date _Sept. 4_			
Please issue a credit memorandum for the following:			
Quantity	Item Description	Unit Cost	Total
2 L	Haut Villages	7.10	14.20
Reason for request for credit:			
Bottles broken			
Delivery driver's signature _____			

Figure 16-2   Credit memorandum.

```
┌─────────────────────────────────────────────────────────────┐
│ Date received _____ │
│ Quantity checked by _____ │
│ Quality checked by _____ │
│ Prices checked by _____ │
│ Listed on receiving report by _____ │
└─────────────────────────────────────────────────────────────┘
```

Figure 16-3   Receiving stamp.

in the case of a bartender, sell its contents at the bar, not record the sales, and pocket the money. In such situations it is management's responsibility to ensure that when bottle discounts are given, these extra bottles received are recorded on the invoices.

Beverage-receiving Report

The final step in receiving beverages is the preparation, from invoices, of a weekly beverage receiving report (see Figure 16-4). In a busy bar operation with daily deliveries, this form may need to be completed and closed off daily, with daily totals transferred each weekend to a summary form (one line for each day), as illustrated in Figure 16-5.

Note that on the receiving reports illustrated in Figures 16-4 and 16-5, purchases are broken down into three categories: liquor, beer, and wine.

Week ending March 9				
Supplier	Liquor	Wine	Beer	Invoice Total
Atlantic Brewers			$214.60	$214.60
Vintage Imports		$125.40		125.40
H & J Agency	$375.48	75.90		451.38
Totals	$375.48	$201.30	$214.60	$791.38

Figure 16-4   Weekly beverage-receiving report.

Week ending March 9				
Date	Liquor	Wine	Beer	Total
March 5	$ 114.10	$213.10	$ 72.35	$ 399.55
6	893.21		315.95	1,209.16
7	132.18	128.06	371.60	631.84
Totals	$1,321.10	$782.16	$1,851.40	$3,954.66

Figure 16-5   Weekly beverage-receiving summary form.

The reason for this is that because the markup (that is, the selling price versus the cost price) for each category is generally quite different, distortions, false assumptions, and erroneous decisions could result if the purchases are not analyzed by category. (This problem is discussed in more depth in Chapter 19.)

Nonalcoholic Beverages

It may also be desirable to record nonalcoholic beverages on the receiving report, on an extra column. In addition, if the establishment is large enough, it may be a good idea to expand this receiving report to include columns for supplies (cleaning, paper, and the like), glassware, and similar items that are purchased fairly frequently and for which it might be advantageous to have a written receiving record.

Invoices

Before any invoices are paid, the bookkeeper should make sure that they match up with the goods received. This is usually done when the goods are received. All arithmetic should be verified, including checking any extensions (quantity of item times item purchase cost) and additions of invoices. All invoices should be paid by check. As each invoice is paid, the check number and date should be written on it so that it will not be paid again. Suppliers sometimes send in, accidentally or otherwise, a second invoice, and the accounts payable system should make sure that this second invoice is not inadvertently paid. This can be done by stapling invoices to be paid to the related receiving report.

A beverage operation manager who does not do the receiving himself or herself should watch for false invoices: A dishonest purchaser may set up a dummy company and make out fictitious invoices for goods never actually purchased.

PAYING FOR PURCHASES

Whenever possible, the purchaser should take advantage of the supplier's billing practices. Most suppliers (other than government agencies) supply beverages as required during each month and, within a few days of the month's end, mail out a statement.

Suppose that a month's supply of inventory is purchased from a supplier at the beginning of each month, using the items as required during the month, and that the terms of the supplier's statement are 2/10, net 30. In other words, there will be a 2 percent discount off the total month's purchases if the statement is paid within ten days of the end of the month; otherwise, the statement is payable within thirty days without discount. The establishment thus can use the supplier's credit for forty days if the discount is taken, otherwise for sixty days. This "free" money can be used to advantage.

On the other hand, suppose that purchases are made from the same supplier but that at the end of each month enough inventory is bought to carry through until the end of the next month. In this case the use of the "free" money is for only ten days if the discount is taken, and otherwise only for thirty days. These two cases are extreme, but they do point out that a wise purchaser can take advantage of a supplier's billing practices in order to increase net profit. Consider the following: A beverage operation makes a $1,000 purchase and the terms are 2/10, net 60. On a $1,000 purchase paid within ten days, this would save $20. This may not seem like a lot of money, but when multiplied many times over on all similar purchases made during a year, it could amount to a large sum. However, in the example cited, the business might have to borrow the money ($980) in order to make the payment within ten days. Let us assume the money were borrowed for fifty days (sixty days less ten days) at 8 percent interest. The interest expense on this borrowed money would be

$$(\$980 \times 50 \text{ days} \times 8\%)/365 = \$10.74$$

In this case, it would be advantageous to borrow the money, because the difference between the discount saving of $20.00 and the interest expense of $10.74 still would provide a saving of $9.26.

DISCUSSION QUESTIONS

1. Discuss the difference between a control or monopoly situation and a license or open situation.
2. In an open situation in which there are several suppliers for the same products, why may there be no pricing competition?
3. Discuss the pros and cons of having only one or two suppliers versus having many suppliers.
4. Explain how kickbacks can occur in liquor purchasing and how they can be controlled.
5. List five factors to consider (other than price) when deciding whether to use a particular supplier.
6. Differentiate between well or house liquor and premium or call liquor.
7. Why is it useful to price liquor products on a cost-per-ounce basis?
8. List two other factors that a purchaser might want to consider, other than cost, when deciding to buy a particular product.
9. What factors determine the quantity of each type or brand of liquor to be carried?
10. What column headings are needed on a liquor order form, and what three purposes does this form serve?
11. Why might it not be a good idea to buy low-cost carbonated beverages (soft drinks)?
12. What factors need to be considered when buying fresh products (for example, dairy products and fruit) for a bar?
13. What items should be checked when alcoholic beverages are received?
14. Discuss how a credit memorandum is used in the receiving process.
15. List the five items that are to be completed on a receiving stamp.
16. Why is it a good idea to mark on the packing cases the date on which the goods were received?
17. On the beverage-receiving report, why should purchases be separated into liquor, beer, and wine?
18. Explain the difference between a weekly beverage-receiving report and a weekly beverage-receiving summary form.
19. List the procedures for paying invoices.
20. Explain how a bar manager can take advantage of a supplier's invoicing practices.

PROBLEMS

1. Calculate the cost per ounce for each of the following:

U.S. Bottle Size	Bottle Cost
a. 1.75 liters	$21.48
b. 1 liter	$18.22
c. 750 milliliters	$12.96

2. For each of the following, calculate the quantity of each item to be ordered:

Item	Consumption Rate	Ordering Frequency	Safety Level	Current Stock	Delivery Time
a.	14 per week	every 2 weeks	3	6	2 days
b.	7 per week	weekly	1	1	1 day
c.	10 cases per month	monthly	1 case	3 cases	1 week

    Note that item c can be ordered only in full cases.

3. You have made a purchase costing $500. The supplier's terms are 2/10, net 60. Assume that to take advantage of the discount you were to borrow the money from the bank at 10 percent on the day the invoice is to be paid. You would repay the bank thirty days later. Would you take advantage of the discount?

4. On June 5, a beverage operation purchased a new item of bar equipment costing $3,200. A 1 percent purchase discount is offered by the supplier if the invoice is paid by June 15; otherwise the invoice is payable in full by July 31. Should the beverage operation borrow the money from the bank at 12 percent interest on June 15 (to be repaid on July 31) to take advantage of the purchase discount? Would your decision change if the amount to be borrowed were only $1,500, the balance coming from the operation's current bank account?

17

Storeroom Control

CHAPTER OBJECTIVES

After studying this chapter the reader should be able to

- Discuss basic storeroom design requirements with particular reference to security.
- Describe how perpetual inventory cards and requisitions aid in storeroom inventory control.
- Describe both the first-in, first-out and last-in, first-out methods of pricing storeroom inventory.
- Explain how "empty-bottle" return control works and under what circumstances a bartender may not be able to conform fully to this practice.
- Define control terms such as *bottle coding* and *par stock*.
- Discuss when and how storeroom inventory should be taken.
- Explain how differences between the actual count of inventory items and perpetual inventory card figures can be tracked down.
- Describe an inventory sheet.
- Describe a storeroom inventory reconciliation form and explain how it is used.
- Define and use the equation for beverage inventory turnover.

There are two main areas for control once products have been received: the storeroom and the bar. After alcoholic beverages and other bar supplies have been received and checked, they should be put into the appropriate storage areas unless they are to be consumed fairly quickly (for example, eggs, fresh fruit, and similar items). All alcoholic beverages and other items in containers (soft drinks) should be put into storage even if some will be used within a day or so. Only in this way can there be complete control over the major products used, not only for reasons of inventory control and security from theft, but also for quality control (for example, proper temperature for wine storage) and proper stock rotation.

BASIC STOREROOM REQUIREMENTS

Storeroom space requirements can vary widely from one bar to another. Beer often requires a great deal of costly space, particularly when related to the revenue it can generate. For example, a case of liquor and a case of beer take up roughly the same amount of space, but the sales from a case of liquor can be as much as twenty times that from a case of beer. And when a great deal of keg or draft beer is served, these space requirements can increase considerably.

The liquor inventory in the storeroom at any one time can amount to several thousand dollars. Liquor is money, and therefore it should be treated like money and with a great deal more security than is often the case in the typical bar. This security begins with good storeroom design. The storeroom should be difficult, if not impossible, for unauthorized persons, and even professional thieves, to enter. Electronic alarm systems may be needed to help prevent unauthorized entry. The storeroom should have no windows. If it has, bricking them up or using steel bars across them—if the local fire code will allow this—may be considered.

To prevent other types of loss (for example, from evaporation or deterioration for wines), the storeroom should be adequately ventilated and the temperature properly controlled. If liquor is ordered once a week—which means the storeroom will usually hold about ten days' supply, the storeroom should be designed to accommodate about two weeks' supply for maximum demand periods.

Shelving

Shelves should be about three feet deep and eighteen inches high, sturdy enough to take the weight of full bottles. If the room is large enough, the center area should be kept free for the temporary storage of deliveries before they are checked and put in their proper storage locations.

When storing case lots, leave some wall area unshelved so that unopened cases can be stacked in columns and rows against the wall. Never leave open cases with bottles in them. When a full case is opened, put all the bottles on shelves. Flatten the cases and then remove them; otherwise it will be easy for unauthorized persons to carry away full bottles in the empty-looking cases. Do not mix stacks of cases of different brands or types, as this can make inventory taking confusing. On the shelves, store major brands of liquor (rye, gin, rum, scotch, vodka, bourbon) in the same area, providing enough space for each brand for the maximum inventory ever needed to be carried. Finally, label the shelves for easy identification of the items on them.

Location

The main beverage storeroom should, if possible, be close to the receiving area. This will decrease the amount of time spent moving products from the receiving area to the storeroom and also will lessen the possibility of losses during the movement of beverages. All beverages should be routed through the storeroom before being distributed to the bar (to allow the use of perpetual inventory cards and requisitions to tighten control of the storeroom).

Keys

Regardless of the number and type of beverage storage areas, only one person should be responsible for and have access to them. For a small bar, this should be the bar owner/manager. For a larger bar, this responsibility may have to be delegated. In either case, storage areas must be kept locked, with the key in the hands of only one person (although for emergencies, there should be backup keys available in a safe location).

The lock should be a deadbolt in a heavy door, and the door must be kept locked when the storekeeper is not present. Employees requiring beverages from the storeroom should not be allowed to enter it and help themselves but, rather, should use a system of requisitions (to be explained later in the chapter). The storeroom lock should be changed periodically in case someone has been able to make a duplicate key. If an employee with a key to the storeroom leaves the establishment's employ without returning that key, the lock should be changed immediately. Or a combination lock could be used whose combination can be changed as frequently as necessary.

Distilled Spirits (Liquor)

The storage of distilled spirits is not a major problem, as little special care is required and shelf life is long. Distilled spirits should be placed in a dry storage room, preferably without direct sunlight or excessive heat.

Once bottled, distilled spirits do not improve or change with age, although they can evaporate if bottles are stored unopened. Any distilled spirits containing sugar (for example, liqueurs) should not be stored for long periods once the bottles have been opened, as they can both evaporate and spoil.

Wine and Beer

Wine and beer require particular care in storage, which was discussed in Chapters 10 and 11.

Deposits

If a deposit is paid on beer bottles and kegs (or any other beverage containers), a system should be established to obtain refunds from the empties—especially for cases of beer, as dishonest employees can easily remove cases of empties and collect the deposit for themselves. Make sure that all empties are returned to the storeroom for proper control and that deposit refunds are collected by the establishment.

PERPETUAL INVENTORY CARDS

Perpetual inventory cards are recommended for all items carried in the beverage storeroom(s). A separate card is required for each type and size of beverage item carried in stock, as shown in Figure 17-1. The In column figures are taken from the invoices delivered with the goods. The figures in the Out column are recorded from the requisitions (to be discussed later in this chapter) prepared and signed by the bartender or bar manager. Obviously, if all In and Out figures are properly recorded on the cards by the person in control of the storeroom, the Balance column figure should agree with the actual count of the items on the shelf. Thus the cards aid in inventory control and also are useful for recording the purchase prices of the various items, thereby allowing the requisitions to be costed out.

Maximum/Minimum Levels

Inventory cards also help ensure that items are not over- or understocked, as they can show the maximum stock to be carried for each individual type or brand and the minimum point to which that stock level can fall before the item needs to be reordered. Without having to count the items on the shelves, the person responsible for purchasing needs only to go through

Item _Chivas Regal_	Supplier _J & H_	Tel. # _432–1981_
Maximum _30_	Supplier _Savory_	Tel. # _436–9181_
Minimum _6_	Supplier _____	Tel. # _____

Date	In	Out	Balance	Requisition Cost Information
March 9			6	$17.10
10	24		30	17.10
11		4	26	17.10
14		6	20	17.10
18		6	14	17.10
20	12		26	14 at $17.10
				12 at 16.85

Figure 17-1   Perpetual inventory card.

the cards once a week, or however frequently it is practical to reorder. At that time, the items for which the balance figure is at or close to the minimum point are listed (for example, on an order form such as that illustrated in Figure 16-1), along with the quantity to be ordered, so as to bring the inventory up to maximum stock, keeping in mind any possible delivery delays.

To assist in contacting suppliers (when there is a choice), the cards can also list the names and telephone numbers of suggested suppliers. And to save on printing costs, consider using standard blank three-by-five (or larger) cards.

REQUISITIONS

Requisitions (sometimes known as issue slips) should be used to allow authorized employees to receive items from the storeroom and to ensure that each bar (if the establishment has several) is correctly charged for its share of liquor costs. A sample requisition is illustrated in Figure 17-2.

Consider having the requisitions preprinted with the descriptions of the items regularly requisitioned. Although this will incur printing costs, it will save time for the bartender. Blank requisitions should be made available,

Department _Main Bar_	Date _Aug. 21_		
Quantity	Item Description	Item Cost	Total
6 L	Old Kentucky	$ 8.10	$ 48.60
3 L	Old South	7.50	22.50
4 L	V.O.	9.60	38.40
5 L	Black Label	13.90	69.50
Total			$382.10
Authorized signature _____			

Figure 17-2   Requisition.

preferably in duplicate, only to those authorized to sign them. The original—listing the items and quantities required—are delivered to the beverage storekeeper. The bartender doing the ordering keeps the duplicates so that quantities received from the storeroom can subsequently be checked. When the stores make deliveries to the bar, the bar manager should sign the original to verify the transfer of the goods and the responsibility for them.

Issues from the main storeroom to the bar should be made only before the bar opens or after it closes, to minimize disruptions to normal bar-operating procedures. Alternatively, issues may be made before or after each shift.

Requisition Costing

Perpetual inventory cards should list the current price of the item in stock: Out column figures are recorded from the requisitions (and the Balance column figure on the card is adjusted), and the price of the item is recorded on the requisition in the Item Cost column.

Frequently, an item in stock may have two or more different delivery dates and prices. In this case, either the first-in, first-out or the last-in, first-out method of inventory pricing should be used.

First-in, First-out (FIFO)

With first-in, first-out (FIFO) pricing, it is assumed that stock is rotated properly (as it should be, regardless of the costing method used) and that the items purchased first are issued first and are issued at the price that was paid for them.

For example, assume that at a particular time five items are on hand, at $10 per item, and a case of twelve more is purchased for $11 each. If six items are then requisitioned, five will be costed on the requisition at $10 and one at $11. The total requisition cost will be $61 (5 × $10 + 1 × $11). Because all the first group of items at $10 have been used up, the $11 price will now be used on requisitions until another shipment arrives at a different price.

In order to use the FIFO pricing method, the related perpetual inventory card must show in the Requisition Cost Information column the number of each item and its price. Alternatively, as the items are received, the price may be written onto the case or, if necessary, onto each bottle. Once costed out, requisitions can later be extended and totaled so that at the end of each accounting period, each bar (in a multibar establishment) will be charged for its proper share of beverage cost.

Issuing to each separate bar blank requisitions of a different color will aid in identifying each bar, and if necessary for control purposes, requisitions can also be numbered. If the establishment has several bars, each requisitioning its own requirements from storage, a specially designed perpetual inventory card may be useful. It may show, for each requisition completed, the particular bar to which the items were transferred. Figure 17-3 illustrates such a perpetual inventory card.

Of course, if the business is large enough to support computerized inventory records, much of the paperwork that would otherwise be required with perpetual inventory cards and requisitions can be handled directly by the computer, including, for example, a daily printout of all items whose level has dropped to the reorder point, and cost information for inventory on hand. Today's microcomputers (commonly called home or personal computers) are remarkably useful even for a small business such as a bar, in helping control inventory and inventory usage.

Last-in, First-out (LIFO)

Another method of perpetual inventory card and requisition costing is last-in, first-out (LIFO), in which the last items received are the first ones issued. In other words, in our example, the six items all would be issued at $11, and the total requisition cost would be $66 (6 × $11). Note that this is $5

		Out						

Date	In	Main Bar	Bar 1	Bar 2	Bar 3	Balance	Requisition Cost Information
March 1	24	6	2		4	12	$17.10
2			2	2	3	5	17.10
3	24	4		2		23	16.85

Item _Chivas Regal_ Supplier _J & H_ Tel. # _432–1981_
Maximum _30_ Supplier _Savory_ Tel. # _436–2732_
Minimum _6_ Supplier _____ Tel. # _____

Figure 17-3 Perpetual inventory card for an establishment with several bars.

more than with FIFO. By the same token, if a value were assigned to the remaining inventory of eleven items, it would be $5 less under LIFO:

$$FIFO: 11 \times \$11 = \$121$$
$$LIFO: (5 \times \$10) + (6 \times \$11) = \$50 + \$66 = \$116$$

Thus the costing and inventory valuation method can affect both the cost assigned to sales made (cost of sales) and inventory value. LIFO is an important method to understand, as many computer costing and inventory programs today use LIFO rather than FIFO or some other method.

OTHER CONTROLS

Other useful storeroom control procedures are discussed next.

Par Stock

As an aid to knowing the quantity of each item to requisition each day, the bar or bars should be given a par stock list, which names the person responsible for requisitioning the quantity of items required to bring the current quantity on hand up to the par, or required, level. Par stock lists are changed when necessary (for example, with a change of season, when customers' drinking habits change, or when bartenders continually run out of a particular brand during a shift).

If the establishment caters to special functions or banquets, greater quantities may be requisitioned than normally required to replenish the listed par stock. The banquet department will then requisition its full-bottle requirements from the bar and, after the function, return to the bar all unopened full bottles, plus any partly used bottles and all empty bottles (Chapter 19 comments further on banquet bar controls).

The par stock lists should be posted at suitable places in the bar. For example, the inside of the door of the beer refrigerator is an ideal place for the beer par stock list.

Full-Bottle Replacement

Even with a par stock list it is not always possible for a bar to replenish its stock each day exactly to the par stock level, as it may still have some partly empty bottles. Therefore, a system of full-bottle requisitioning is often used for each empty bottle that the bartender turns in.

Empty bottles are returned to the storeroom with the requisitions and are then matched up, bottle for bottle, with the full ones. The empty bottles should then be destroyed (unless there is a refundable deposit for them from the supplier) in accordance with local or other laws. The empty bottles should be disposed of to prevent their being returned to the bar by a dishonest bartender who could exchange them again for full bottles. For the same reason, make sure that bartenders are not bringing in their own empty bottles to exchange them for full ones. Coding bottles is one way to make this less likely, along with checking the bar's par stock from time to time. Also check for deviations from normal levels of activity. For example, if the normal daily requisition for gin is five or six bottles and it suddenly jumps to eight or nine, determine whether there is a good explanation.

Some bars require bartenders to requisition a full bottle of liquor for a bottle that is less than half-full, turning in the empty bottle the following day when it is empty. But the extra bookkeeping and control for this may not be worth the effort; it might simply be better to increase by one bottle the par stock for fast-moving brands, to compensate for the half-empty bottle of that brand at the bar.

Bottle Coding

Some establishments issue full bottles only after they have been coded with a difficult-to-duplicate coding device, and in such cases, empty bottles returned for replacement with full ones should be checked to ensure that they have this code. An establishment with more than one bar should use a separate code for each bar.

This control does not, however, prevent a dishonest bartender from bringing in privately purchased bottles, selling the contents, not recording the sales, and pocketing the cash. However, it does reduce that likelihood, as spot control checks by management will show whether all the bottles at the bar have been properly coded. But even with that spot check, be alert to a bartender transferring the contents of a privately purchased bottle to an empty, coded one before selling the contents and keeping the cash.

After the empty bottles have been replaced each day with full ones, the stock at the bar should be at par, adjusted, when necessary, for partly full bottles. This par stock should be checked from time to time immediately after it has been replenished to make sure that the levels are correct.

Full-Bottle Sales

Note that when bars are associated with hotels (or in similar circumstances) that sell full bottles, thereby making it difficult for bartenders to return empties for full bottles, an adjustment must be made to compensate for any such full-bottle sales.

Such an adjustment means that the bar should be issued extra bottles equivalent to those sold as full bottles. Obviously this equivalent number must be supported by sales checks proving that those empty bottles are not available, as they were sold as room service or off-premise full ones.

STOREROOM INVENTORY RECONCILIATION

An important part of storeroom inventory control is ensuring that the invoices for beverages purchased have been properly recorded on the beverage-receiving report. At the end of each control period, each item in inventory should be counted.

Taking Storeroom Inventory

A bar operation usually takes inventory monthly, although it can be taken more frequently if desired, for example, weekly. Indeed it is preferable to take inventory weekly, as that allows better inventory control and also provides inventory information useful for weekly purchasing requirements. Taking inventory is sometimes referred to as taking an actual inventory or taking a physical inventory.

A person other than the person who controls the storeroom should take inventory. In larger operations, it is easier and faster if two people perform this task. One person counts the quantity of each item on the shelves, and the second person verifies that this count agrees with the perpetual inventory card balance figure.

Inventory Differences

If the two figures do not agree, the items should be recounted. If the figures still do not agree, then the figures recorded from invoices and requisitions on the cards should be traced back to the related invoices and requisitions, and the arithmetic of the card balance should be checked. Items whose count does not agree should not be checked during the actual inventory taking, as it will slow down the entire process.

If discrepancies between actual counts and perpetual inventory card figures cannot be resolved, then the card balance figure should be corrected to the actual figure so that the card figure will at least be correct from that point on.

The actual count and the card balance may also differ if deliveries have been made to the storeroom on inventory day but have not yet been recorded on cards, or if invoice information has been recorded on the cards but the items have not yet been put onto storeroom shelves. Similar differences can occur with items requisitioned on inventory-taking day. These possibilities should be checked out and corrected before the inventory is taken.

It is sometimes useful to spot check the perpetual inventory cards between inventory periods (particularly if inventory is taken only once a month, making tracking down differences more difficult). Periodically spot checking each day a few of the major brands means that any errors will be discovered more quickly after they occur.

Inventory Sheets

To speed the inventory taking, the items listed on the perpetual inventory cards and the inventory sheets should be in the same order the items are placed in on the shelves. This will reduce the possibility of missing items and is, obviously, more efficient. A typical partial inventory sheet is illustrated in Figure 17-4.

The inventory sheets should be kept in three sections, one each for liquor, beer, and wine. In this way the inventory value for each of these categories can be totaled up separately. (The importance of keeping separate these three category costs and their related sales revenue is discussed in Chapter 19.)

When costing items on the inventory sheets, make sure that the cost recorded is for the correct size of bottle. And cost figures must be recorded consistently. That is, if FIFO is being used for costing requisitions, it should also be used for costing inventory. One should not switch back and forth from one method to the other.

If the storekeeper is also the same person who completes the perpetual

Period ending Jan. 31				
Item	Size	Quantity	Item Cost	Total Value
Ballantine	L	21	$ 7.10	$149.10
Bell	L	8	9.48	75.84
Red Label	L	6	9.76	58.56
Black Label	L	11	12.14	133.54

Figure 17-4   Storeroom inventory sheet.

inventory cards from invoices and requisitions, he or she could purposely fail to record certain information on the cards, remove items from the shelves for personal use, and still have the card balance and the actual count agree. Spot checking the cards against invoices and requisitions thus helps eliminate that possibility. And much of inventory control can be computerized.

Final Reconciliation

Once storeroom inventory taking has been completed, the final figures for the period can be recorded on the beverage storeroom inventory reconciliation form, such as that illustrated in Figure 17-5. In this figure the Opening inventory figure is the actual Closing inventory from the previous period. The Purchases for period figure is transferred from the beverage-receiving report(s) for that period. The Requisitions for period figure is simply the total cost information from all relevant requisitions completed for that period. Opening inventory plus Purchases for period less Requisitions for period provides the Closing inventory amount, which can be compared with the Actual inventory figure for the end of the period taken from the inventory sheets. Note again that the Requisitions for period and Closing inventory figures will be affected by the costing method used (FIFO, LIFO, or some other method). However, regardless of the method used, the Difference figures will still be largely the same.

Period ending _April 15_	Beer	Wine	Liquor	Total
Opening inventory	$241.40	$305.79	$ 659.60	$1,206.79
Add: Purchases for period	807.80	492.73	1,378.24	2,678.77
Deduct: Requisitions for period	(716.10)	(516.05)	(1,288.18)	(2,520.33)
= Closing inventory	333.10	282.47	749.66	1,365.23
Actual inventory	335.40	281.10	752.90	1,369.40
Difference	2.30	(1.37)	3.24	4.17

Figure 17-5   Beverage storeroom inventory reconciliation.

Differences

The difference figures for the two sets will be largely—but not exactly—the same because the item cost figures taken from the invoiced amounts are rounded to the nearest cent on the perpetual inventory cards and requisitions. However, differences of more than a few dollars should be investigated. With this type of reconciliation in effect, management can be sure that there is good control over the beverage storeroom.

BAR INVENTORY

The inventory taking that we have discussed has been for storeroom control purposes only. For complete beverage control, all inventory should be taken, both in the storeroom and at the bar.

Inventory at the bar, unlike that in the storeroom, cannot be double checked against perpetual inventory cards. Instead, it is necessary only to count each full and part bottle by type of liquor and to record and add it to the quantity on hand in the storeroom. Part bottles are usually estimated in tenths rather than in exact ounces (or the equivalent metric measure)—for example, a half-bottle would be 0.5. Some bars use metering devices to dispense liquor. The meters count each drink dispensed, thus making inventory taking easier. If a bar does use dispensing devices, do not forget to add to the liquor content still in the bottles the amount of liquor leading

Period ending	February 28					
			Quantity on Hand			
	Size	Storeroom	Bar	Total	Item Cost	Total Value
Ballantine	L	6	2.2	8.2	$10.28	$ 84.30
Bell	L	8	3.9	11.9	11.10	132.09
Red Label	L	4	1.5	5.5	10.76	59.18
Black Label	L	1	4.1	5.1	13.87	70.74

Figure 17-6   Storeroom and bar inventory sheet.

from the bottlenecks to the dispensing heads. When the equipment is installed, the supplier can provide that quantity. The bar inventory should, obviously, be taken when the bar is closed. A combined storeroom/bar inventory sheet is illustrated in Figure 17-6.

INVENTORY TURNOVER

It is important in any business not to have too much money tied up at any one time in inventory, as it is not earning interest. At the same time, it is also important not to have too few items in inventory and to risk running out of them and disappointing the customers. One way to achieve a balanced inventory is to use perpetual inventory cards, and another is to calculate (usually monthly) the beverage inventory turnover rate. The equation for this is

$$\frac{\text{Beverage cost for the month}}{\text{Average inventory for month}}$$

The beverage cost for the month is

Beginning of the month inventory + Purchases during
month − End of the month inventory

and the average inventory is

$$(\text{Beginning of the month inventory} + \text{End of the month inventory}) \div 2$$

Assuming the following figures:

Beginning of the month inventory	=	$2,000
End of the month inventory	=	$3,000
Purchases during the month	=	$3,500

the inventory turnover rate for the month will be

$$\frac{(\$2,000 + \$3,500 - \$3,000)}{(\$2,000 + \$3,000)/2}$$

$$= \frac{\$2,500}{\$2,500} = 1 \text{ time}$$

The turnover rate in a typical bar will normally range from one-half to one time a month, or from six to twelve times a year. Each beverage operation's management should establish the appropriate turnover for its own needs and then compare the actual one with this standard from time to time to see whether there are any major deviations.

Note also that a particular establishment's turnover rate can be affected by factors such as geographic location. For example, if a beverage operation is located on a resort island that receives liquor deliveries only once a month, it must carry much more in inventory at any one time, and so its turnover rate will be much lower. Similarly, if a beverage operation decides to purchase three or four times a week, rather than only once, it will carry much less in inventory, and so its turnover rate will increase.

DISCUSSION QUESTIONS

1. Briefly describe the basic requirements for bar storeroom security.
2. Why should empty liquor cases be flattened before being removed from the storeroom?
3. Explain why all alcoholic beverages, when received, should be routed through the storeroom, even when the bar will need them in a day or so.
4. Briefly describe how perpetual inventory cards and requisitions are used in storeroom control.
5. Explain why the bartender(s) should return empty liquor bottles to the storekeeper and why these bottles should be destroyed immediately.

6. Describe the first-in, first-out method of pricing items in the storeroom.
7. Describe the last-in, first-out method of pricing items in the storeroom.
8. What does the term *par stock* mean, and how is it useful in bar control?
9. Discuss the value of bottle coding in bar control.
10. Under what circumstance may a bar not return an empty bottle for a full one? What needs to be done to control this?
11. Why is it often preferable to take inventory weekly rather than monthly?
12. How can differences between perpetual inventory card balances and the actual count of the stock be resolved?
13. List the column headings that appear on an inventory sheet.
14. Explain the risk in allowing the storekeeper to record figures on the perpetual inventory cards.
15. Explain the process of completing the beverage storeroom inventory reconciliation form.
16. On a beverage storeroom inventory reconciliation form, where does the Opening inventory figure come from?
17. What is the equation for calculating beverage inventory turnover, and what is the normal turnover in a typical bar?
18. How is beverage cost for the month calculated for use in the beverage inventory turnover equation?
19. How is average inventory for the month calculated for use in the beverage inventory turnover equation?

PROBLEMS

1. The Swizzle Stick Bar uses the first-in, first-out method of issuing liquor from the beverage storeroom to the bar. On December 4 it had on hand three bottles of a particular brand of scotch at $12.30 each. On that date, two dozen more bottles were purchased and received at a price of $151.20 a case (twelve bottles to a case). On December 5 the manager submitted a requisition for eight bottles of this brand of scotch to be delivered from the storeroom to the bar. Calculate
    a. The total cost that will appear on the requisition for this transaction.
    b. The inventory value at the end of December 5.
2. Recalculate parts a and b of Problem 1 using the last-in, first-out inventory method.
3. The beverage inventory figures for a storeroom reconciliation showed the following:

Opening inventory:	liquor	$2,421.08
	beer	615.12
	wine	394.87
Purchases for period:	liquor	672.68
	beer	221.58
	wine	152.07
Requisitions for period:	liquor	579.41
	beer	241.40
	wine	446.12
Actual inventory:	liquor	2,498.10
	beer	593.87
	wine	101.22

Prepare a beverage storeroom inventory reconciliation form like that in Figure 17-5, using the above information. Comment about any differences you discover.

4. A club lounge had an opening inventory of $4,116.20 on April 1. Its closing beverage inventory was $3,917.80 on April 30. During April its beverage cost of sales was $5,011.15. Calculate the beverage inventory turnover rate for the month.

5. The January 1 opening inventory for a beverage operation was $5,126.40. Purchases during January were $4,232.20, and the closing inventory on January 31 was $5,006.20. Calculate the beverage inventory turnover rate for the month.

18

Bar Control Methods

CHAPTER OBJECTIVES

After studying this chapter the reader should be able to

- Discuss some of the many ways in which bar fraud can occur.
- Define the term *standard recipes* and list the three advantages of using them.
- Describe a simplified method of drink costing and explain its main disadvantage.
- Describe the two main types of measuring devices used in bars.
- Describe an interbar transfer form.
- Define the term *spillage allowance*.
- Describe how the requisition control method works and explain its pros and cons.
- Describe how the standard cost control method is used and explain why, with the standard cost control method, the standard cost percentage figure changes from one period to the next.
- Describe how the quantity control method works, what its main disadvantage is, and how it can be most effectively used.
- Describe how the standard revenue control method works, define the term *standard revenue per bottle,* and explain how it is calculated using the weighted average method.
- Explain what tolerance would normally be allowed between actual and standard revenue with the standard revenue control method and also what impact the sales of full bottles of liquor may have on this method.
- Describe a shortcut method of calculating the total standard revenue for use with the standard revenue control method.
- Discuss the control problems that "happy hours" can create.

METHODS OF THEFT OR FRAUD

As discussed in the preceding chapter, controlling the beverage storeroom is relatively easy using the procedures outlined. Unfortunately, controlling the bar is not as easy, particularly when the bartender is also responsible for handling cash from beverage sales. Many situations may permit theft or fraud if a bartender or beverage server is dishonest:

1. Underpouring five drinks by, say, one-sixth the normal measure, not recording the sale of each sixth drink, and pocketing the cash from that drink.
2. Using personal drink-measuring devices (shot glasses or jiggers) that are smaller than the house ones, with the objective of achieving item 1.
3. Diluting liquor with water and keeping the cash from the additional drinks sold. This is particularly easy to do with gin, vodka, and tequila, as there will be no color change. With the brown liquors any color change can be reversed by also adding a little tea. And if the bartender uses these diluted brands only with mixed drinks, the customers are highly unlikely to notice any minor taste change. The only effective way to check for this is by chemical analysis.
4. Bringing in liquor purchased personally, selling the contents, not recording the sales, and pocketing the cash.
5. Not recording the sales of individual drinks until they add up to the normal number of drinks from a full bottle, recording the sale as a cash sale of a full bottle, and disposing of the bottle. Because the full-bottle sale price is usually less than the accumulated sales of individual drinks, the bartender can pocket the difference.
6. Substituting a house brand for a call brand (which usually sells at a higher price), charging for the call brand, and pocketing the difference; or filling an empty call brand bottle with a house brand. In this case, no one will notice that the wrong bottle is being used.
7. Selling drinks; recording them as spilled, complimentary, or a walk-out; and pocketing the cash.
8. Overcharging the number of drinks served to a group of customers who are running up a tab to be paid later.
9. If automatic drink-measuring and -dispensing devices are used (see Chapter 19), obtaining the contents for, say, five drinks, spreading this content into six glasses, and pocketing the cash from the sixth drink.
10. Overpouring drinks (and underpouring others to compensate) to influence a larger tip or a guest to "buy" the bartender a drink.
11. Using private sales checks rather than those authorized by the establishment.

12. Reusing an already paid sales check.
13. "Losing" sales checks after the guest has paid.
14. Changing sales check items and prices after the customer has paid.
15. Bringing in empty bottles, exchanging them from the storeroom for full ones, and selling from the full ones without recording the sales.
16. Using a fraudulently obtained credit card to convert cash sales into charge sales and pocketing the cash.
17. Using a customer's legitimate credit card, running through some blank charge vouchers with that card, and later transferring cash sales to those vouchers. A bartender doing this (as well as item 16) usually is eventually caught when the credit card–issuing company receives complaints about the fraudulent charges.
18. At "hosted" banquet functions (at which the hosting organization pays for all drinks that customers consume), removing unsold bottles for personal use or transferring them for sale at the regular bar, and charging the customer for those bottles.
19. Recording the sale of every drink, but from time to time showing and registering the sale as a beer rather than a more expensive highball or cocktail, and removing the difference in cash.
20. Prerecording and registering the sale of drinks (which have not actually been sold) at lower than normal prices during the "happy" hour and pocketing the cash difference when these drinks are actually sold at normal higher prices later on. Alternatively, unsold drinks can be recorded as sales during normal periods, and when actually sold at higher prices during an entertainment period, a bartender can again pocket the difference in cash. The use of different-colored guest checks during these special periods could help prevent this.
21. Not recording sales of straight soft drinks, as the sales revenue from these is often not controlled in many bars.
22. Breaking a used empty bottle and claiming it was an "accident," and receiving a replacement full one that can be sold for the benefit of the bartender.
23. Short-pouring cocktails that contain a number of different alcoholic ingredients and filling up the cocktail with extra amounts of nonalcoholic ingredients such as cream, egg white, or lemon juice.

Management Awareness

These are only some of the many common dishonest practices that have been observed. Management awareness and supervision can help prevent them. In particular, management should look for collections of toothpicks, matches, small coins, or similar items that a bartender may have at the working station to keep track of how much to remove in cash at the end of the shift.

But even using all of the control procedures detailed in this book will not guarantee that nothing will go wrong. For example, consider the par stock control procedure. If a par stock policy is in effect, any bottles brought in by bartenders will mean that there are more bottles of that brand at the bar than there are supposed to be. But having a par stock policy cannot help unless the par stock is checked from time to time. This means that the number of bottles at the bar should be randomly counted and checked by management against the par stock list. Without this spot check, the par stock policy will not be very effective. Similarly, in order for bottle coding to be effective, the bottles at the bar must be spot checked to ensure that they have the proper codes.

If necessary, contact one of the many security firms that provide trained "spotters" who are expert at posing as regular bar customers and observing common forms of bartender theft. If such people are employed to help determine whether the bar is being properly run, make sure in advance that they are familiar with the operation's policies, systems, rules, and prices, so that they know what to look for.

PRELIMINARY CONTROL REQUIREMENTS

The following control methods concentrate on controlling liquor, rather than beer or wine. The reason is that in the typical bar, liquor sales account for the greatest part of the total revenue derived, and losses, theft, and fraud are therefore more likely to occur with liquor than with other beverages. However, the control techniques described for liquor can be applied equally as well—often in a simplified form—to the control of items such as wine and beer. Accordingly, make sure that the sales register breaks down sales into at least the three basic categories of liquor, beer, and wine.

Standard Recipes

Regardless of the type of bar and control method to be used, standard recipes must first be established for each type of drink. It may seem strange to talk about recipes for liquor control, but even defining the amount of liquor to be served in a standard measure constitutes a "recipe." Because most drinks in the typical bar are just a standard portion of liquor—usually measured by some type of pouring or measuring device—the recipes are generally easy to prepare. A standard recipe should specify the amount of ice, water, or soft drink or mineral water to include. Note, however, that the term *drink size* usually refers to the amount of the principal liquor, and not to the total amount of liquid in the finished drink.

Cocktail recipes are more complicated, as they specify the quantities of all liquid ingredients and, when required, the garnish (such as a cherry, olive, or fruit slice) to be included. These food ingredients are usually considered part of beverage cost and so must be part of the recipe.

The type and quantity of ice in cocktails and the mixing method used are also important (and therefore should be included in the recipe), as they will help determine the drink's final quantity and quality.

Glassware

The type and size of glass for the drink should also be part of the recipe. The drink's appearance is important. For example, a two-ounce martini served in a six-ounce glass may look like a short measure. Alternatively, a highball drink served in too small a glass, with too little mixer, may taste too strong.

The glass size does not control the quantity of liquor in a drink; drink-measuring devices do that. The glass size does, however, control the appearance of the finished drink. For example, a footed glass often gives a drink more appeal than does the same drink in a tumbler or in a small glass filled to the brim.

Advantages of Standard Recipes

The major advantages of having standard recipes are

- Drinks will be consistent; therefore, regardless of when they are made and which bartender makes them, they will look, taste, and, most important, cost the same.
- Written recipes and drink-mixing procedures simplify training new employees.
- Management may reduce its supervision.
- Bottles of liquor will yield a predictable amount.

Costing Drinks

When recipes have been prepared, the cost of each drink can be calculated, and selling prices can be established that will yield an appropriate beverage cost percentage. A recipe showing the standard cost for a Rye Alexander is illustrated in Figure 18-1.

Notice that the procedure for making the drink is included in the recipe. The standard cost of each drink is what it should be if all procedures are

Drink: Rye Alexander					
Ingredient	Quantity	Cost	Cost	Cost	Cost
House rye	3/4 oz.	$0.25	$0.28		
Crème de cacao, dark	3/4 oz.	0.30	0.32		
Cream	3 oz.	0.10	0.11		
Total cost		$0.65	$0.71		
Selling price		2.50	2.75		
Cost percentage		26.0%	25.8%		
Method: Shake all ingredients with small-cubed ice. Pour through strainer into 6 oz. champagne glass. Sprinkle with nutmeg.					

Figure 18-1   Drink recipe.

correctly followed. Accordingly, the standard costs should be updated when the ingredients' costs change.

A simplified method of costing drinks is to cost out only the main alcohol ingredient or ingredients (house rye and crème de cacao in our example) and then to add an allowance (for example, 10 percent) for any other ingredients. Obviously this method is easier than costing out all the ingredients, but it may not provide the true cost for the drinks and thus could then lead to an incorrect evaluation of the actual performance at the bar.

Measuring Devices

Standard recipes will be useless unless bartenders are given appropriate measuring devices. Allowing bartenders to free-pour liquor is asking for trouble even if bartenders complain that using measures slows them down.

There are two types of measuring device (apart from those attached to automatic or electronic dispensing equipment): shot glasses and jiggers. Shot glasses are used primarily for basic "highball" drinks—for example, one ounce or one and one-quarter ounces, or their equivalent in metric measure. Shot glasses can be purchased with or without engraved lines below the top rim, but lined glasses are preferable because one can see whether a full measure is being served.

Jiggers are used to measure smaller quantities of ingredients, for example, a quarter or a third of an ounce, or their equivalent in metric. Because jiggers are usually made of stainless steel, they are not very effective for controlling underpouring. These jiggers often have an inverted cone shape, and so it is easy for a dishonest bartender to fill the jigger to just below the rim and quickly pour the contents into a serving glass. Because most of the volume is at the wide top of the cone, even a slight deficit can provide significant extra liquor for the bartender's own profit. Thus bartenders' measuring devices must be checked from time to time to ensure they have not been substituted for devices that contain a smaller measure.

Sales Checks

Regardless of the type of bar and the type of sales register, both bartenders and servers should use sales checks unique to the establishment. It is important to institute a policy that all drinks must be recorded on sales checks before the drinks are prepared and served. But even with this policy it is still necessary to ensure that all employees follow it. This may not be easy to do, but with proper sales-check control, management can be more confident that it is receiving all the money it should be.

Sales checks should be used in conjunction with a sales register that will not operate without a sales check inserted in it. (Sales checks and sales registers are covered in more detail in Chapter 21.)

Keeping Full-Bottle Sales Separate

In some jurisdictions, bars are allowed to sell full bottles of liquor for off-premise consumption or to room guests in a hotel. The price to the customer of the full bottle is generally quite a bit less than the price of an equivalent number of individual drinks. For this reason the sales revenue from full-bottle sales should be separated from that from individual drink sales.

Interbar Transfers

Some establishments may have several bars under one roof (for example, a hotel). In such situations it may be necessary to transfer bottles of beverages from one bar to another. In such cases, an interbar transfer form is useful, as it ensures that each bar's costs will be kept separate for later analysis. An interbar transfer form is illustrated in Figure 18-2.

Spillage Allowance

A bar manager may want to permit a spillage allowance, because without mechanical or electronic dispensing/measuring devices, the liquor from

From _Main bar_				
To _Service bar_			Date _March 10_	
Item	Size	Quantity	Unit Cost	Total Cost
House rum	_L_	_3_	_$10.20_	_$30.60_
Ordered by _____			Filled by _____	

Figure 18-2   Interbar transfer form.

each bottle cannot be accounted for down to the last drop. Also, drinks can be wrongly mixed and have to be discarded. Or there can be some inadvertent overpouring.

To compensate for such errors, a spillage allowance for each bottle of liquor may be permitted. For example, if thirty-four standard drinks can be made from a particular bottle of liquor if they all are correctly measured, the spillage allowance may be one drink per bottle, and so management would expect only thirty-three drinks per bottle. But if a generous spillage allowance is made known to bartenders, they may be tempted to take advantage of it for individual gain.

In this chapter we will look at some of the most frequently used liquor control methods:

1. Requisition control
2. Standard cost control
3. Quantity (ounce) control
4. Standard revenue control

REQUISITION CONTROL

One of the easiest control methods to use is that based on daily requisitions. The daily requisitions are costed, extended, and totaled, and that total becomes the total cost of sales for the day. That cost can then be divided by sales and multiplied by 100 to arrive at a cost percentage.

Each daily cost and sales figure can be summed to find the To-date figure, as shown in Figure 18-3. For example, on June 2 the To-date Cost figure is the sum of the Today amounts for both June 1 and June 2, or $252.75 + $201.76 = $454.51. On June 3, the June 2 To-date Cost figure is brought forward and added to the June 3 Today Cost figure of $384.58, to yield the

Date	Cost		Sales		Cost (%)	
	Today	To-date	Today	To-date	Today	To-date
June 1	$252.75	$ 252.75	$1,001.50	$1,001.50	25.2%	25.2%
2	201.76	454.51	963.10	1,964.60	20.9	23.1
3	384.58	839.09	1,401.90	3,366.50	27.4	24.9
4	280.25	1,119.34	1,096.55	4,463.05	25.6	25.1
5	651.06	1,770.40	2,711.05	7,174.10	24.0	24.7
6	503.78	2,274.18	2,118.75	9,292.85	23.8	24.5

Figure 18-3   Requisition cost and sales record.

June 3 To-date amount of $839.09. The To-date Sales figures are calculated using the same technique.

The Today Cost percentage figures are calculated by dividing the Today Cost figure by the Today Sales figure and multiplying the result by 100, or by dividing the To-date Cost figure by the To-date Sales figure and multiplying the result by 100. For example, on June 6 the Today Cost percentage figure is

$$(\$503.78/\$2,118.75) \times 100 = 23.8\%$$

and the To-date Cost percentage figure is

$$(\$2,274.18/\$9,292.85) \times 100 = 24.5\%$$

The main advantage of this method is that it is fast and simple and does not require an inventory to be taken, as it assumes that the bar is operating with a par stock system.

The main disadvantage of the method is that it may not be accurate, as it also assumes, unless this is adjusted for, that there are no partly empty bottles of liquor in the bar at the end of each day. Because that is highly unlikely, the cost figure could be considerably off (either too high or too low) on a daily basis.

However, over time the daily highs and lows tend to even out, and the accumulated average by the end of the week should fairly accurately reflect the bar's actual cost of sales for each period. This actual cost can be compared with previous periods' costs to see whether it is within "normal" limits.

Another problem with this method is that despite its simplicity and the fact that it shows what the cost actually was, it provides no information about what the cost should be! That is, there is no means of comparing the result with a standard. The standard cost control method, discussed next, rectifies that problem.

STANDARD COST CONTROL

One of the easiest and most accurate bar control methods is the use of a standard cost. A standard cost is what the cost should be for a given level of sales, and it is based on recipes that have been correctly costed out.

The standard cost control method simply compares the standard cost for a bar over a period of time with the actual cost for that same period. If an operation has more than one bar, the cost information should be kept separate for each.

The cost comparison can be in either dollars of cost or percentage of cost (cost of sales as a percentage of revenue). The actual count of each type of drink sold during the period is multiplied by its recipe or standard cost and by its selling price. With the electronic sales registers currently available to bar operators, a tally of drinks by type is easy to maintain. Figure 18-4 demonstrates how the total standard cost and the total standard cost percentage are calculated.

The actual cost figure for the same period is calculated as follows:

> Inventory at bar at beginning of period
> + Value of requisitions filled during period
> − Inventory at bar at end of period

The actual cost figure may need to be adjusted for any interbar transfers.

Differences

Using the standard cost control method, the difference between the standard and the actual cost percentages should usually be no larger than one-half of 1 percent. (Note that it is 0.4 percent in Figure 18-4.) Any difference greater than one-half of 1 percent should be checked. Management can expect the actual cost to be higher than the standard cost because the standard cost is based on what the cost should be if no errors, inadvertent or otherwise, are made.

Drink	Drink Cost	Drink Selling Price	Quantity Sold	Total Standard Cost	Total Standard Sales
House rye	$0.35	$1.80	830	$ 290.05	$1,494.00
House gin	0.30	1.50	420	126.00	630.00
House rum	0.32	1.80	315	100.80	567.00
Totals				$1,218.10	$4,937.70

Standard cost percent $\dfrac{\$1,218.10}{\$4,937.70} \times 100 = 24.7\%$

Actual cost percent $\dfrac{\$1,237.80}{\$4,937.70} \times 100 = 25.1$

Difference   0.4%

Figure 18-4   Standard cost control calculation.

Full-Bottle Adjustment

If any bottles are sold as full bottles during this period, for less revenue than they would if sold by the individual drink, then both the cost and the revenue figures for these full-bottle sales must be adjusted.

Sales Mix Change

Finally, note that with the standard cost control method, the standard cost percentage for each period will change slightly. The reason is that for each period, the actual quantities sold of each drink are used in the calculation. Unless these quantities (often referred to as the sales mix) stay the same each period (and it is highly unlikely that they ever would), each subsequent period's standard cost percentage will be affected by the difference.

QUANTITY (OUNCE) CONTROL

Quantity control is a useful bar control method; it ignores cost dollars and concentrates on the quantities used and sold. This method compares the number of ounces of each type of liquor used according to inventory records with the number used according to sales records.

Consider Table 18-1 for just one type of liquor, house rum. Suppose that a bar served, in addition to rum highballs, four other drinks that contained rum and that the following figures show the Rum Quantity and the number of Drinks Sold for each of these five drinks during a certain period. The Total Amount of Rum Sold figure is calculated by multiplying, for each of the drinks, the Rum Quantity figure by the Drinks Sold figure. As can be seen from the table, 1,178 ounces were sold. Inventory records show that the opening inventory of rum was 4.6 bottles, 46 bottles were issued by requisition, there were no interbar transfers, and the closing inventory was 3.7 bottles. Assuming that 750-milliliter (25-ounce) bottles of rum were used, inventory records show that 1,172 ounces were consumed:

$$4.6 + 46.0 - 3.7 = 46.9 \times 25 \text{ oz.} = 1,172 \text{ oz.}$$

The difference between the two figures is 6 ounces. This would normally be quite satisfactory, because part bottles are estimated in tenths and a mistake in estimating a part bottle by one-tenth represents 2.5 ounces in a 25-ounce bottle.

If a spillage amount were permitted in this bar, the inventory usage figures must be adjusted to compensate. For example, if there were a one-ounce spillage per bottle, the 46.9 bottles used according to inventory would be multiplied by 24 instead of 25.

Even though we demonstrated the quantity control method using ounces, it can just as easily be used with metric numbers. Note also that quantity control is not dependent on percentage figures. The cost percentage can go up and down daily, but as long as the ounce (or metric) numbers are in line, there is no need for concern.

Table 18-1   Quantity control (rum).

Drink	Rum Quantity	Drinks Sold	Total Amount of Rum Sold
Rum highball	1.5 oz.	336	504 oz.
Drink 2	1.25	208	260
Drink 3	1	106	106
Drink 4	1.75	128	224
Drink 5	1.5	56	84
		Grand Total:	1,178 oz.

Time Problem

We demonstrated the quantity control method for only one type of liquor. Many argue that it is too time-consuming to complete an entire inventory control using this method, unless the sales register can provide sales quantities converted into total ounces sold by brand or type of liquor. Today's microcomputers can also be easily programmed to handle this control method.

Alternatively, because the typical bar sells 80 percent to 90 percent of all liquor from the basic house brands of the most common liquors (rye, rum, scotch, gin, vodka, and bourbon), it may be possible to use this method only for those half-dozen brands, for if loss or fraud is likely, it will be in the high-selling items.

One suggestion is to control each of these high-selling brands on a rotational basis, or to use this quantity control method in conjunction with either the standard cost method (discussed earlier) or the standard revenue method (to be discussed in the next section), both of which show a higher than normal variance for any particular period. In other words, one can use the quantity control method to isolate the variance (shown by either of the other two methods) to a particular type of liquor.

STANDARD REVENUE CONTROL

The standard revenue control method is sometimes referred to as the potential revenue (or sales) control method. It is not concerned with cost percentages and, for this reason, is sometimes considered a monitoring, rather than a control, tool. However, it is probably the most commonly used method in practice, because most beverage operations do not have the detailed record of every different type of drink sold that the standard cost control and quantity (ounce) control methods require.

The standard revenue control method converts the quantity of liquor used, according to inventory records, into standard revenue, which is then compared with the actual revenue from sales. The method assigns a standard sales or revenue value that each type or brand of liquor should produce per bottle used.

Standard Revenue per Bottle

In a simple situation it is easy to calculate the standard revenue per bottle. For example, if basic 1-ounce bar drinks are sold, a 750-milliliter (25-ounce) bottle of house gin should produce twenty-five drinks (assuming no spillage allowance). If a gin highball sells for $1.80, then the standard revenue for house gin will be

$$25 \times \$1.80 = \$45.00$$

If metric measures are used, the approach is the same. For example, if gin is purchased in liter (1,000-milliliter) bottles and if the standard drink calls for 30 milliliters of gin with a selling price of $1.80, the standard revenue for that liter bottle of gin will be

$$\frac{1,000}{30} \times \$1.80 = \$60.00$$

Unfortunately, the contents of a bottle of house gin (or other types of liquor) are seldom dispensed in the same quantities for all drinks served. For example, even though the basic portion of gin in a highball is 1 ounce, it may be served in 1.5-ounce portions in Martinis, and in different portion sizes in other cocktails. To solve this dilemma, a weighted average can be used to calculate the standard revenue per bottle for each type of liquor used.

Weighted Average Method

With the weighted average method it is necessary to tally up all the various kinds of drinks sold during a test period. The sales register (particularly if it is one of the newer electronic types) should be able to provide this information readily.

The test period should be at least one week long, in order to even out the ups and downs caused by changes in the sales mix. Suppose that five gin drinks are served during the test period (see Table 18-2). The next step is to multiply the quantity of each drink sold by the amount of gin it contains. The total amount of gin used is therefore 3,325 ounces, and if 750-milliliter (25-ounce) bottles are used, 133 bottles (3,325 ounces divided by 25 ounces) will have been used.

At this point we must then find out the total sales derived during the test

Table 18-2 Weighted average method (gin).

Drink	Number Sold	Quantity of Gin	Total Amount of Gin
Highball	1,600	1.25 oz.	2,000 oz.
Martini	600	1.75	1,050
Drink 3	100	1	100
Drink 4	50	1.5	75
Drink 5	80	1.25	100
		Grand Total:	3,325 oz.

period for gin drinks. This can also be provided from the sales register, or it can be calculated as in Table 18-3. The final step is to divide total sales by the number of bottles sold to obtain the standard revenue for each 25-ounce bottle of gin:

$$\frac{\$5,093}{133} = \$38.29$$

If metric measures are used, the approach will be the same.

Similar types of calculations are made for each type of liquor carried in inventory. Once the calculations are made, the standard revenue control method is then quite easy to use. Simply add the inventory at the bar at the beginning of the control period (a week, ten days, a month, depending on management policy) to the number of bottles requisitioned from the storeroom during that period, and then deduct the inventory at the bar at the end of the period. Figure 18-5 shows how the calculations are made. Note that part bottles of liquor are measured in tenths, as accuracy in ounces is not necessary. The quantities used of each type of liquor are simply multiplied by their previously calculated standard revenue figures. Finally, the total standard revenue is compared with actual revenue.

Differences Allowed

Any difference between the total standard revenue and the actual revenue (from the sales register) should be no more than 1 percent of the standard revenue. In other words, management should expect the actual revenue to range from 1 percent below standard to 1 percent above.

In our case, 1 percent of standard revenue of $2,502.20 is $25.02, and our calculated difference in Figure 18-5 is only $11.30. The difference, therefore, is acceptable.

A difference is to be expected because the standard revenue per bottle calculations are based on a past sales mix for each type of liquor used during the test period, and it is unlikely that the sales mix will stay exactly the

Table 18-3   Total Sales.

Drink	Quantity Sold	Selling Price	Total Sales
Highball	1,600	$2.00	$3,200
Martini	600	2.50	1,500
Drink 3	100	1.75	175
Drink 4	50	1.80	90
Drink 5	80	1.60	128
		Grand Total:	$5,093

	Opening Inventory	Added per Requisitions	Total	Closing Inventory	Used	Standard Revenue per Bottle	Total Standard Revenue
House rye	2.6	18.0	20.6	2.9	17.7	$40.20	$ 711.54
House rum	4.1	9.0	13.1	4.2	8.9	41.80	372.02
House gin	0.9	6.0	6.9	1.4	5.5	35.90	197.45

Total standard revenue	$2,502.20
Total actual revenue	2,490.90
Difference	$ 11.30

Figure 18-5   Calculation of total standard revenue.

same in all future periods. Therefore, it might be a good idea to test the sales mix periodically for various types of liquor so that the standard revenue figures per bottle do not drift too far out of line. This will be particularly important if the bar is in a seasonal area where customer tastes, and therefore the sales mix, will change with the season. And obviously, if recipe portions or selling prices change, the standard revenue per bottle figures must be recalculated.

Shortcut Method

A shortcut standard revenue control method multiplies the requisitioned quantities by the standard revenue per bottle to arrive at the total standard revenue. However, this shortcut has the same disadvantage as does the requisitions-only cost control method outlined at the beginning of this chapter. That is, it can be inaccurate because it takes no account of part bottles of liquor in inventory at the bar. Nevertheless, even though this inaccuracy may exist on a daily basis, the part bottle overages and shortages tend to even out over time.

Full-Bottle Adjustments

If any full bottles are sold at less than the standard revenue per bottle, this must be adjusted for in the total standard revenue calculations. The easiest way is to bring into line the total standard revenue figure with the actual revenue (including full-bottle sales). In other words, if the standard revenue per bottle of a particular liquor is $35, and a full bottle of that liquor is sold during the period at $20, simply deduct $15 from total standard revenue so that it can be compared correctly with the total actual revenue.

Happy Hours

At certain times of the day when this is allowed by law, some bars reduce the prices of drinks during the so-called happy hour. (At other times the prices may be increased to help pay for entertainment provided.) In such cases the calculations for the standard revenue per bottle must take this into consideration. An alternative is to separate the costs and sales for these special periods, but that can create a great deal of extra work.

One problem associated with reducing drink prices during certain hours is that earlier sales made at regular prices may not yet have been fully recorded and rung up. Thus they are held over and shown as sales made at the reduced prices, with the bar employees keeping the cash difference between the regular and the lower prices. Preventing this requires management supervision. In addition, management should regularly calculate the amount of sales made during the happy hour or entertainment period as a percentage of total sales each day and should watch for deviations.

DISCUSSION QUESTIONS

1. Explain how a bartender can profit from a situation in which full-bottle sales are allowed.
2. How can a customer's credit card be used by a bartender to commit fraud?
3. What could a collection of toothpicks, matches, or small coins at a bartender's work station signify?
4. What is meant by the term *standard recipe?*
5. Discuss the role that proper glassware plays in drink preparation.
6. List three of the advantages of using standard recipes.
7. Describe a simplified method of drink costing, and its main disadvantage.
8. What is a shot glass, which is the best type to use, and why?
9. Define a jigger, and explain how it can be used to underpour drinks.
10. Describe an interbar transfer form.
11. Discuss the term *spillage allowance.*
12. Briefly describe how the requisition control method works and explain its main advantage as well as its two main disadvantages.

13. Briefly describe the standard cost control method. How is the actual cost figure calculated for comparison with the standard cost percentage in the standard cost control method?

14. With the standard cost control method, why does the standard cost percentage normally change from period to period?

15. Briefly explain how the quantity (ounce) control method works and what its main disadvantage is. How might management be able to use the quantity control method with one of the other control methods?

16. Briefly describe the standard revenue control method.

17. What is meant by the term *standard revenue per bottle* in reference to the standard revenue control method?

18. Briefly describe how the weighted average method is used to calculate the standard revenue per bottle for use with the standard revenue control method.

19. With the standard revenue control method, how much difference is usually allowed between the total standard revenue and the total actual revenue?

20. Briefly describe the shortcut method of calculating total standard revenue using the standard revenue control method.

21. Why is it necessary, with the standard revenue control method, to adjust for any full-bottle sales?

22. Briefly discuss possible control problems in a bar that has a happy hour.

PROBLEMS

1. The Local Lounge sells only a limited variety of types of drinks. Its individual drink cost and selling prices, as well as quantity sold, for the week ending March 14 are as follows:

Drink	Cost	Selling Price	Quantity Sold
Gin	$0.60	$2.50	680
Rye	0.64	2.60	556
Scotch	0.74	2.80	720
Bourbon	0.70	2.70	905
Rum	0.58	2.60	380
Manhattan	0.80	3.00	1,058
Martini	0.70	3.00	1,382

The actual beverage cost for the week ending March 14 was $4,025.00, and the actual revenue was $15,911.65.

a. Calculate the standard cost percentage and the actual cost percentage for the week. Round all dollar figures to the nearest dollar.

b. For the week ending March 21, because of a special purchase, the cost per drink for scotch dropped to $0.70. There was no change in the selling price. Quantities sold during the week of March 21 were gin 657, rye 608, scotch 708, bourbon 963, rum 425, Manhattan 1,158, Martini 1,299. The actual beverage revenue for the week ending March 21 was $16,283.30. Recalculate the standard cost percentage and the actual cost percentage for the week ending March 21, and explain why the percentage changed from that of the preceding week.

c. Would you, as the Local Lounge manager, be satisfied with the results for each of the two weeks? Explain.

2. The Coconut Club uses the quantity (ounce) control method. The manager wishes to spot check the rum sales records for comparison with the rum inventory records on November 25. The opening rum inventory on that date was 6.4 bottles, and the closing inventory was 4.1 bottles. Five full bottles of rum were requisitioned from the storeroom on November 25. The bottles contain 750 milliliters (25 ounces). An analysis of the sales checks revealed the following:

Drink	Quantity Sold
Straight rum (1 oz. rum)	144
Daiquiri (1.5 oz. rum)	8
Cuba Libre (1.25 oz. rum)	8
Rum Swizzle (1.125 oz. rum)	8

Use these figures to compare the ounces used with the ounces sold. As the manager, would you be satisfied with this analysis?

3. The Limited Lounge serves only the drinks listed. Alongside each drink listed is the quantity sold on December 11, according to a tally of the sales checks used on that day.

Drink	Quantity Sold
Bourbon	244
Gin	36
Rye	24
Scotch	84
Vodka	44
Martini	64
Manhattan	48

Drinks made with the five basic bar brands each contain 1.25 ounces of liquor. The Martini contains 1.75 ounces of gin and 0.25 ounces of dry vermouth. The Manhattan contains 1.75 ounces of bourbon and 0.25 ounces of sweet vermouth. Inventory records for December 11 indicate the following:

Item	Opening Inventory	Added	Closing Inventory
Bourbon	5.1	16.0	4.5
Gin	4.2	4.0	2.0
Rye	9.7	none	8.5
Scotch	2.6	3.0	1.4
Vodka	3.8	1.0	2.6
Dry vermouth	2.4	none	1.9
Sweet vermouth	3.5	none	3.1

All bottles contain the equivalent of 25 ounces except the two types of vermouth, which each contain 34 ounces. Using the quantity (ounce) control method, analyze these results and comment.

4. You are the beverage comptroller for the Flamboyant Lounge and have the following information about the operation of the bar for November 20:

Item	Opening Inventory	Added	Closing Inventory
Bourbon	3.1	12.0	2.4
Gin	5.2	8.0	3.7
Rum	6.0	8.0	5.5
Scotch	3.8	5.0	3.3
Vermouth	0.5	1.0	1.1

The standard revenues per bottle have been calculated as follows:

Bourbon	$27.00
Gin	27.50
Rum	25.00
Scotch	27.50

a. The actual revenue for the day is $940.57. Calculate the total standard revenue, compare it with the actual revenue, and comment about the result.

b. You decide to investigate further by using the quantity (ounce) control method to determine what differences there are, if any, between the usage and sale of each type of liquor. An analysis of sales checks showed the following:

Item	Drinks Sold
Bourbon	270
Gin	195
Rum	197
Scotch	126
Martini	24
Manhattan	16
Double Martini	4
Daiquiri	12
Scotch Sour	8

Bourbon, gin, rum, and scotch drinks each contain 1 ounce of liquor. A Martini contains 1.25 ounces of gin and 0.25 ounce of vermouth. A double Martini contains double the quantities of the single drink. A Manhattan contains 1.25 ounces of bourbon and 0.25 ounce of vermouth. A Scotch Sour contains 1.5 ounces of scotch. A Daiquiri contains 1 ounce of rum. All bottles contain 25 ounces, except vermouth bottles, which have 34 ounces. Comment on the results obtained.

5. The Cabaña Club uses the standard revenue control method. The following are the standard revenues per bottle of the only types of liquor that it sells:

Bourbon	$40.00
Gin	36.00
Rum	44.00
Scotch	50.00
Vodka	38.00

An analysis of the bar is being made for a particular day, on which the inventory figures are as follows:

Item	Opening Inventory	Added	Closing Inventory
Bourbon	6.2	12.0	5.8
Gin	4.1	5.0	3.6
Rum	5.4	7.0	3.9
Scotch	4.8	6.0	4.4
Vodka	2.5	8.0	8.5

The total actual revenue for the day was $1,450. However, included in that revenue was a full bottle of bourbon that was sold, as a full bottle, for $20. Calculate the total standard revenue, and explain why you would or would not be satisfied with the result.

6. The Bongo Bar uses the standard revenue control method, calculating the standard revenue per bottle using the weighted average technique. Calculate the standard revenue of a 750-milliliter (25-ounce) bottle of gin given the following information:

Item	Number Sold	Amount of Gin	Selling Price
Straight gin	860	1 oz.	$3.00
Dubonnet cocktail	60	0.75	3.75
Gimlet	80	1.5	3.75
Pink Lady	20	1.25	3.75
Martini	360	1.25	4.05

7. The Elbow Bar uses the standard revenue control method and calculates the standard revenue of each of its 750-milliliter (25-ounce) bottles of rye using the weighted average technique. From the following information, calculate the standard revenue per bottle of rye:

Item	Number Sold	Amount of Rye	Selling Price
Rye straight	500	1 oz.	$3.00
Manhattan	40	1	4.00
Rye Alexander	50	1.25	5.00
Rye Sour	20	1.5	5.00
John Collins	100	1.5	5.40

19

Other Control Considerations

CHAPTER OBJECTIVES

After studying this chapter the reader should be able to

- Differentiate between a host and a no-host bar, describe how tickets can be used for control in a no-host bar, and explain how the ticket seller and the bartender can work together fraudulently.
- Explain why sometimes the hosting organization is charged for drinks on an hourly basis.
- Describe some of the controls necessary for selling keg (draft) beer.
- Explain why it is important to separate the revenue and costs for liquor, beer, and wine.
- State the equation for separating the tax amount from the net revenue when the tax is included in the total revenue.
- Explain how the cost of mixes, food, and garnish ingredients can be controlled.
- List five advantages and five disadvantages of using liquor-dispensing systems.
- List three "information" benefits that a liquor-dispensing system can provide, and three basic questions that management should ask when investigating the purchase of such a system.

BANQUET CONTROL

If a business has a banquet department with its own liquor storage area, it can control its storeroom and the banquet bar using one or more of the methods described in Chapter 18. If the banquet department does not have its own controlled, locked storage room, it must requisition the needed beverages for each banquet function from the main storeroom or bar, returning any unused quantities to that storeroom or bar at the end of the banquet. This is a double interbar transfer, and a specially designed form can be used to control these transfers and calculate the banquet beverage cost.

Such a form is illustrated in Figure 19-1; it has space for the signatures of those responsible for both issuing and returning bottles. The Bottle Cost column figures are taken from the related perpetual inventory cards (see Chapter 17) so that the Total Cost information can be calculated. The Total Drinks column figures are calculated by multiplying the Bottles Used column figure and the Drinks per Bottle figure, rounded to the nearest whole number. The figure assumes one-liter bottles and thirty drinks per bottle. Total Standard Sales is the result of Total Drinks and Drink Selling Price multiplied together.

Ticket Sales

The total number of drinks sold can be compared with the total number of tickets sold in a no-host banquet bar. (A no-host bar is one in which each customer pays for his or her own drinks, as opposed to a hosted bar, in which the association, group, or company organizing the function picks up the tab.) The total standard sales should agree with the cash collected from ticket sales.

If tickets are sold for drinks, the bartender may have difficulty selling the tickets, handling cash, and even ringing up sales all at the same time. Thus it may be a good idea to have a separate person, located away from the bar, selling the tickets. The bartender then simply exchanges the tickets for drinks. The tickets may be color coded to differentiate various-priced drinks. The cost of hiring a ticket seller will more than likely be offset by the bartender's increased efficiency and the reduced possibility of errors and/or dishonesty.

However, the ticket seller and bartender can still work together for dishonest purposes. For example, the bartender can hand back "used" tickets to the ticket seller so that they can be resold, with the two employees then splitting the profits. To help prevent this, the bartender should be given a locked box with a slot on top into which used tickets must be immediately inserted when exchanged for drinks. Management supervision is also required.

A hosted bar will require no direct ticket or cash handling, in which case

Room Central		Function Abbott Corp.		Date Nov. 27						
Item	Size	Bottles Issued	Bottles Returned	Bottles Used	Bottle Cost	Total Cost	Drinks per Bottle	Total Drinks	Drink Selling Price	Total Standard Sales
Bourbon	L.	12	4.1	7.9	$15.10	$119.29	30	237	$3.00	$ 711.00
Scotch	L.	3	1.4	1.6	17.80	28.48	30	48	3.25	156.00
Rum	L.	6	0.7	5.3	15.30	81.09	30	159	3.00	477.00
					Totals	$228.86		444		$1,344.00

Cost percent $ $\dfrac{228.86}{1,344.00} \times 100 = 17.0\%$

Ticket (drink) Prices

	$3.00	$3.25	$3.50	$3.75	$4.00	$4.25	$4.50	$4.75
Ticket information:								
A. Closing number								
B. Opening number								
C. Tickets used (A minus B)								
D. Less: voided tickets								
E. Tickets sold (C minus D)								
F. Drinks sold								
G. Difference (E minus F)								

Figure 19-1 Banquet liquor control.

the Total Standard Sales figure from Figure 19-1 will be the amount billed to the customer. Note that in some host bars the host organization is charged for all full bottles used and also for those opened. In other words there is an agreed-upon charge per bottle, rather than per drink, and the host pays full price for any partly used bottles.

Another variation is for the host to be charged a fixed fee per person per hour, regardless of how many drinks of any kind are consumed; thus the average number of drinks that the typical person will consume per hour must be estimated. A rule of thumb is that guests will typically have three drinks each during the first hour, two in the second, and one in the third (or an average of $6 \div 3 = 2$ drinks per hour). Thus, if a three-hour reception has one hundred guests in attendance and the drink selling price is $3.00, the organization will be charged

$$100 \times \$6 \times 3 \text{ hours} = \$1,800$$

regardless of how many drinks are actually consumed.

BEER AND WINE

Beer

For bottled or canned beer, any of the control methods described in Chapter 18 (requisition control, standard cost control, quantity or ounce control, or standard revenue control) can be used. For keg beer the problem is a little more complicated and offers opportunities for theft because beer is often not controlled as well as are distilled spirits.

The first step in control is to convert the keg container into ounces of beer. The total number of ounces is then divided by the number of ounces served in the bar's standard beer glass. This will give the number of servings that should be obtained from a keg. The number of servings is then multiplied by the selling price of a glass to find the total standard revenue from a keg. However, beer kegs (because of their design) do not yield 100 percent of possible revenue because there is always a small amount of beer that cannot be extracted and problems such as line pressure can cause excessive foam and beer loss at the dispensing tap. For these reasons the actual cash from a keg can be expected to be as much as 5 percent less than the standard revenue.

It thus is important to make a daily, or even a shift, calculation of the number of kegs used and to compare this figure with revenue. Indeed, some operations take a register reading after each keg is emptied, in order to find the amount of revenue per keg. Even when two or more different beers are on tap at different prices, control can still be maintained by having a separate sales register, or a separate key on the register, for each type of beer. When beer from the same keg is sold in different-sized glasses at different prices, control is more complicated.

One item in particular to monitor is the size or depth of the head desired. The larger the head is, the less beer there will be in the glass. A dishonest bartender can thus significantly increase the number of servings per barrel (and make a personal gain as a result) by increasing the size of the head.

Wine

The sale and cost of full bottles of wine can be controlled in the same way that liquor and canned or bottled beer are. However, one variable to be considered is bottled wine sold by the glass, particularly if the establishment buys large glass containers (jug wine) and sells it as house wine by the liter, the half-liter, or the glass. The best way to handle house wine is to use the standard revenue control method, using the weighted average approach to establish the standard revenue for each type or brand of house wine carried.

SALES MIX

We have already discussed the need to keep separate the purchase costs and sales of liquor, wine, and beer. See also Figure 19-2 and note that from Month 1 to Month 2, the overall beverage cost declined from 36.6 percent to 36.3 percent. On the surface this might seem desirable, but an analysis of the cost percentage by category (beer, wine, and liquor) shows that in each case it increased, despite the decline in the overall percentage.

Change in Sales Mix

The decline in the overall percentage was caused solely by a change in the sales mix (that is, the relative amounts of each category of alcoholic beverages that customers consumed). Month 2 shows a large shift in the amount of beer sold, relative to wine (with little change in liquor revenue). Because beer has a lower cost percentage than wine does, this shift encouraged the overall percentage downward, even though the cost percentage of all three categories went up. Only an analysis by category can show this.

But also note that the cost percentage is not necessarily a good indicator of profit. Even though the overall cost declined from Month 1 to Month 2, so did gross profit, from $91,600 to $90,000—and this would not normally be a desirable trend, because if all other costs remained constant, the net profit would also have declined.

Generally in most bars, because liquor has the lowest cost percentage of

	Month 1			Month 2		
	Cost	Revenue	Cost Percent	Cost	Revenue	Cost Percent
Beer	$ 4,800	$ 12,200	39.3%	$ 9,600	$ 24,200	39.7%
Wine	23,600	48,000	49.2	16,400	33,200	49.4
Liquor	24,400	84,200	29.0	25,200	83,800	30.1
Totals	$52,800	$144,400		$51,200	$141,200	
Overall cost	$\dfrac{\$52,800}{\$144,400} \times 100$ = 36.6%			$\dfrac{\$51,200}{\$141,200} \times 100$ = 36.3%		
Gross profit	$144,400 − $52,800 = $91,600			$141,200 − $51,200 = $90,000		

Figure 19-2   Sales mix analysis by cost category.

the three categories, if wine and/or beer sales are increased at the expense of liquor sales, the overall profits will decline. However, if wine and/or beer sales can be made in addition to normal liquor sales, the profits will increase.

SALES TAX

To this point we have not included any sales tax in the sales revenue. But because any government tax collected on liquor sales does not belong to the beverage establishment, it must be separated from the sales revenue earned. If sales registers record net revenue and tax revenue separately, this will eliminate the problem. In other cases, the prices on drink menus include the sales tax and are registered in this way, and thus the total register revenue also includes the amount of tax collected. In such cases the tax needs to be separated out so that only net sales revenue is compared with costs. Simply add the tax rate percentage to 100, divide the result into gross sales including tax, and multiply the result by 100. In other words,

$$\text{Net sales revenue} = \frac{\text{Total revenue including tax}}{100 + \text{tax rate}} \times 100$$

For example, assume that gross revenue is $21,000, including a 5 percent sales tax. The net sales revenue will be

$$\frac{\$21,000}{105} \times 100 = \$20,000$$

We can easily verify this answer:

Net sales revenue	$20,000
Tax at 5%	1,000
Gross sales revenue	$21,000

This method can also be used for a single drink price. For example, assume that the $3.00 selling price of a drink includes a 5 percent tax. The net revenue will be

$$\frac{\$3.00}{105} \times 100 = \$2.86$$

and again the proof is

Net drink revenue	$2.86
Tax at 5%	0.14
Total drink price	$3.00

MIXES AND GARNISHES COST

Most bars include the cost of mixes (carbonated beverages), food (for example, sugar, syrup, eggs), and garnishes (orange slices, maraschino cherries, and similar items) as part of the overall beverage or liquor cost. However, it can be useful to establish an overall percentage of these "other" ingredient costs as compared with total liquor sales. This is simple to do because the cost of these items purchased, requisitioned, and used can be added up over a period of, say, a month and be divided by total liquor sales for that month.

For example, if these other ingredient costs for a typical month were $1,000 and liquor sales were $50,000, the ingredient costs would be

$1,000/$50,000 \times 100 = 2\%$ of liquor sales

If liquor sales the next month were $60,000, the ingredient costs that month would be

$2\% \times \$60,000 = \$1,200$

It is useful to compare the actual ingredient costs from time to time with the forecast so that any variations from "normal" can be detected.

EQUIPMENT

Many different types of automatic and electronic beverage-dispensing equipment are available for both alcoholic and nonalcoholic beverages, from individual dispensing heads that attach to each bottle and require the bottle to be raised for pouring, to dispensing devices that are linked electronically to a sales register.

With the more expensive models, the dispenser will operate only if a sales check is inserted in the sales register before the appropriate sales keys are depressed. Bottles as large as a half-gallon (approximately 1.75 liters) can be stored, inverted, in a remote storeroom that is controlled by lock and key.

Using larger (and cheaper) liquor bottles with liquor-dispensing equipment should result in a cost-per-ounce saving. The same saving, however, is not feasible with a manual pouring system because the weight of the glass containers makes it too difficult to pour from them.

With dispensing equipment the storage location can be several hundred feet away and even on a different floor, and one location can even serve several different bars. Beverages are pumped through flexible plastic hoses. Sales can be recorded for each separate bar by brand, and even by bartender, on individual counters. For bars operating in resort properties, mobile, independent, and completely self-contained and motorized controlled bars are available.

Advantages

Some of the other advantages of liquor-dispensing devices are as follows:

- Bartender errors from spillage and over- or underpouring will be reduced or eliminated.
- Losses from liquor theft may be fewer, particularly if the bar inventory is far from the bar and accessible only to management.
- Drinks can be prepared faster, and so fewer bartenders may be needed.
- Bartenders can be trained more easily, and so employee turnover problems may be reduced.
- Bartenders require less manual dexterity.
- Back bar space is freed up.
- Sales control is improved, particularly if a drink cannot be served without going through the system. If this can be achieved, a critical control problem has been overcome. In such a situation, management does not need to worry about bartenders' bringing in their own bottles, because the sales will be recorded and the establishment will be entitled to the revenue! Cash control will thus be far more effective.

- Accurate inventory information is available, with records of drinks sold by category and inventory constantly being updated.
- Some systems monitor and even pour draft beer.
- Employees do not make pricing decisions (for example, when the happy hour begins). And with many of the new systems, management can change the prices from a control panel in an office remote from the bar.

Although the more sophisticated and expensive electronic bar control models do provide both direct cost savings—such as accurate drink measuring and complete draining of all bottles—and labor cost savings, as well as indirect benefits—such as ease of control, as each drink dispensed is recorded by a remote drink counter, resulting in less loss of liquor—it is a mistake to presume that a dishonest bartender cannot find a way around the system.

Management should never assume that equipment can provide absolute control and that other controls and management supervision are no longer required. Bars installing this type of equipment thus should continue to rely on some of the traditional manual controls outlined in this and the previous chapter, using as an aid the inventory information provided by the dispensing equipment drink counters.

Disadvantages

Consider also the disadvantages of automatic dispensing equipment:

- In some cases this equipment can slow drink service.
- Not all drinks can be dispensed through the equipment; some will still need to be mixed by hand.
- The atmosphere of the bar and the customers' attitudes may not be conducive to using dispensing equipment. In particular, customers may complain that they can no longer see the bottle from which the product is being poured.
- Employees may resist the change when the equipment is installed.
- In the event of the equipment's malfunctioning, it may be necessary to return to manual dispensing until the equipment is repaired.
- The cost of repair must be considered and added to the initial equipment costs.

Benefits of Information

The modern sales registers available to bars today can provide information for rational and effective management decision making and control. Some of the ways in which an establishment can benefit from this equipment are

- The numbers of customers and menu (beverage) selections can be translated into order quantities, for effective inventory investment. Eventually it may be possible to link suppliers directly to such systems, thereby eliminating some of the paperwork required by manual ordering systems.
- Continually updated inventory printouts are available, and purchases can be added to inventory at the time of delivery.
- Storeroom requisitions can be produced automatically, based on the amount of liquor used at the bar; that is, automatic requisitioning is available each day (or even each shift) to replenish par stock.
- Drink recipes can be cost updated automatically if the purchase price of any ingredient changes.
- Statistical information regarding what is and is not selling is available, thus allowing dead stock to be removed or special promotions to be introduced to use up that stock.

The availability of this information should be viewed not only as an asset to management (that is, more data on which to make decisions) but also as the opportunity to free up workers. They can then be put to more creative use (improving the bar's ambiance, devising new drinks, paying more attention to customers' needs, and so on). Employees would probably like this, as it would give them time to develop their skills by implementing positive control!

Evaluating Systems

To evaluate the value of installing an automated system, management should answer the following questions:

1. What is the bar's current liquor cost percentage?
2. What liquor cost saving is the system likely to provide?
3. Can most of the drinks sold be routed through the system, or will many of them still have to be hand poured or mixed?
4. How are the physical facilities (storage and bar areas) likely to be affected?
5. How will employees' productivity be improved, and will this affect management's productivity and the overall labor cost in the bar operation?
6. Does the system do more than the bar really needs?
7. How reliable is the manufacturer, in regard to repairs and service?
8. How reliable is the equipment? That is, what has been its performance in other establishments?

Each bar manager must carefully analyze his or her own bar to make sure that the investment costs can be more than adequately covered by benefits.

DISCUSSION QUESTIONS

1. How does a no-host bar differ from a hosted bar at a banquet?
2. How are tickets used for control in a no-host bar, and how can a bartender and a ticket seller work together for personal gain in such a situation?
3. In some hosted bars, the hosting organization is charged by the hour for drinks. How is this calculated?
4. Explain some of the controls necessary in bars that sell keg or draft beer.
5. Why is it important to separate the costs and sales of liquor, beer, and wine?
6. What is the equation for separating tax from net revenue when sales tax is included in total revenue?
7. Explain how the cost of mixes, food, and garnishes used in drinks can be controlled.
8. What are five advantages of using a liquor-dispensing system?
9. What are five disadvantages of using a liquor-dispensing system?
10. What are three "information" benefits from using an electronic liquor-dispensing system?
11. What are three questions that need to be answered before investing in a liquor-dispensing system?

PROBLEMS

1. The Relax Inn's banquet liquor control form indicated the following concerning a function held on May 6:

Item	Number of Bottles Issued	Number of Bottles Returned	Bottle Cost
Bourbon	20.0	4.3	$ 9.50
Rye	16.0	2.2	10.00
Gin	4.0	1.0	10.50
Rum	8.0	3.6	11.00
Scotch	6.0	0.9	13.00
Vodka	7.0	2.4	9.00

All bottles contain 750 milliliters (25 ounces); all drinks contain 1 ounce of liquor. The banquet liquor-selling prices are $2.40 each, except for scotch, which is $3.00. Calculate the liquor cost percentage for this function.

2. For each of the following situations, calculate from total revenue (including tax) the net revenue and the amount of tax:
   a. Total revenue $5,322.40, tax rate 7 percent.
   b. Total revenue $4,122.95, tax rate 5 percent.
   c. Total revenue $8,904.63, tax rate 6 percent.
3. The Hasting Hotel's cocktail lounge has the following sales and beverage cost percentage results for two successive months:

	January		February	
Item	Sales	Cost	Sales	Cost
Liquor	$24,321	30.0%	$25,840	29.0%
Beer	5,107	45.0	6,405	50.0
Wine	4,211	60.0	4,104	65.0

   a. Calculate, for each month, the overall beverage cost percentage.
   b. Comment on the results for any changes between January and February.
   c. Calculate the gross profit for each month.
4. Sales, including a 5 percent tax, in the Liquid Lounge for one week were $5,746.20. Opening inventory was $431.31, and closing inventory was $554.85. Purchases during the week were $1,744.20. Only five types of liquor are sold in the bar:

Item	Bottle Cost
Bourbon	$13.80
Gin	13.80
Vodka	13.65
Rum	14.10
Scotch	15.75

All bottles are 750 milliliters (25 ounces). All drinks, whether straight or in cocktails, contain only 1 ounce of liquor. It is estimated that 90 percent of all drinks sold are straight, with the following individual prices, including a 5 percent tax:

Drink	Price
Bourbon	$2.10
Gin	2.10
Vodka	2.10
Rum	2.10
Scotch	2.25

Approximately equal quantities of each are sold. Any carbonated mixers (soft drinks) served with a drink are priced at $0.15 extra. All cocktails are priced at $3.00 including tax.

a. Calculate the bar's actual liquor cost percentage for the week.

b. Using the other information given, explain whether or not this is a satisfactory actual result, supporting your comment with calculations.

20

Beverage Pricing

CHAPTER OBJECTIVES

After studying this chapter the reader should be able to

- Explain the concept that profit is a form of cost.
- Calculate the annual sales required for a bar to cover all its forecast costs (including profit), and convert this sales figure into an average drink price.
- Calculate, given appropriate information, an average drink price.
- Explain the effect that the beverage sales mix can have on the average drink price.
- Discuss the variables to be kept in mind when pricing beverages and explain the value of knowing the beverage cost percentage when pricing beverages.
- Discuss some of the other important considerations in pricing, such as a bar's elasticity of demand, cost structure, and the competition and product differentiation.

INTRODUCTION

Total alcoholic beverage sales are made up of the number of drinks sold times their price. It is important to control sales, that is, to control the prices of the drinks offered. Because there is a relationship between prices charged and total sales, prices must also affect the bar's general financial results, such as its ability to cover all operating costs and provide a profit that yields an acceptable return on investment. Price levels also affect budgeting, working capital, cash management, and equipment and furniture investment decisions.

Profitable pricing requires that individual drink prices be set to maximize the difference between total sales and total costs. This includes the cost of each drink, the contribution of each drink to total sales, the effect of price on demand for that drink, and the effect of the sales mix on profits.

The traditional method of looking at a budgeted income (profit and loss) statement is from the top down, that is, by calculating forecast sales and the costs associated with those sales in order to determine whether there is likely to be a profit. A different approach might be to start with the profit required, to calculate the costs, and to determine what sales are required and what prices need to be charged in order to achieve the desired profit. This "bottom-up" approach assumes that profit is a cost of doing business, which indeed it is. If a bank lends money at a particular interest rate to a bar, the interest expense will be considered a cost. The bank is an investor. Another group of investors are the owners of the bar. They too expect interest on their investment of money and/or time, except that their interest is called profit. Therefore, profit is just another type of cost. This concept, and the bottom-up approach to calculating sales, can be useful in setting prices.

AN EXAMPLE OF PRICING

Consider the following beverage operation with one hundred seats that wishes to determine its average drink price for the next year. We will use the following information about its fixed or overhead costs:

Administrative and general	$ 25,600
Marketing	12,200
Energy	6,800
Maintenance	5,400
Rent	42,000
Depreciation	23,000
Income tax	25,000
Profit required	25,000
Total	$165,000

In addition, the beverage cost is 25 percent of sales, labor cost is 40 percent, and other operating costs are 15 percent—totaling 80 percent for its variable costs, or costs that go up and down as sales go up and down.

Because the total fixed costs, including profit, are $165,000 and beverage, labor, and other variable costs are 80 percent of sales, then the fixed cost, including profit, must represent the other 20 percent of sales (sales 100 percent − variable costs 80 percent = fixed costs 20 percent). Therefore, the sales level required can be calculated as follows:

If 20% of sales = $165,000
Then 100%   = $165,000/20% = $825,000

We can verify this by preparing a traditional income statement:

Sales	$825,000
Variable costs 80% × $825,000	− 660,000
Contribution to fixed costs	165,000
Fixed costs (including profit)	165,000

Now that we know—assuming our cost projections are correct—we need $825,000 in annual sales in order to have a $25,000 profit next year, we can consider this $825,000 in relation to the individual drink price.

For example, what must our average drink price be, assuming that the bar is open six days a week (6 × 52 = 312 days a year) and on average 950 drinks are sold a day? The equation for the average price is

$$\text{Average price} = \frac{\text{Total annual sales}}{\text{Drinks sold} \times \text{Days open in year}}$$
$$= \$825,000/(950 \times 312)$$
$$= \$825,000/296,400 = \$2.78$$

Note that the figure of $2.78 does not tell us what every drink must be priced at—only what the average drink price should be. Some drinks will be more and some less than $2.78. Nevertheless, it gives us some idea of what the pricing structure of our drink menu should be, with a balance of prices, some higher than the average and some lower. The average drink price also tells us, as the year progresses, whether or not we will achieve the profit required. If we see that our actual average drink price is less than required, and all other items have not changed (days open, average number of drinks sold per day), we will know that something must be changed if we are not to have a shortfall in profit. Selling prices might have to be increased; costs might have to be decreased; or a combination of these variables might be required. If there is a sales tax on beverage sales, and prices on drink lists are to include the tax, then prices will have to be raised to accommodate it.

Note also that we assumed that the operation's only revenue was from selling drinks. But many bars make additional profit from music box receipts, video games, and miscellaneous sales. To reflect this additional profit in the average drink prices, the total annual sales required from drink sales should be decreased by the profit from other sales, thereby reducing the average drink price required.

Average Drink Price by Period

Because some bars have an average drink price that differs by period (for example, daytime versus nighttime), it might be desirable and useful to calculate the average drink price by period rather than for the entire day. To do this we need to know the proportion of sales derived from each period and the usual number of drinks sold during each period. In an ongoing bar, our own historical records will provide this information. In a new venture, these figures would need to be forecast. Let us assume our records tell us that 40 percent of our total sales is from daytime business and the other 60 percent from nighttime business and that 400 drinks are sold in the daytime and 550 at night on average. The equation is

$$\frac{\text{Period percentage of total sales} \times \text{Total sales}}{\text{Drinks sold} \times \text{Days open}}$$

Therefore in the daytime the average drink price will be

$$(40\% \times \$825,000)/(400 \times 312)$$
$$= \$330,000/124,800 = \$2.64$$

At night the average price will be

$$(60\% \times \$825,000)/(550 \times 312)$$
$$= \$495,000/171,600 = \$2.88$$

We can verify the accuracy of our average price calculation as follows:

Daytime: 400 drinks × $2.64 average price × 312 days =	$329,472
Nighttime: 550 drinks × $2.88 average price × 312 days =	494,208
Total sales	$823,680

Our original calculated sales total was $825,000, the difference caused by rounding the average drink prices to the closest cent.

Even though the illustration was for two periods, we can use the same approach for more than two periods. For example, we might want a separate calculation for the cocktail-hour period when special lower prices prevail or for the late-night entertainment time when higher prices are in effect. Note again that the average price by period is not the price of all drinks for that period: Drink menus generally have a range of prices.

Pricing Individual Drinks

One of the most common approaches to individual drink pricing is to calculate—given the drink recipes and specific ingredient purchase costs—the standard cost (what the cost should be) for each different drink. This cost is then multiplied by a factor obtained by dividing the overall beverage cost percentage desired into one hundred to get the selling price.

For example, we know from earlier that we wish to have an average cost of 25 percent. One hundred divided by 25 equals 4, which is our multiplication factor. To illustrate its use, suppose we had a drink that has been costed out to $0.70. Then $0.70 × 4 would give us the selling price of $2.80.

However, it may not be practical to do this across the board for all drinks. When developing drink prices, one must keep in mind what the average drink price needs to be, to what market one is selling (what the customers will pay and what they expect to pay for certain drinks), and what competitive bars are charging for the same drinks. It becomes a bit of a juggling act, with some items having a higher markup, some having a lower. In other words, some will have more than a 25 percent beverage cost, and some will have less than 25 percent.

Also, keep in mind that the individual beverage cost percentage of a drink is not as important as is the gross profit (selling price less beverage cost). Table 20-1 illustrates. All other things being equal, it is more profitable to sell drink 2, with a 40 percent cost and a $2.40 gross profit, than drink 1, with a 25 percent cost and a $1.50 gross profit. In fact, it would be better if all customers chose drink 2, for if they did, we would have more sales, because the selling price is higher. Both gross and net profit would be greater (assuming labor and other costs did not change). In other words, the sales volume, not the cost percentage, determines profit. A high beverage cost by itself is thus neither good nor bad.

Table 20-1   Cost percentage versus gross profit.

Item	Cost Price	Selling Price	Cost Percentage	Gross Profit
1	$0.50	$2.00	25%	$1.50
2	1.60	4.00	40%	2.40

Categories of Drinks

Many bars break down their drinks into categories such as the following:

Highballs—well brands
Highballs—call brands
Cocktails—well brands
Cocktails—call brands
Brandies and liqueurs
Frozen and ice-cream drinks
Specialty drinks
Beers—regular
Beers—premium
Wine

Their prices are then set within a narrow range within each category, thereby recognizing that there is an interdependence among categories and their prices. For example, if the prices of call-brand cocktails are raised, people may switch to well-brand cocktails. Alternatively, if some new, high-priced specialty drinks are created, people might switch to them, but in total (because of the higher prices), fewer of those drinks will probably be sold. Generally, specialty drinks yield a low cost percentage and a high gross profit.

Remember also that some drinks will always have a higher cost percentage and a lower gross profit, because if prices are raised above what the customers think is "normal," demand will drop drastically owing to elasticity of demand (to be discussed in more detail later). An example is bottled wine. Often wine will sell at twice its cost, or at about a 50 percent beverage cost. If this price were raised to four times cost (yielding a 25 percent beverage cost), then few bottles might be sold, and customers might switch to wine by the glass which yields a high gross profit but lower total sales.

Sales Mix Problem

What people choose from a variety of drink selections is known as the *sales mix*. When pricing, it is a good idea to keep in mind the likely sales mix because the average check, and ultimately profit, can be influenced by a change in the sales mix. Table 20-2 illustrates this, showing a sales mix for a bar offering an average drink price of $2.52. Let us suppose that through a promotion, the sales mix was changed, with one hundred people no longer drinking well highballs. Fifty switch to call highballs, and the other fifty switch to specialty drinks. The new average drink price is $2.62, as shown in Table 20-3. The higher drink price will result in higher sales, higher gross

Table 20-2   Example of sales mix.

Category	Quantity Sold	Selling Price	Total Revenue
Highballs, call	100	$2.50	$ 250.00
Highballs, well	300	2.00	600.00
Cocktails, well	200	2.25	450.00
Cocktails, call	240	2.75	660.00
Specialties	160	3.50	560.00
Totals	1,000		$2,520.00

Average price $2,520.00/1,000 = $2.52

profit, and higher net profit. Because of all these variables, drink pricing can be a complex task for the bar manager.

OTHER PRICING CONSIDERATIONS

The method demonstrated in this chapter for determining drink selling prices to ensure an adequate profit and for basing prices on costs has its shortcomings, however. It ignores many factors that must be considered when establishing prices. For that reason the drink-pricing methods used should be used as a reference point only, and not be the only determinant in setting the final prices.

Elasticity of Demand

Elasticity of demand pertains to the responsiveness of demand to a product or service when prices are changed, that is, the relationship between price and number of drinks sold. When there is a large change in demand resulting from a small change in prices, this is referred to as an elastic de-

Table 20-3   Another example of sales mix.

Category	Quantity Sold	Selling Price	Total Revenue
Highballs, call	150	$2.50	$ 375.00
Highballs, well	200	2.00	400.00
Cocktails, well	200	2.25	450.00
Cocktails, call	240	2.75	660.00
Specialties	210	3.50	735.00
Totals	1,000		$2,620.00

Average price $2,620.00/1,000 = $2.62

mand. When there is a small change in demand following a large change in prices, it is referred to as an *inelastic demand*.

Perhaps the easiest way to find out whether the demand for a product is elastic or inelastic is to note what happens to total sales revenue when prices are changed. If the demand is elastic, a decline in price will result in an increase in total revenue, because even though each drink receives a lower price, enough additional drinks are now being sold to more than compensate for a lower price.

For example, assume that average drink price is $3.00 and that an average of 6,000 drinks per week are sold. Total revenue per week is $18,000. If the average drink price is reduced by 5 percent, to $2.85, and the average number of drinks sold goes up by 10 percent, to 6,600, total revenue will rise to 6,600 × $2.85, or $18,810—which is $810 more than before. Thus, demand is elastic.

Generally, if demand is elastic, a change in price will cause total revenue to change in the opposite direction. If demand is inelastic, a price decline will cause total revenue to fall. The small increase in sales of drinks will not be sufficient to offset the decline in drink prices. Again, one can generalize and say that if demand is inelastic, a change in price will cause total revenue to change in the same direction. In other words, when demand is inelastic, a drink price change will have little or no effect on the number of drinks sold, but it will affect total revenue. If drink prices are increased, total revenue will increase, and if prices are decreased, total revenue will decrease. Therefore, when demand is inelastic, there is little value in cutting drink prices because revenue and net profit will decline.

Influencing Factors

One of the factors that influences elasticity of demand is the availability of substitutes. Bars that charge the highest prices usually are able to do so because there are few substitutes. For example, an elite bar with little competition can charge higher prices because its customers expect to pay higher prices, can afford to do so, and probably would not move to a lower-priced, less luxurious bar even if prices were increased. Demand is inelastic. A successful, high-priced bar also will usually find less customer resistance to an increase in prices.

On the other hand, a bar that is one of many in a particular neighborhood catering to the working trade would likely lose a lot of business if it raised its prices out of line with its competitors'. Its trade is very elastic, for its price-conscious customers will simply take their business to another bar. One can therefore say that the lower the income levels of a business's customers are, the more elastic will be their demand, and vice versa.

Closely related to income levels are the habits of a bar's customers. The more habitual the customers are, the less likely they will be to resist some upward change in prices, as customers tend to have loyalties to bars just as they do to the drink brands they buy. Bars that need to count on repeat business thus must be conscious of the effect that price changes may have on that loyalty. Note also that the demand for a bar's products tends to be more elastic over time. That is, even though customers are creatures of habit and do develop loyalties, those habits and loyalties can change over time.

Each bar operator must be familiar with the elasticity of demand of the market in which he or she operates, as well as with the customers' loyalty; in other words, he or she must have a market-oriented approach to pricing. This market orientation is particularly important to short-run decision making such as offering happy-hour prices to help increase business, or special prices during slow periods. These reduced prices are particularly appropriate when demand is highly elastic.

Cost Structure

A bar's specific cost structure is also a major factor influencing pricing decisions. Cost structure in this context means the breakdown of costs into fixed and variable. Fixed costs are those that normally do not change in the short run, such as a manager's salary or insurance expense. Variable costs are those that increase or decrease depending on sales volume, such as the cost of drink ingredients and the cost of napkins (coasters) and similar items.

If a bar has high fixed costs relative to variable costs, its profits are likely to be less stable as the volume of sales increases or decreases. In such a situation, having the right prices for the market becomes increasingly important. In the short run, any price above the variable cost will contribute to fixed costs and net profit, and the lower the variable costs are, the wider will be the range of possible prices.

For example, if the variable costs to sell an extra drink are $0.50 and that drink normally sells for $3.00, any price between $0.51 and $3.00 will contribute to fixed costs and profit. In such a situation the person who sets prices has at his or her discretion a wide range of possibilities for imaginative marketing and pricing to bring in extra business and maximize sales and profits. Note that this concept of variable costing is valid only in the short run. Over the long run, prices must be established so that all costs (both fixed and variable) are covered in order to produce a long-run net income.

The Competition

A bar's competitive situation is also critical to pricing. Very few bars are in a monopolistic situation (although some are, such as a bar operator who has the only concession at an isolated airport).

In a monopolistic, or near monopolistic, situation the operator has greater flexibility in determining prices and may, indeed, tend to charge more than is reasonable. But the customer still has the freedom to buy or not buy a drink. Also, in a monopolistic situation in which high prices prevail, other new entrepreneurs will soon be attracted to offer competition.

In a more competitive, but not completely competitive, situation there often exists an oligopoly, in which there tends to be one major or dominant bar and several smaller, competitive ones. In an oligopoly the dominant business is often the price leader. Thus when the price leader raises or lowers prices, the other businesses raise or lower their prices in tandem. An oligopolistic situation may arise in a resort area where there is one major resort hotel bar, surrounded by several independent bars catering to a slightly lower income level of customer.

Most bars, however, are in a purely competitive situation in which the demand for the drinks of any one establishment is highly sensitive to the prices charged. In such situations there is little to choose—from a price point of view—from one establishment to the next. When there is close competition, competitive pricing will often prevail, with little thought to other considerations. For example, an operator practicing competitive pricing may fail to recognize that his or her particular products or services are superior in some ways to his or her competitors' and thus could command a higher price without reducing demand.

In a highly competitive situation, an astute operator will look at the strengths and weaknesses of his or her own situation, as well as those of competitors. In analyzing strengths and weaknesses, operators should try to differentiate themselves and their products and services from their competitors'. The establishments that are most successful in differentiating themselves then have more freedom in establishing their prices. This differentiation can be in such matters as ambiance and atmosphere, decor, location, entertainment, development of special drinks, and similar things. Indeed, with differentiation, psychological pricing may be practiced, in which prices are established according to what the customer expects to pay for the "different" drinks or services offered. The greater the differentiation is, the higher the prices can be set. For example, this situation prevails in fashionable bars in which a particular market niche has been created and, at this point, a monopolistic or near monopolistic situation may prevail.

Other Pricing Methods

For most successful bars there is no doubt that the prices charged are those that are reasonable and fair under the circumstances, or what the customer believes is value for his or her money. Some bars will achieve this by trial and error, or by guessing, which can lead to constant price changes and confusion in the customers' minds.

Others will practice "what the traffic will bear" pricing, or the highest price that they can get under the circumstances. Others will always offer prices that are lower than any of their competitors', hoping to attract business away from the competition and to make up in volume what they lose on lower prices. Sometimes these lower prices are offered only on popular drinks as a form of loss leader. Still other bars will go to the other extreme and offer higher prices than any of their competitors do, hoping to attract a more select clientele that will spend more money in that bar than would lower-income customers.

In summary, there is no one method of establishing prices for all bars. Each establishment will have somewhat different long-run pricing strategies related to its overall objectives and will adopt short-run pricing policies appropriate to its cost structure and market situation.

DISCUSSION QUESTIONS

1. Why is profit just another cost of running a bar?
2. If sales for a bar are forecast to be a certain figure, how can a manager use this figure to determine the average drink price?
3. If a certain level of sales is wanted in a bar and the number of drinks sold is expected to go down, must the average drink price go up or down to reach the desired level of sales? Explain.
4. Define the term *sales mix,* and explain what influence it can have on an average drink price.
5. What factors would a bar manager need to consider when establishing individual drink prices?
6. Why do you, or do you not, think that the beverage cost percentage figure is important to drink pricing?
7. Define elasticity of demand, and using your own figures, show how a reduction in a bar's average drink price, and the resulting change in total revenue, would indicate an inelastic demand.
8. What implications does the breakdown of a business's costs into fixed and variable costs have for the pricing decision?
9. Discuss the concept of product and/or service differentiation in a bar.

PROBLEMS

1. The Belle Bar has annual fixed costs (including the profit required) of $193,000. Beverage cost of sales is 30 percent; labor cost is 35 percent; and other costs are 12 percent. Calculate the total sales required.

2. Assume that the Belle Bar is open seven days a week and that it sells, on average, 740 drinks per day. Calculate the average drink price required.

3. Assume that 35 percent of the Belle Bar's total sales are from the daytime and 65 percent from the nighttime. On average, 240 drinks are sold during the day and 500 at night. Calculate the day and night average drink prices, and prove your answer.

4. The Lincoln Lounge has fixed costs, including the profit required, of $378,000 a year. Beverage cost of sales is 28 percent; labor cost is 33 percent; and other costs are 12 percent. Assume that the lounge is open seven days a week and that on average, 1, 520 drinks are sold per day. Assume further that 30 percent of total sales are from the daytime and 70 percent from nighttime. On average, 480 drinks are sold during the day and the balance at night.

    a. Calculate the total sales required.

    b. Calculate the overall average drink price required.

    c. Calculate the daytime and the nighttime average drink prices, and prove your answer.

21

Sales Control

CHAPTER OBJECTIVES

After studying this chapter the reader should be able to

- Describe a sales check and list the basic controls required for it.
- Describe the three methods of sales control that can be used with a cash register–only system.
- List the five management control procedures that should be carried out daily when a cash register–only system is used.
- Differentiate a precheck from a preset–precheck sales register.
- Explain why the bartender's cash drawer should be kept closed between transactions and why bartenders should not be allowed to take register readings.
- Define the term *drop deposit*.
- Explain the procedures for cash floats and banks and also why a float should not be transferred from one employee to another on the next shift.
- Explain why cash registers should have sufficient tape in them each day for a full day's transactions and why management should take surprise, random register readings and cash counts.
- Explain why frequent cash overages from the same employee should be investigated.

The largest part of most bars' sales revenue is in the form of cash. It is therefore important that if costs are to be in line with what they should be for an achieved sales level, sales must be properly controlled. Management must be sure that it receives all the income due for the costs incurred. To achieve this, standard procedures must be implemented to control sales, analogous to the standard procedures used to control costs.

SALES CHECKS

If there is a complete detailed written or machine-printed record of every drink served in a bar, there should be few concerns about control. But this complete control may not be easy to achieve; thus sales checks are required.

Sales checks are available in many styles and varieties, but mainly it is a space for writing down the quantities of drinks ordered, names of drinks, prices, extensions (quantities times prices), and total dollar amount and tax, if any. It may also have space for recording the bartender's or server's identifying number or letter and the number of guests served. Sales checks should be sequentially prenumbered.

Record of Checks Issued and Returned

All prenumbered checks should be controlled. Blank pads of checks can be issued to bartenders and servers by the bar manager at the beginning of each shift. Unused blank checks should be locked away. These sales checks should be unique to the bar (for example, with the bar's name and/or logo on them) to make it more difficult for bar employees to bring in their own supply of sales checks, use them, and pocket the cash from sales. Sales checks should be printed on erasure-proof paper, as this makes it more difficult to change a sales check after a sale is made, without the change's being noticed. Pens, rather than pencils, should be used on handwritten sales checks. Mistakes should be crossed out and not erased. Indeed, it is a good procedure to have the bar manager initial all error corrections on sales checks. Bartenders and servers should return both used and unused sales checks at the end of their shift.

Missing Sales Checks

Bartenders and servers should be made responsible for ensuring that no sales checks inadvertently leave the premises with customers. A control book or form should be used to indicate which bartender or server is responsible for missing sales checks (see Figure 21-1).

Date Oct. 1				
Checks Issued	Employee Signature	Last Number Used	Checks Used	Management Signature
1026–1050		1043	18	
1051–1075		1074	24	
1201–1250		1246	47	
Total checks used Total checks turned in			321 321	

Figure 21-1   Check number issue control form.

Each missing sales check should be discussed with the responsible employee. Even if this does not result in the check's being found, it will act as a psychological control, and employees will know that the sales checks are being accounted for. For example, an employee might test the system by "losing" a used sales check and holding back the cash. If management does not question the loss, the employee may continue to "lose" used checks and pocket the cash. Unless all sales checks are accounted for, management has no control.

It is not normally necessary to count each bartender's and server's used sales checks and match that count against each issue control form. Rather, management only has to compare the total number of all checks used (according to the check number issue control form) with the total number of used checks turned in each day. If the two figures balance, all checks will have been accounted for.

BANKS OR FLOATS

Most bars issue their bartenders and servers a bank or float at the beginning of each shift. This bank is a change-making fund, a fixed amount counted out in front of each bartender and server, each of whom should sign for receipt of that fund. At the end of the shift the fund is turned back to the bar manager, who signs a receipt that is given to the employee.

CASH REGISTER–ONLY SYSTEM

Some bars' sales control system requires only a cash register (a register for ringing up each sale) with a cash drawer that opens for making change as each sale is recorded (rung up) on the register. There are two common systems of such cash control and a third, less common system.

In the first system the bartender serves and collects cash for the customers served at the bar itself, and also collects cash from the servers as they pick up the drinks. In other words, the bartender acts as the cashier for the servers. These servers then collect the cash from the customers at tables. With this system, the bartender turns in all cash from each day's (or shift's) sales, along with all sales checks, to the bar manager or a designated accounting office employee. The cash turned in should correspond to the register reading.

In the second system the servers do not pay the bartender for drinks picked up but act as their own cashiers and, at the end of their shift, turn in their total remittance to the bar manager or the accounting office. The bartender turns in only the cash and sales checks from sales made to customers served at the counter. If servers handle their own cash from sales and do not have access to a sales register to record those sales, they should have access to an adding machine. The servers add up all sales checks at the end of the shift and turn in the sales checks, adding-machine tape, and cash to correspond.

In the third system—although it is rarely used today, as it requires an additional person on the payroll—neither the bartenders nor the servers handle cash. Instead, the customers at both the bar and tables are presented with sales checks and pay a separate cashier on leaving the bar. The cashier then turns in all cash and all sales checks.

Drinks Served at Tables

Whatever cash-handling system is used, table servers should give the original sales check for each customer, or group of customers, to the bartender so that drinks can be prepared; the server then gets back this sales check when picking up the drinks. A good precaution with this method is to have the bartender stamp the check or draw a line underneath the last drink picked up, so that if the server again presents the sales check to the bartender for another round of drinks, he or she will know that all drinks listed above the stamp or line have already been picked up.

Drinks at Bar

For drinks sold at the bar, the bartender simply places the original sales check in front of the customer at the bar until he or she pays. At the time of payment the total sale should be rung up on the bartender's register and the cash placed in the cash drawer. In some bars the bartender is required to place the sales check in a slotted locked box so that it cannot be used again, with the bartender's pocketing the cash from the second sale. The bar manager should watch for and question the bartender if at any time there is no sales check in front of any guest at the bar.

At no time should a sales check be rung up in the register before payment has been received, because this would allow a bartender to use the same sales check more than once. This procedure may be modified if the register is the kind that has one set of keys for recording the sale and another set (which also opens the cash drawer) for recording the payment of cash.

No Sales Check at Bar

The requirement for bartenders to complete the sales checks for each sale at the bar counter can be a drawback during peak periods if it slows down service and loses sales. To overcome this problem, some bars eliminate the sales check. The bartender records in the register each drink served. The register provides a simple printed cash receipt for that drink, and the receipt is placed in front of the customer. Bartenders should be instructed to tear up the receipt when the customer pays, to prevent reuse of the receipt with another customer. However, note that if this system is used, there will be no detailed written record of what is sold, as there are no sales checks, and so there will be much less control of sales.

If servers pay for the drinks when picking them up, the bartender should ring up those sales in the bar register at that time, on a separate server key to separate those sales from sales at the bar counter.

Accounting Office Responsibilities

If a cash register system is used, management should daily

1. Spot check prices, extensions, and additions of sales checks.
2. Ensure that each check has been register machine validated and thus properly recorded in the sales register for drinks served and paid for at the bar, or on the adding machine tape if each server acts as his or her own cashier.
3. Reconcile each bartender's and server's cash remittances with the register or adding machine tape total.
4. Ensure that no sales checks are missing. Watch particularly for missing numbers between the last one in each series used on the preceding day and the first one used on the current day.
5. Follow up any errors or questionable items, by discussing them with

the employee(s) involved to determine how the error occurred and, if necessary, set up new control procedures to prevent that type of error from happening again. Talking to employees about errors is a good form of psychological control and shows them that management expects them to be careful.

MACHINE SYSTEMS

Most bars today use sales machines that go far beyond the control offered by a simple cash register system.

The Precheck Machine

The precheck register is a printing sales register without a cash drawer. Precheck machines or registers are generally designed to operate only when a sales check is inserted in the machine. Each server has his or her own machine-operating key. To operate the machine with a check inserted, the server depresses drink description keys, amount keys, and finally his or her own machine-operating key. This last operation causes the machine to issue a duplicate that the server can then use to obtain drinks from the bar. If any errors are made, these checks should be voided with the approval of the bar manager or his or her delegate.

For each transaction, the machine also prints a sequential number on both the original sales check and the duplicate, so that the two can be cross-referenced if questions arise later. Indeed, because the machine prints a sequential number on each sales check, it is possible to eliminate the cost of preprinting numbers on sales checks. If a sales check numbered by the register is used again (for the same customer or group of customers for another round of drinks), the employee enters its number in the machine so that the machine does not print a new number on the check. As a result, the machine holds a record of all transactions for each sales check. Thus, if a sales check is missing, management will know how much it totals and which bartender or server is responsible. The machine adds up the amount of sales that each server makes. It also records all transactions on a continuous audit tape that can be removed from the machine only at each day's end, by the bar manager, at the time the machine is cleared (reset to zero).

The advantage of a precheck system is that it makes out the sales check and records the amount of the sale before (thus the use of the prefix *pre*) the items are ordered from the bartender. The machine also has a balance pickup feature that records a running total on each check for customers running a tab. At the end of each shift or day, machine readings can be taken to determine the total dollar sales by each server. This amount—adjusted for any corrections (or voided checks) and reduced by the value of any charge sales handled by that server—is the amount of cash that must be turned in.

Some minor problems with the precheck machine are that servers can make mistakes in pricing drinks or in picking up running balances. Also, if machine drink keys are not descriptive, the server may have to do some additional writing on machine duplicates to give the bartender more specific instructions about preparing a drink.

The Preset–Precheck Machine

An improvement over the basic precheck machine is the preset–precheck machine. The keyboard of this machine has additional keys that enable automatic pricing on the sales check and additional descriptive wording to reduce the amount of handwriting required by the servers. The price is preprogrammed into the machine for each drink item, thus eliminating pricing errors. A remote control panel, kept under lock and key, allows management to change the price of drink items. The machine can also keep a running count of each type of drink sold.

Today's electronic precheck machines also have an automatic price lookup feature, which makes it unnecessary for the server to refer to drink lists for prices of special promotion items. Automatic price changes during periods such as happy hours are also possible. By entering a special code number when the sales check is being prepared, the server can instruct the machine to change the normal preset price to a special price that the machine has stored in its memory.

When applicable, tax can also be calculated automatically when it is not included in the drink price.

Machines can also operate with remote printers. For example, the register might be located at the server's working station, rather than at the bar, and operation of the register causes a printer at the bar to issue a requisition telling the bartender what drinks are required. In busy bars this means that a server can order drinks for several tables without having to walk back and forth to the bar for each table's order, other than to pick up the drinks when they are ready. In this way the server is in more constant contact with customers and also has more time to watch for possible walkouts.

Some of the more advanced integrated bar systems have networked all sales registers in use to the manager's office, where price changes can be preset and register readings can be taken remotely. The most sophisticated systems can also be integrated into automatic drink-dispensing devices, as detailed in Chapter 19.

CASH HANDLING AND OTHER SECURITY SUGGESTIONS

To ensure that all cash from sales is received, the following rules should be implemented:

1. The bartender's cash drawer should be kept closed between transactions. If this rule is enforced, there will be a record on the register tape of every sales transaction as well as of every other time that the cash drawer is opened. However, this rule is often broken, as bartenders say they can work faster if the drawer is left open, but this also allows cash from unrecorded drink sales to be removed more easily from the cash drawer without a record of the drawer's opening appearing on the tape. If the drawer needs to be opened between sales transactions (for example, when making change for a customer), the bartender should use a special card or a specific sales check to do this. This special card or sales check should be dated, signed, and turned in with all other checks at the end of the shift. In this way management will know the number of times that the cash drawer was opened for a "no sale" reason.

2. Do not allow bar personnel to clear the cash register (reset it to zero). If a bartender can do this, he or she may clear it well before closing and later turn in the requisite cash to correspond. After clearing the register, the bartender is in business for himself or herself and at regular closing time can once again clear the register and keep that cash. In some bars the bar personnel are not even allowed access to the key that allows them to take "readings" during the day. If there is no choice but to let the bartender clear the register, then make sure that each transaction on the register tape has a sequential number on it and that the starting number each day follows the closing number of the previous night.

3. If possible, do not allow cash-handling bar personnel to know how much cash to turn in. That is, do not tell bar employees the end-of-shift register reading. A management person should take all readings and keep them confidential in order to determine how much cash should be turned in, compared with the amount actually turned in. The manager should be present at the end of each shift to count out each cash-handling employee's bank or float, to give the employee a receipt for it, and to take all the rest of the cash for deposit in the safe until it is later counted, verified against the machine's sales transaction record, and then deposited in the bank. This procedure makes it more difficult for a dishonest person to remove cash (for unrecorded sales) at the end of a shift. An alternative method is for the bar manager to count the cash remittances in the presence of each employee and to give a receipt to the employee for that amount. Either way, any unexplained serious overages and shortages should be noted and discussed with the employee(s) involved. Depending on management policy and the relevant laws, employees may be required to make up shortages. Under no circumstances should any overages be given back to them.

4. It may be a good idea to have "drop" deposits if the business warrants it. A drop deposit can be established at, say, $500 of sales above the starting bank. As soon as this much cash accumulates in the cash drawer, the bartender/cashier should turn it in (drop deposit it) to a management person to be put in the safe. The employee should receive a receipt for each drop deposit. If nothing else, this will offer some protection in the event of a robbery.

5. Make sure that each sale is rung up separately on a sales check even when a customer does not pay immediately. Do not allow a bartender to run a tab in his or her head to be recorded as a lump-sum sale on a check when the customer is ready to pay.

6. Start *each* employee on shift with his or her own bank or float to make each employee accountable. Do not allow employees to transfer their bank to another employee on the next shift.

7. Make sure that each register has enough blank tape in it at the beginning of each day. If the tape runs out during the day, drinks can still be registered, but there will be no printed record in the machine, thereby making fraud easier.

8. At no time should the bar personnel's tip glass be near the cash register. This is necessary to eliminate the possibility of a bartender's making change from the tip glass, to prevent the transfer of money from the cash drawer to the tip glass, and to reduce the possibility of cash from sales' being deposited in the tip glass rather than in the cash drawer.

9. Bills from customers should remain on the register shelf until after a sales check has been paid and the customer is satisfied that he or she has received the correct change.

10. Whenever possible, each person handling cash should have a separate register or at least a separate cash drawer.

11. If more than one employee is using the same register, each should have a separate key that must be depressed to operate the register. This key can be coded with a number or letter and should appear on the register tape alongside each transaction.

12. Take random, surprise register readings and cash counts. If cash has been received and put into the cash drawer (to be removed later by a bar employee for personal gain), there will temporarily be more cash in the drawer than the register reading indicates there should be. Alternatively, the bartender might remove money from the drawer early in the shift to be compensated later with cash received and put in the drawer from unrecorded sales. In this case there will be a cash shortage.

13. Do not allow the bartender to give away drinks "on the house." Any drinks given away should be recorded on a sales check signed by the manager.

14. Any overrings or voided checks should be approved with the bar manager's signature on the check at the time of the transaction.

15. Frequent cash overages should be checked out. The register user may be underringing and removing only part of the cash, so as to avoid a shortage that otherwise might alert management.

16. Registers should be left empty, unlocked, and with cash drawers left open when the bar is closed (to prevent damage to the machine during any attempted theft).

17. Do not allow bartenders to accept postdated checks or IOUs without the bar manager's approval.

18. Do not allow money to be taken from the cash drawer for petty cash purchases without the bar manager's authorization in advance. Be sure that any petty cash payment is supported by a sales slip or written voucher signed by the manager. Better yet, do not permit the daily receipts to be used for petty cash or for COD deliveries, but set up a separate petty cash fund for this.

19. Deposit all receipts each day in the bank.

20. Make sure the register's display indicating prices rung up is in full view of the customers (and management) and that the register itself is well lit.

21. Put bar control policies into writing, and make sure that each employee receives a copy, reads it, and understands it. For example, management might want to have the right to inspect any packages brought in or taken out by employees. If so, put this policy in writing.

22. Bond all employees who handle cash.

23. Ensure that management employees closely watch the cash register and its operation as part of their day-to-day supervisory responsibilities.

24. If absolutely necessary—because theft is suspected—use profes-

Employee name _____		
Date	Comment
Feb. 1	Cash over $2.10
2	Check #3016 missing
7	Cash short $7.85
10	Cash short $10.00
12	Check #3927 missing

Figure 21-2 Employee record book.

sional spotters. Even though a bar cannot afford to have spotters permanently, if employees know that spotters will be randomly used, they are more likely to stay honest. Some bars use video cameras that record a certain number of frames per minute, thereby placing the bar under virtually continuous observation (just as many banks are today). But as with many other controls, this control is of no value unless the manager takes the time to view the video frames each day.

25. Keep an employee record book, as illustrated in Figure 21-2. Such a record allows management to be aware of which employees are consistently losing checks or making errors that need to be discussed.

DISCUSSION QUESTIONS

1. To control a bar, what initial documentation is essential, and what basic controls over this documentation are required?

2. When using a cash register–only sales control method, what are the three systems for cash collection that can be used?

3. Why should bartenders not be allowed to ring up a sales check in the bar's cash register before payment is received? Under what circumstances might this be allowed?

4. What five control procedures should management carry out daily when a cash register–only system is used?

5. Differentiate a precheck from a preset-precheck machine.

6. Why is it a good policy to require bartenders to keep the cash drawer closed between transactions?

7. Why should bartenders not be allowed to clear cash registers (reset them to zero)?

8. What is a drop deposit?

9. Why should cash banks or float not be allowed to be transferred from an employee finishing a shift to one just starting?

10. Why should management make sure there is enough tape in each register at the start of each day?

11. Why is it a good idea to take random, surprise register readings and cash counts?

12. Why should management investigate frequent cash overages from the same employee?

APPENDIX A

Cocktail Recipes

These sixty-six recipes are the standard ones used in many beverage operations, although some bars may have adapted them to their own particular needs.

ALEXANDER
Ingredients: 1 oz. liquor of choice
                 1/2 oz. crème de cacao (light with gin, vodka, and tequila; dark with rum, brandy, and whiskey)
                 2 oz. cream
Method: Shake/blend
Glass: Cocktail, rocks, or champagne
Garnish: Grated nutmeg

BACARDI
Ingredients: 1 oz. light rum
                 1 oz. sweet/sour mix
                 1 oz. lime juice
                 3 dashes grenadine
Method: Shake/blend
Glass: Champagne
Garnish: None

BANANA DAIQUIRI
Ingredients: 1 oz. light rum
                 1/2 oz. banana liqueur
                 1 oz. lime juice
                 1 medium banana
Method: Shake/blend
Glass: Champagne
Garnish: Banana slice

BETWEEN THE SHEETS
Ingredients: 1/2 oz. light rum
                 1/2 oz. brandy
                 1/2 oz. Cointreau
Method: Shake/blend
Glass: Cocktail
Garnish: None

BLACK RUSSIAN
Ingredients: 3/4 oz. vodka
                 3/4 oz. dark crème de cacao or Kahlua
Method: Build
Glass: Rocks/Old Fashioned
Garnish: None

BLOODY MARY
  Ingredients: 1 oz. vodka
                1 dash Tabasco
                2 dashes Worcestershire sauce
                Top with tomato juice
  Method: Build
  Glass: Highball
  Garnish: Celery stick + lemon wedge

BUCK
  Ingredients: 1 oz. liquor of choice
                Lemon wedge squeezed in glass, shell in
                Fill with ginger ale
  Method: Build
  Glass: Highball
  Garnish: None

CHAMPAGNE COCKTAIL
  Ingredients: 1/2 oz. brandy
                1 cube sugar
                1 dash Angostura bitters
                Fill with champagne
  Method: Build
  Glass: Champagne
  Garnish: None

CHI CHI
  Ingredients: 1 oz. vodka
                1 oz. coconut syrup
                3 oz. pineapple juice
                4 oz. cream
  Method: Shake/blend
  Glass: Hurricane
  Garnish: Pineapple wedge

CUBA LIBRE
  Ingredients: 1 oz. dark rum
                1/2 oz. lime juice
                Fill with cola
  Method: Build
  Glass: Highball
  Garnish: Lime wedge

DAIQUIRI

Ingredients: 1 oz. light rum
1 oz. lime juice
1 oz. sweet/sour mix
Method: Shake/blend
Glass: Cocktail
Garnish: Lime wheel

EGGNOG

Ingredients: 1/2 oz. rum
1/2 oz. Tia Maria
1 whole egg
4 oz. cream
Method: Shake/blend
Glass: Highball
Garnish: Grated nutmeg

FLIP

Ingredients: 1 oz. liquor of choice
3/4 oz. sweet/sour mix
1 whole egg
Method: Shake/Mix
Glass: Cocktail
Garnish: None

FOGHORN

Ingredients: 1 oz. gin
1 oz. lime juice
Top with ginger ale
Method: Build
Glass: Highball
Garnish: Lime wedge

FRAPPÉ

Ingredients: 1 oz. liquor of choice
Crushed ice
Method: Build
Glass: Rocks
Garnish: None

FREDDY FUDPUCKER

Ingredients: 1 oz. tequila
Fill with orange juice
Circle with Galliano
Method: Build
Glass: Rocks
Garnish: Cherry + orange slice

FRENCH 75
Ingredients: 1 oz. gin
1 oz. lemon juice
1 oz. sweet/sour mix
Top with champagne
Method: Shake/blend
Glass: Champagne
Garnish: None

GIBSON
Ingredients: 1 1/2 oz. gin
2 dashes dry vermouth
Method: Stir
Glass: Cocktail
Garnish: Onion

GIMLET
Ingredients: 1 oz. gin
1 oz. lime juice
1 oz. sweet/sour mix
Method: Shake/blend
Glass: Cocktail
Garnish: Lime wheel

GIN FIZZ
Ingredients: 1 oz. gin
1 oz. lemon juice
1 oz. sweet/sour mix
Method: Shake/blend
Glass: Sour
Garnish: Cherry

GOLDEN CADILLAC
Ingredients: 1/2 oz. dark crème de cacao
1 oz. Galliano
2 oz. cream
Method: Shake/blend
Glass: Champagne
Garnish: None

GOLDEN DREAM
Ingredients: 1/2 oz. dark crème de cacao
1 oz. Galliano
1 oz. orange juice
2 oz. cream
Method: Shake/blend
Glass: Champagne
Garnish: None

GOLDEN FIZZ
Ingredients: 1 oz. gin
1 oz. lemon juice
1 oz. sweet/sour mix
1 egg yolk
Method: Shake/blend
Glass: Fizz
Garnish: None

GRASSHOPPER
Ingredients: 1 oz. green crème de menthe
1/2 oz. white crème de cacao
2 oz. cream
Method: Shake/blend
Glass: Champagne
Garnish: None

HARVEY WALLBANGER
Ingredients: 1 oz. vodka
Fill with orange juice
Circle with Galliano
Method: Build
Glass: Highball
Garnish: None

HOT TODDY
Ingredients: 1 oz. liquor of choice
1/4 oz. simple syrup
Fill with hot water
Method: Build
Glass: Mug or Old Fashioned
Garnish: Sprinkled nutmeg + cinnamon stick

HURRICANE
Ingredients: 1/2 oz. brandy
1/2 oz. light rum
1/4 oz. coffee liqueur
1 oz. pineapple juice
2 oz. cream
Method: Shake/blend
Glass: Hurricane
Garnish: Pineapple + cherry

JOHN COLLINS
Ingredients: 1 oz. rye
1 oz. sweet/sour mix
1 oz. lemon juice
Soda out

Method: Build
Glass: Collins or Highball
Garnish: Cherry + orange slice

MAI TAI
Ingredients: 3/4 oz. light rum   *Creme de almond*
1/2 oz. Amaretto
3/4 oz. dark rum
Top with pineapple/orange juice
Method: Build
Glass: Brandy snifter
Garnish: Cherry + orange slice

MANHATTAN
Ingredients: 1 1/2 oz. rye
2 dashes sweet vermouth
Method: Stir
Glass: Cocktail
Garnish: Cherry

MARGARITA
Ingredients: 1 oz. tequila
1/2 oz. Triple Sec
2 oz. lime juice
1/2 oz. sweet/sour mix
Method: Shake/blend
Glass: Champagne
Garnish: Salt glass rim + lime wheel

MARTINI
Ingredients: 1 1/2 oz. gin
2 dashes dry vermouth
Method: Stir
Glass: Cocktail
Garnish: Olive

MINT JULEP
Ingredients: 1 1/2 oz. Southern Comfort
1/2 oz. white rum
1/2 oz. brandy
Fill with 7-Up
Method: Build
Glass: Sling
Garnish: Cherry + mint sprigs

MOSCOW MULE
Ingredients: 1 oz. vodka
Squeeze of lime
Fill with ginger beer
Method: Build
Glass: Rocks
Garnish: Lime wedge

OLD FASHIONED
Ingredients: 1 oz. rye
1/2 oz. sweet/sour mix
1 drop Angostura bitters
Soda out
Method: Build
Glass: Old Fashioned
Garnish: Cherry + orange slice

ORANGE BLOSSOM
Ingredients: 3/4 oz. gin
1/4 oz. Cointreau
3 oz. orange juice
Method: Shake/blend
Glass: Champagne
Garnish: Orange wheel

PIÑA COLADA
Ingredients: 1 oz. light rum
1 oz. coconut syrup
3 oz. pineapple juice
4 oz. cream
Method: Shake/blend
Glass: Hurricane
Garnish: Pineapple wedge

PINK LADY
Ingredients: 1 oz. gin
1/2 oz. sweet/sour mix
1/2 oz. grenadine
2 oz. cream
Method: Shake/blend
Glass: Champagne
Garnish: None

PLANTER'S PUNCH
Ingredients: 1 oz. dark rum
Fill with pineapple/orange juice
Top with apricot brandy

Method: Build
Glass: Sling
Garnish: Cherry + orange slice

POUSSE CAFÉ
Ingredients: 1/4 oz. Cognac
1/4 oz. Cointreau
1/4 oz. green crème de menthe
1/4 oz. dark crème de cacao
1/4 oz. grenadine
Method: Build
Glass: Pony
Garnish: None

RAMOS FIZZ
Ingredients: 1 oz. gin
1 oz. lemon juice
1 oz. sweet/sour mix
1 oz. cream
Method: Shake/blend
Glass: Fizz
Garnish: None

RICKEY
Ingredients: 1 oz. liquor of choice
Squeezed 1/2 lime, shell in
Fill with soda
Method: Build
Glass: Highball
Garnish: None

ROB ROY
Ingredients: 1 1/2 oz. scotch
2 dashes sweet vermouth
Method: Stir
Glass: Cocktail
Garnish: Cherry

ROYAL FIZZ
Ingredients: 1 oz. gin
1 oz. lemon juice
1 oz. sweet/sour mix
1 whole egg
Method: Shake/blend
Glass: Fizz
Garnish: None

RUSSIAN BEAR

Ingredients: 3/4 oz. vodka
　　　　　　3/4 oz. Kahlua or dark crème de cacao
　　　　　　2 oz. cream
Method: Shake/blend
Glass: Champagne
Garnish: None

RUSTY NAIL

Ingredients: 3/4 oz. scotch
　　　　　　3/4 oz. Drambuie
Method: Build
Glass: Rocks
Garnish: None

SCARLETT O'HARA

Ingredients: 1 oz. Southern Comfort
　　　　　　1 oz. lime juice
　　　　　　1/2 oz. grenadine
　　　　　　1 dash sweet/sour mix
Method: Shake/blend
Glass: Champagne
Garnish: Lime wheel

SCORPION

Ingredients: 3/4 oz. brandy
　　　　　　1/2 oz. dark rum
　　　　　　2 oz. orange juice
　　　　　　1 oz. lime juice
Method: Build
Glass: Collins
Garnish: Cherry + orange slice

SCREWDRIVER

Ingredients: 1 oz. vodka
　　　　　　Fill with orange juice
Method: Build
Glass: Highball
Garnish: None

SIDECAR

Ingredients: 1 oz. brandy
　　　　　　1/2 oz. Triple Sec
　　　　　　1 oz. lemon juice
　　　　　　1 dash sweet/sour mix

Lime wedge
Sugar rim

Method: Shake/blend
Glass: Champagne
Garnish: Sugar glass rim

SILVER FIZZ
Ingredients: 1 oz. gin
1 oz. lemon juice
1 oz. sweet/sour mix
1 egg white
Method: Shake/blend
Glass: Fizz
Garnish: None

SINGAPORE SLING
Ingredients: 1 oz. gin
1 oz. sweet/sour mix
1 oz. lemon juice
1 oz. orange juice
1 dash grenadine
Fill with soda
Top with cherry brandy
Method: Build
Glass: Sling
Garnish: Cherry + orange slice

SOUR
Ingredients: 1 oz. liquor of choice
1 oz. sweet/sour mix
1 oz. lemon or lime juice
Method: Shake/blend
Glass: Sour
Garnish: Cherry

SPRITZER
Ingredients: 6 oz. white wine of choice
Top with soda
Method: Build
Glass: Wine or Highball
Garnish: Lime wedge

STINGER
Ingredients: 1 oz. brandy
1/2 oz. white crème de menthe
Method: Stir/build over ice
Glass: Champagne or rocks
Garnish: None

STRAWBERRY DAIQUIRI
Ingredients: 1 oz. light rum
3 oz. lime
3 oz. strawberries
Method: Blend
Glass: Wine
Garnish: Fresh strawberry

SWIZZLE
Ingredients: 1 oz. liquor of choice
1 oz. lime juice
1 oz. simple syrup
2 dashes Angostura bitters
Fill with soda
Method: Build
Glass: Collins
Garnish: None

TEQUILA SUNRISE
Ingredients: 1 oz. tequila
Fill with orange juice
Circle with grenadine
Top with 1/4 oz. Triple Sec
Method: Build
Glass: Highball
Garnish: Cherry + orange slice

TOM AND JERRY
Ingredients: 1 oz. rum
1 oz. whiskey or brandy
1 T Tom and Jerry mix
Fill with hot water or milk
Method: Build
Glass: Mug
Garnish: Sprinkled nutmeg

TOM COLLINS
Ingredients: 1 oz. gin
1 oz. sweet/sour mix
1 oz. lemon juice
Soda out
Method: Build
Glass: Collins or Highball
Garnish: Cherry + orange slice

VELVET HAMMER
Ingredients: 3/4 oz. Kahlua
1/2 oz. Triple Sec
3 oz. cream
Method: Shake/blend
Glass: Champagne
Garnish: None

VODKATINI (VODKA MARTINI)
Ingredients: 1 1/2 oz. vodka
1/4 oz. dry vermouth
Method: Stir
Glass: Cocktail
Garnish: Lemon twist or olive

WARD 8
Ingredients: 1 oz. rye
1 oz. lemon juice
1 oz. orange juice
1 oz. sweet/sour mix
1 dash grenadine
Method: Shake/blend
Glass: Fizz
Garnish: Cherry

WHITE CADILLAC
Ingredients: 1 oz. Galliano
1/2 oz. Cointreau
2 oz. cream
Method: Shake/blend
Glass: Champagne
Garnish: None

WHITE RUSSIAN
Ingredients: 3/4 oz. vodka
3/4 oz. Kahlua or dark crème de cacao
2 oz. cream
Method: Build
Glass: Rocks
Garnish: None

ZOMBIE

Ingredients: 1 oz. light rum
1 oz. dark rum
1 oz. overproof rum
1/3 oz. apricot brandy
1/2 oz. pineapple juice
1/2 oz. orange juice
1/2 oz. grenadine
1/2 oz. lemon juice

Method: Build
Glass: Sling
Garnish: None

APPENDIX B

Wine-tasting Terms

Although this book does not cover the topic of wine tasting, many of the terms are nevertheless useful to know and are used throughout this book to describe certain wines. The most commonly used descriptive words are summarized as follows:

Acidic. A sharp taste caused by acids in the grapes. The right amount of acidity makes a wine fresh and crisp tasting.

Aroma. The smell of a young, fresh wine. Sometimes also referred to as **nose.** Do not confuse aroma with **bouquet.**

Astringent. A taste derived from tannin dissolved from the grape skins, making the wine taste rough. Usually characteristic of young red wines. An astringent wine may mellow as the wine matures.

Balanced. Refers to a perfectly constituted, but probably rare, wine with a balance of sugars, acids, tannins, and alcohol, with no one element predominant or out of harmony with the others.

Bitter. A disagreeable taste that may wear off in time as the wine matures.

Body. The feel of the wine in the mouth. The feel of a wine with body is often described as chewy. A light-bodied wine is referred to as a light wine and is low in one or more of the body components (alcohol, sugar, and glycerine) formed during fermentation. A full-bodied wine is typically high in those components and normally has a higher alcohol content.

Bouquet. A pronounced fragrance resulting from a wine's maturity. Sometimes also referred to as **nose.**

Character. The positive, distinctive, unmistakable taste of a particular wine.

Clean. A natural fresh flavor with no negative smell or taste.

Complex. A variety of fragrances and subtle tastes found only in quality wines.

Corked. Refers to a wine that has declined in quality because of a rotten cork whose smell affects both the taste of the wine and its bouquet.

Dry. Refers to wine with almost no residual sugar, that is, less than 1 percent. No absolutely dry wine would taste very good.

Dull. Without character.

Earthy. A flavor and smell derived from the wine's soil.

Elegant. Class or exceptional character used in reference to an outstanding wine.

Fine. Light and delicate.

Finish. The aftertaste of a wine. A good wine should have a pleasant aftertaste.

Flat. Insipid, lacking character and acidity.

Flinty. A dry, stony, crisp taste, often characteristic of a young dry wine.

Flowery. Leaves an impression of a flower smell.

Foxy. The aroma, bouquet, and flavor of wines made from the labrusca vine varieties.

Fruity. The fresh flavor of grapes, especially the particular grape variety used.

Full. Rich.

Generous. Rich in color, strength, and warmth.

Grapey. A smell typical of certain grape varieties.

Green. Acidic and either made too young or from unripe grapes.

Hard. Undissolved tannins, indicating a wine, usually a red, that needs further aging to soften it.

Light. Low in alcohol, acid content, and body. This may be a good characteristic for a jug wine, but is not desirable in a quality wine.

Lively. Young, fresh, and vigorous.

Maderized. Refers to an old or badly corked wine that has oxidized (sometimes because of excess heating) and whose color and taste resemble Madeira (a sweet dessert wine). If the wine is white, its color will also turn brown.

Mellow. The opposite of **astringent**, that is, softened with age.

Musty. A moldy smell or flavor resulting from unclean casks or the use of rotten grapes.

Nose. See **aroma** and/or **bouquet**.

Oaky. An aroma, reminiscent of vanilla, derived from aging in oak casks.

Oxidized. Refers to a wine that has been affected by exposure to air, which can prematurely age a wine and spoil it.

Powerful. Generous, with good strength and body.

Raisiny. The smell and flavor of sun-dried grapes. Often found in a wine made in a hot climate.

Ripe. At the peak of maturity, mellow and perfect.

Robust. A predominating alcohol flavor, creating a rich and vigorous yet well-rounded wine.

Rough. A hard, harsh tannic taste.

Round. Harmonious, full, and without any rawness.

Sharp. A high acid content, typical of a tart wine.

Silky. A good soft feel, found in mature quality wines.

Soft. Mellow, well rounded, and lacking in tartness. Usually used to describe a mature wine. See also **tart**.

Spicy. A predominantly fragrant smell and taste of herbs.

Sweet. A high residual sugar content, characteristic of some dessert wines, but should be balanced with acidity and alcohol content.

Tannic. Refers to the tannin (an astringent element derived from the skins, stalks, and seeds of grapes), which is necessary for a wine that needs long aging. Tannin can also be added during fermentation or aging. If present in young wines, they can be rough and unpleasant but may soften with age. Sediment in old red wines results from tannin deposits.

Tart. A sharp, acid taste, not to be confused with **dry**. Tartaric acid is one of the four basic grape acids, along with ascorbic, citric, and malic. Some tartness may be a good characteristic, but a wine tart to the point of tasting vinegary is not good. If a white wine is chilled, some tartaric acid can precipitate as crystals but will not affect the wine's taste.

Weak. Low in alcohol.

Well balanced. A harmonious blend of taste and smell. Fruit, acid, tannin, and alcohol all are in balance.

Woody. A detrimental flavor derived from the oak barrel in which the wine has matured. Do not confuse with **oaky**, which is a positive flavor as long as it is not overwhelming.

Yeasty. Smelling of the fermented yeast still present in young wines. This smell disappears in time.

Glossary

Abboccato. Italian for semisweet.

Abfüller. German for bottler.

Absinthe. Bitter high-proof wormwood-flavored spirit that is now illegal.

Adjunct. Grain product added to malted barley in making beer.

Advocaat. Eggnog-flavored Dutch liqueur.

Aging. Storing wine or distilled spirits in casks or other containers to improve flavor.

Aguardiente. Spanish type of Marc. See **Marc**.

Ale. Type of beer made by top fermentation.

Almacenista. Type of extremely well aged unblended sherry.

Amabile. Italian for semisweet.

Amaretto. Almond/apricot-flavored liqueur.

Amer Picon. Type of French bitters. See **Bitters**.

Amontillado. Pale, dry sherry with a mellow flavor made in Spain.

Amoroso. Golden rich dessert sherry made in Spain.

Amphora. Ancient container in which early wine makers, such as the Greeks and Egyptians, stored their wine.

Amtliche Prüfungsnummer (A.P.Nr.). German term for an officially tested wine that has a number on its bottle label.

Anbaugebiet. German for an official wine region, of which there are eleven in Germany.

Angostura. Type of bitters made in Trinidad. See **Bitters**.

Anisette. Licorice-flavored liqueur.

Annata. Italian for vintage year.

AOC. Abbreviation for *Appellation d'Origine Contrôlée*—the top French wine quality designation.

Aperitif. A fortified wine flavored with one or more herbs and spices, usually consumed before a meal.

Apfelschnapps. German brandy made from apples.

Appellation contrôlée. French term meaning a controlled place name and appearing on bottle labels to show that the wine conforms to government standards. See also **AOC** and **VDQS**.

Applejack. U.S. brandy distilled from apple cider.

Apricot brandy. Brandy distilled from apricots, or an apricot-flavored liqueur.

Aquavit (Akvavit). Scandinavian distilled spirit flavored with caraway.

Aqua vitae. An early term, meaning water of life, for a distilled spirit.

Arak. See **Arrack**.

Armagnac. Brandy made in the Armagnac region of France.

Aromatized wine. Fortified wine to which aromatic flavorings have been added. For example, vermouth.

Arrack. Strong spirit made from the fermented juices of palm leaves and/or other products. Also known as **Arak**, **Rack**, or **Raki**.

Asciutto. Italian for dry.

Astringent. Sharp, acidic flavor in a wine.

Audit tape. Continuous, chronological register tape that records all beverage sales made for a specific period—usually a day.

Aus dem Weingut. German term meaning from the estate or vineyard.

Aus eigenem Lesegut. German term meaning grower's own harvest, and the equivalent of estate bottled.

Auslese. German term meaning that the wine grapes have been selectively picked in ripened bunches. Used with Q.m.P. wines.

Azienda agricola or **Azienda agraria.** Italian terms for a farm, vineyard, or agricultural holding.

Back bar. Part of a cocktail bar that is behind the bartender(s) and that faces the customers sitting at a bar's counter.

Bagaceira. Portuguese Marc. See **Marc**.

Bank. See **Float**.

Barley. Main ingredient in quality beer and Scotch whisky.

Bar spoon. Teaspoon-sized spoon with a long handle used for stirring certain drinks before they are poured into glasses.

Bar strainer. Round metal strainer surrounded by a wire spring and with a handle, used for straining certain mixed drinks before they are poured into glasses.

B & B. Benedictine liqueur with cognac or brandy added. See **Benedictine**.

Beer. Alcoholic beverage made from malted grain flavored with hops. See also **Distiller's beer**.

Beerenauslese. German term meaning that the wine grapes have been selectively picked one by one. Used with Q.m.P. wines.

Benedictine. Herb/spice-flavored liqueur.

Bentonite. Fine clay sometimes used to help filter or clarify a wine.

Bereich. German word meaning a district within one of West Germany's eleven official wine-growing regions (**Anbaugebiete**).

Beverage cost percentage. Beverage cost of sales for a particular period, divided by sales for that same period.

Beverage-receiving report. Report showing the dollar amount of goods received from each supplier each day or period, usually broken down into beer, wine, and liquor.

Bianco. Italian for white.

Bitters. Spirits flavored with herbs or spices and with no added sugar.

Blackberry brandy. Blackberry-flavored liqueur.

Blanc. French for white.

Blanc de blancs. French term meaning white wine made entirely from the juice of white grapes and usually used to describe a champagne made in this way.

Blanc de noirs. French term describing a white wine (generally champagne) made entirely from the juice of black grapes.

Blanco. Spanish for white.

Blended straight whiskey. In the United States, a blend of several straight whiskeys of the same type. See also **Straight whiskey**.

Blender. Mechanical mixing device with blades for cutting up ice and solid food items used in some cocktails.

Blending. Process of mixing wines or spirits of different ages and/or personalities, before bottling.

Blush wine. Rosé wine.

Bock beer. Rich, heavy, dark beer with a high alcohol-by-volume content.

Bocksbeutel. Distinctively shaped gourdlike bottle used for German Franken (Franconia) wines.

Bodega. Spanish wine cellar or warehouse. Also used in Spain to mean a bar.

Body. Amount of flavor and aroma of an alcoholic beverage.

Bottle coding. Special code put on each full bottle of liquor issued from the storeroom to the bar. No bottles are allowed at the bar, or empties returned to the storeroom, that do not have this code.

Bottle well. Heavy-duty plastic containers surrounded by ice to keep fruit juices and other liquids refrigerated at the front bar.

Bottom fermentation. Method of fermenting a lager beer in which yeasts act at a low temperature at the bottom of the fermenting tank.

Bouquet. Clean and pleasing fragrance found in the best wines.

Bourbon. Whiskey made with at least 51 percent corn plus other grains.

Branco. Portuguese for white.

Brandy. Distilled spirit made from wine or other fermented fruit juice. See also **Cognac.**

Brandy glass. Footed glass with a large bowl allowing release of the brandy's bouquet. See **Snifter.**

Brewing. Stage in beer making in which the wort is boiled with hops.

Brown sherry. British term for a type of dark sweet sherry.

Brut. On a champagne label, means dry and signifies that little sugar has been added.

Buck. Type of cocktail.

Bulk process. Method of making sparkling wine in a large closed tank or container to which carbon dioxide is introduced under pressure before bottling rather than created in the bottle itself. Also known as the **Charmat process.**

Byrrh. Type of French aperitif wine.

Call brand. Brand of liquor named by the customer when ordering.

Calvados. Apple brandy made in France.

Campari. Type of Italian bitters. See **Bitters.**

Cantina. Italian for cellar.

Cantina sociale. Italian for cooperative cellar.

Carbon dioxide. Gas released when a product is fermenting and producing alcohol.

Carbonic maceration. Process of removing acids from grape juice during initial fermentation to produce a lighter, fruitier wine.

Casa vinicola. Italian for winery.

Cava. Spanish word meaning that a sparkling wine has been made using the champagne method.

Cave. French for cellar.

Chai. French term meaning an above-ground storage place for wine in casks, as distinct from a cellar below ground.

Champagne. Sparkling wine made in the Champagne district of France.

Champagne process. Method used to produce sparkling wine in which a second fermentation occurs in the bottle and carbon dioxide is produced to give the wine its effervescence.

Chaptalization. Process of adding sugar to crushed grapes at vintage time to raise the wine's alcohol content.

Charmat process. See **Bulk process.**

Chartreuse. Herb/spice-flavored liqueur with brandy base.

Château. French word for castle, but often used to mean a vineyard or estate. Many of the wines produced in the Bordeaux region carry the word *château* on the label followed by the vineyard name.

Château bottled. Wine bottled at the vineyard and made exclusively from grapes grown at that vineyard.

Cherry brandy. Cherry-flavored liqueur with brandy base.

Cherry whiskey. Cherry-flavored liqueur with whiskey base.

Claret. English term for a red Bordeaux wine, sometimes also used in the United States as a generic term for a light red wine.

Clarete. Portuguese light red wine.

Clarifying. See **Filtering**.

Classico. Italian wine from a special district within a DOC zone.

Clos. French for vineyard.

Cocktail. Mixed drink consisting of a type of alcohol (usually a distilled spirit) mixed with one or more liquids and/or other ingredients.

Cocktail glass. Stemmed glass with a flared three- to five-ounce bowl.

Coffee drink. Coffee with a liquor and/or liqueur and/or other ingredients added.

Cognac. Name given to brandy made exclusively in the Cognac region of France.

Cointreau. Orange-flavored liqueur.

Colheita. Portuguese for vintage.

Collins. Type of cocktail.

Collins glass. A ten- to twelve-ounce tall tumbler.

Column still. Tall still in which distilled spirits are vaporized by steam.

Commune. French for village municipality.

Congeners. Products present in very small amounts in fermented and distilled beverages and providing a unique flavor and aroma.

Consorzio. Italian for a cooperative.

Control state. State in which all alcoholic beverages are sold from government stores. Also known as a **Monopoly state**.

Cooler. Tall glass holding about fifteen to sixteen ounces. Also the name of a type of wine-based cocktail.

Cordial. See **Liqueur**.

Cordial glass. See **Liqueur glass**.

Corn whiskey. Whiskey made from at least 80 percent corn.

Cosecha. Spanish for vintage.

Cost percentage. See **Beverage cost percentage**.

Cost per ounce. Method of comparing the relative costs of different alcoholic beverages by analyzing them on a per-ounce basis.

Côte. French for riverbank or slope.

Coteaux champenois. Light, still wine produced in the Champagne region of France.

Crackling. Term sometimes used to describe a sparkling wine.

Cream of coconut. Coconut-flavored syrup used in some cocktails.

Cream sherry. Sweetened blend of well-aged oloroso sherry.

Credit memorandum. Document crediting the purchaser with goods invoiced but not received or else returned to the supplier for some reason.

Crémant. French term for a slightly sparkling Champagne.

Crème de bananes. Banana-flavored liqueur.

Crème de cacao. Chocolate/vanilla-flavored liqueur.

Crème de cassis. Black currant-flavored liqueur.

Crème de menthe. Mint-flavored liqueur.

Criado y embotellado por. Spanish for "grown and bottled by."

Cru. French for growth, or the product of a vineyard producing wine of a definite quality and standard.

Cru bourgeois. A quality of French Bordeaux wine lower than a *cru classé*. See **Cru classé**.

Cru classé. French term referring to wines from vineyards that have been classified by the government as being of excellent quality.

Crusted port. Type of vintage port.

Curaçao. Orange-flavored liqueur.

Cuvaison. French for vatting. See **Vatting**.

Cuve. French for vat.

Cuvée. French for blending several grape varieties.

Dash. About three drops of a liquid (for example, a bitters) used in a cocktail.

Decant. To pour wine carefully from one bottle to another bottle or carafe so that the sediment in the original bottle is not disturbed.

Dégorgement. French for disgorging or removing sediment from a bottle of champagne before its final corking.

Demi-sec. On a champagne bottle label, literally means half-dry, but actually refers to the sweetest type of champagne made.

Denominación de origen. Spanish for an officially regulated wine region.

Denominazione di origine controllata (DOC). See **DOC**.

Denominazione di origine controllata e garantita (DOCG). See **DOCG**.

Designaçao. Portuguese for an officially regulated wine region.

Dessert wine. Type of fortified wine, such as port, that is usually sweet and is served at the end of a meal.

Deutscher Tafelwein. German table wine.

Diastase. Enzyme in a grain malt that changes the starch into fermentable sugar.

Distillation. Use of heat to separate the alcohol vapors from a fermented product which are then condensed to produce a distilled alcohol or spirit.

Distilled spirit. Fermented beverage that has been heated to evaporate its alcohol which is then collected as a distilled spirit. Also commonly referred to as **Liquor**.

Distiller's beer. Fermented grain mixture from which whiskey or some other spirit is to be distilled.

DOC. Abbreviation that appears on Italian wine bottle labels to indicate that the wine comes from the controlled district named and meets appropriate standards. See also **DOCG**.

Doce. Portuguese for sweet.

DOCG. Abbreviation that appears on Italian wine bottle labels to indicate that the wine comes from the controlled district named and is the highest-quality wine that meets government standards.

Dolce. Italian for sweet.

Domaine. French for estate or vineyard.

Doux. On a champagne bottle label, indicates a quite sweet wine.

Draft beer. Unpasteurized beer drawn directly from a keg or barrel into a glass. Also known as **Keg beer** or **Tap beer**.

Drambuie. Scotch whisky and honey-flavored liqueur.

Dry. Term used to describe a wine's lack of sweetness.

Dry gin. British-style gin. See also **Dutch gin**.

Dubonnet. Type of French aperitif wine.

Dulce. Spanish for sweet.

Dummy invoice. See **Memorandum invoice**.

Dutch gin. Gin distilled with a heavy genever berry flavor. Also known as **Geneva**, **Genever**, **Hollands**, and **Schiedam**.

Eau de vie. French translation of *aqua vitae,* water of life. Eau de vie is often used in France as a synonym for brandy. See **Aqua vitae.**

Edelfäule. German term for noble rot and the equivalent of the French **Pourriture noble.** See **Noble rot.**

Einzellage. German for vineyard.

Eiswein. Unique top-quality (Q.m.P.) German wine made from grapes that have been partly frozen.

Elastic demand. Change in customers' demand for a product when its price is altered.

Empty-bottle return. Control method whereby new full bottles of liquor are issued from the storeroom only if an empty bottle is returned. See also **Bottle coding.**

Engarrafado na origen. Portuguese for estate bottled.

Enology. See **Oenology.**

Erzeugerabfüllung. German for an estate-bottled wine. See **Estate bottled.**

Espumante. Portuguese for sparkling wine.

Espumoso. Spanish for sparkling wine.

Estate bottled. Term on a wine bottle label indicating that the wine was bottled at the vineyard by the owner and made exclusively from grapes grown at that location.

Extra sec. On a champagne bottle label, literally means extra dry, even though the wine is slightly sweet.

Falernum. Sweet alcohol syrup with an almond-based flavor used in some cocktails.

Fattoria. Italian for estate.

Fermentation. The action of yeast on a sugar solution that causes the sugar to convert into alcohol and carbon dioxide.

Fernet Branca. Type of French bitters. See **Bitters.**

Fiasco. Straw-covered flask-shaped bottle in which certain types of Italian Chianti are sometimes sold.

Filtering. Process of removing fine particles during wine making to help clarify the wine. Also known as **Fining.**

Fine champagne. French Cognac (brandy) made from grapes 50 percent of which are from the Grande Champagne district and 50 percent from the Petite Champagne district.

Fining. See **Filtering.**

Fino. Spanish term used to describe a fine, light, dry, pale sherry.

First-in, first-out (FIFO). A method of issuing and costing requisitions that ensures that the bottles received first are issued first to the bar. See **Last-in, first-out (LIFO).**

Fixed cost. Cost that does not change as sales go up and down. For example, rent.

Fizz. Type of cocktail.

Float. Cash fund advanced to bartenders and servers for change-making purposes.

Flor. Spanish word for flower, but describing a special yeast that completely covers the surface of wine in vats or tanks during the last stages of sherry fermentation.

Flute glass. Footed or stemmed champagne glass with a long, narrow bowl flared slightly at the top.

Footed glass. Glass whose bowl sits directly on a foot or base with a very short stem.

Fortified wine. Wine to which brandy or other spirits have been added to stop any further fermentation and/or to raise its alcoholic strength.

Framboise. Brandy distilled from raspberries.

Frappé. Liquor served on crushed ice.

Frizzante. Italian term for a slightly sparkling wine.

Front bar. Part of the bar where customers can sit. On the bartender's side of the front bar is the underbar. See **Underbar**.

Frozen-drink dispenser. Machine that freezes large quantities of premixed frozen drinks to a slush in a few minutes.

Fruit squeezer. Hand tool used to squeeze oranges or lemons and to strain the desired liquid away from the unwanted pulp and seeds.

Galliano. Licorice/vanilla-flavored liqueur.

Garantia de Origen. Spanish for a guaranteed origin of a wine.

Garnish. Ingredient (such as an olive, maraschino cherry, or orange slice) added to some cocktails.

Garrafeira. Portuguese for a specially selected wine.

Gaseoso. Spanish for sparkling wine.

Gemeinde. German for a village or parish.

Generic wine. A general type or style of U.S. wine whose name is based on a European wine such as Chablis.

Geneva, Genever. See **Dutch gin**.

Gin. Distilled spirit flavored with juniper berries (Dutch gin) or other flavorings (British dry gin). See also **Dutch gin** and **Dry gin**.

Glass chiller or **froster.** Device that frosts the surfaces of glasses.

Glayva. Scotch whisky and honey-flavored liqueur.

Grain whisky. Scotch whisky made from more than one grain, as opposed to a malt whisky. See **Malt scotch**.

Grand cru. French for great growth. See also **Cru classé**.

Grande Champagne or **Grand Fine Champagne.** On a French Cognac label, indicates brandy distilled from grapes grown in the Grande Champagne area of the Cognac region.

Grand Marnier. Orange-flavored liqueur with a Cognac base.

Gran Reserva. Top-quality Spanish wine.

Grappa. Type of brandy made in Italy from the residue of grapes after the juice is drawn off to make wine. See also **Marc**.

Grenadine. Sweet red cocktail-flavoring syrup made from pomegranates.

Grosslage. German for vineyard collective.

Gross profit. Sales less cost of sales.

Halbtrocken. German for medium dry.

Handgun. Flexible hose, connected to carbonated mixer tanks, with a dispensing head used to serve a variety of different soft drinks.

Hand shaker. Stainless steel shaker and a heavy mixing glass used for hand shaking certain cocktails.

Happy hour. Evening period in a bar when the regular price of drinks is reduced.

Head. Collar of foam on a poured glass of beer.

Highball. Cocktail comprising liquor on ice with water or a carbonated mixer added.

Hochgewächs. German for wine made from grapes grown high on a hill.

Hock. Word used by British to describe any German Rhine wine.

Hollands. See **Dutch gin**.

Hops. Blossom or flower of the hop vine used to flavor beer.

Hosted bar. A bar at a banquet whose entire bill for serving drinks to the guests is paid by the host organization. See also **No-host bar.**

House wine. Wine that a restaurant serves by the glass, half-carafe, or full carafe.

Hybrid. Two vines grafted together to create a new type.

Ice bin. Container on the front part of the bar containing ice to be used in cocktails.

Ice bucket. Metal container filled with ice into which white wine bottles are immersed to chill.

Ice machine. Machine that makes ice for use in mixed drinks or cocktails.

Imbottigliato. Italian for bottled.

Inelastic demand. No change in demand when a beverage operation increases (or decreases) its drink prices.

Inventory. The amount of stock on hand at any time. See also **Physical inventory.**

Inventory sheet. For each item carried in stock, a sheet on which the amount on hand, cost price, and total value are recorded.

Inventory turnover. The rate at which inventory is turned over or replaced. Calculated by dividing the cost of sales for a specific period (a week, or a month) by the amount of average inventory during that period.

Invoice. Document sent by a supplier that shows the quantities of alcoholic beverages shipped to an establishment, their prices, and the total inventory amount.

Irish cream. Chocolate-flavored liqueur with an Irish whiskey base.

Irish mist. Honey-flavored liqueur with an Irish whiskey base.

Irish whiskey. Whiskey made in Ireland that has been triple distilled.

Jigger. Pouring device sized in ounces or fractions of ounces, used for measuring ingredients for cocktails.

Jug wine. Inexpensive U.S. wine available in containers usually larger than a liter.

Juniper. Flavoring ingredient used in gin.

Kabinett. German wine label designation and one of the five categories of Q.m.P. wines.

Kahlua. Coffee-flavored liqueur.

Keg. Draft beer container containing the equivalent of half a full barrel.

Keg beer. See **Draft beer.**

Keller. German for cellar.

Kellerabfüllung, Kellerabzug. German terms meaning bottled in the cellar of the grape grower, or a proprietor or merchant who also is a grower.

Kellerei. German for wine cellar.

Kickbacks. Fraudulent arrangements between a supplier and purchaser or receiver in which, for example, an establishment is billed for more goods than it actually received.

Kirsch, Kirschwasser. Colorless cherry-flavored brandy made in some Western European countries.

Kirsch liqueur. Cherry-flavored liqueur with a Kirsch base.

Krausening. Method of making beer in which a small amount of newly fermenting wort is added during the lagering (aging) stage to encourage additional fermentation and production of carbon dioxide.

Kummel. Caraway-flavored liqueur.

Labrusca. See **Vitis labrusca.**

Lager beer. Beer made by having the yeast ferment at the bottom of the fermenting vat.

Lagering. Storing or aging beer (either ale or lager) in order to mellow it.

Landwein. German for country wine or a better quality of Tafelwein (table wine).

Last-in, first-out (LIFO). Method of costing inventory and requisitions; an alternative to first-in, first-out (FIFO). See **First-in, first-out (FIFO).**

Late harvest wine. Wine produced in the United States from grapes with noble rot. See **Noble rot.**

Lees. Sediment in a newly fermented wine.

License state. State in which a retail outlet may buy from a licensed supplier (rather than from the state).

Liebfraumilch. German Rhine-region generic Qualitätswein that is not from a particular vineyard.

Light beer. Beer with a lower alcohol content and fewer calories than regular beer.

Light whiskey. U.S. whiskey distilled at higher proof, therefore lighter in flavor and body, though not in alcohol.

Lillet. French aperitif wine.

Liqueur. A flavored and sweetened distilled spirit. Also known as a **Cordial.**

Liqueur glass. Small, stemmed glass in which a liqueur, or cordial, is normally served. Also known as a **Cordial glass.**

Liquor. See **Distilled spirit.**

Liquoroso. Italian for sweet.

London dry gin. A British-style gin without any sweet flavoring.

Madeira. Sweet dessert wine made on the island of Madeira.

Maduro. Portuguese for any matured wine that is not a **Vinho verde.**

Magnum. Bottle size equivalent to two regular bottles.

Malaga. Type of sweet dessert wine produced in Spain.

Malt. Grain that is sprouted (germinated) to help convert its starch into sugar for easier fermentation.

Malt beer. Beer with a higher alcohol content than regular beer.

Malt scotch. Unblended Scotch whisky made in the Highlands of Scotland entirely from malted barley.

Malt whisky. See **Malt scotch.**

Manhattan. Type of cocktail.

Manzanilla. Spanish pale, dry sherry with a tart flavor.

Maraschino brandy. Cherry/almond-flavored liqueur.

Marc. French brandy distilled from the grape stalks, pips, and skins left after the juice has been pressed out.

Marsala. Type of sweet dessert wine produced in Sicily.

Martini. Type of cocktail; also a brand of vermouth.

Mash. Malt (sprouted grain) cooked in water to convert the starch into sugar. In beer making, this process is known as mashing.

Maturing. See **Aging.**

Memorandum invoice. Dummy invoice made out by an establishment to take the place of the actual invoice, which has not been received with the goods.

Metaxa. Type of Greek brandy.

Méthode champenoise. French term describing the method of making champagne wine, in which the second fermentation is produced in the bottle.

Mezcal. Mexican distilled spirit; a type of tequila.

Microfiltration. Process of clarifying wine in order to remove any traces of bacteria and yeast.

Mirabelle. Brandy with a plum base, made in some Central European countries.

Mise au château, mise du château, mise en bouteille au château, mise au domaine, mise du domaine, mise en bouteille au domaine, mise du propriétaire, mise à la propriété. French terms for estate-bottled wines.

Mise en bouteille dans nos caves. French term for "bottled in our cellars," generally meaning that it is not an estate-bottled wine.

Mixer. Machine for mixing certain types of cocktails instead of hand shaking them.

Mixing cup or **steel.** See **Hand shaker.**

Mixing glass. See **Hand shaker.**

Molasses. Residue left after sugar has been made from cane. Used for distilling rum.

Monopole. French term for a wine brand name exclusive to the producer.

Monopoly state. See **Control state.**

Moselblümchen. Generic German wine produced in the Moselle region.

Moseltaler. Generic German wine produced in the Moselle region.

Mousseux. French for foamy or sparkling, as in *vin mousseux*—sparkling wine. Used for sparkling wine not made by the champagne process.

Must. Juice crushed from grapes before fermenting.

Nature. On a champagne bottle label, means dry (little or no added sugar); the equivalent of the French term **Brut.**

Neat. Cocktail made without ice.

Négociant. French term for a merchant, shipper, or wine handler.

Neutral spirit. Spirit distilled at 190 proof (95 percent alcohol by volume) or higher.

Noble rot. Condition of grapes allowed to ripen in the sun so that they shrivel, concentrate their sugar and juice, and develop a mold on their skins.

No-host bar. A bar at a banquet at which each customer must pay for each drink that he or she consumes. See also **Host bar.**

Nouveau. French for new, as in Beaujolais Nouveau.

Oenology. The science and study of wine.

Oloroso. Spanish full-bodied, rather sweet sherry.

On the rocks. Cocktail poured over ice.

Open state. See **License state.**

Orange bitters. Orange-flavored bitters. See **Bitters.**

Order form. Form used to record the items ordered from each supplier, thereby serving as a check to verify what is received.

Orgeat. Sweet, almond-flavored syrup used in certain cocktails.

Ounce control method. See **Quality (ounce) control.**

Ouzo. Greek licorice-flavored distilled spirit.

Paring knife. Small, sharp-pointed knife used for cutting up limes, lemons, oranges, and other cocktail ingredients.

Par stock. Quantity of each product to be on hand at the bar at the beginning of each day's business.

Passion fruit. Mixture of tropical juices used in some cocktails.

Pasteurization. Heating beer and some wines to a high temperature and then cooling them rapidly to kill any bacteria that might be in the bottle or to help stabilize the product.

Peach brandy. Peach-flavored liqueur.

Pear brandy. Brandy distilled from pears. Also known as **Pear William** or **Poire Williams.**

Pear William. See **Pear brandy.**

Peppermint. Mint-flavored liqueur.

Pernod. Licorice-flavored distilled spirit.

Perpetual inventory card. Document showing the ongoing balance of each product in the beverage storeroom at all times.

Peter Heering. Cherry-flavored liqueur with a brandy base.

Pétillant. French term meaning that a wine is slightly sparkling or crackling.

Petite Champagne. Type of Cognac made with at least 50 percent grapes from the Grande Champagne district of France's Cognac region.

Petty cash. Small cash fund used in a beverage operation for making minor purchases of needed supplies.

Peychaud's. Type of bitters produced in New Orleans. See **Bitters**.

Phylloxera. Root-eating disease that destroyed nearly all the vineyards in Europe and North America in the late nineteenth century.

Physical inventory. Count of the actual inventory on hand.

Pilsner. Mild, dry type of beer with about 4 to 5 percent alcohol by volume.

Pimm's. Premixed type of sling drink produced in England.

Pisco. Type of brandy made in Peru.

Plum brandy. Brandy distilled from plums.

Poire Williams. See **Pear brandy**.

Port. Type of sweet dessert wine originally made in Portugal.

Porter. Dark type of ale, usually with more than 5 percent alcohol by volume.

Postmix. Carbonated beverages purchased in syrup form. Water and carbon dioxide are mixed with the syrup at the time the beverage is dispensed. See also **Premix**.

Poteen. Illegally made Irish whiskey. See **Irish whiskey**.

Potential revenue or **sales control**. See **Standard revenue control**.

Pot still. Pot-shaped still in which certain spirits are distilled by heat from below.

Pourer. Device fitted into the neck of a liquor bottle that controls the speed of pouring and may or may not allow a measured amount to be poured.

Pourriture noble. French for noble rot. See **Noble rot**.

Pousse café. Specialty drink in which different types of liqueurs and other ingredients are layered on top of one another for an unusual, colorful effect.

Precheck–preset register. Type of sales register that holds drink prices in its memory, thereby eliminating pricing errors. See also **Precheck register**.

Precheck register. Type of sales register used in a beverage operation, in which the drink sale is recorded in the machine before being made and served.

Premier cru. French term for first growth, given to the top classification of Bordeaux wines.

Premium brand. Higher-priced brand of liquor, also known as a call brand. See also **Well brand**.

Premix. Carbonated beverages purchased in large containers in which syrup and water are already mixed. See also **Postmix**.

Prohibition. Period from 1919 to 1933 when alcoholic beverage sales were banned in the United States.

Proof. Measure of alcoholic content of a distilled spirit. In the United States, alcohol content is half the proof. For example, 80 proof equals 40 percent alcohol by volume.

Propriétaire. French for proprietor or grower.

Propriété. French for property or estate.

Pure alcohol. Colorless, tasteless, odorless, 200 proof distilled spirit. See also **Neutral spirit** and **Proof**.

Q.b.A. See **Qualitätswein bestimmter Anbaugebiete**.

Q.m.P. See **Qualitätswein mit Prädikat**.

Qualitätswein. German term meaning quality wine and often used to describe either a Q.b.A. or a Q.m.P. wine.

Qualitätswein bestimmter Anbaugebiete (Q.b.A.). German term for a quality wine from a controlled growing district.

Qualitätswein mit Prädikat (Q.m.P.). German term meaning a quality wine with special attributes, given to the highest quality of wines.

Quantity (ounce) control. Method of bar cost control in which the quantity sold according to sales records of each brand of liquor is compared with the quantity used according to inventory records.

Quetsch. Brandy distilled from plums, made in some Central European countries.

Quinta. Portuguese for an estate, farm, or vineyard.

Rack. See **Arrack**.

Racking. Transferring wine from one container to another, leaving the lees (sediment) behind.

Raki. See **Arrack**.

Raspberry brandy. Raspberry-flavored liqueur.

Receiving report. See **Beverage-receiving report**.

Receiving stamp. Inked stamp placed on an invoice that must be initialed by various responsible people to indicate that all receiving steps have been properly carried out.

Recioto. Italian for a wine made from partly dried grapes.

Rectification. Alteration of a distilled spirit by redistilling it, blending it, or adding other ingredients to it.

Remuage. French term meaning shaking, a technique used in making champagne.

Requisition. Form authorizing designated individuals to request specific items and quantities of inventory from the beverage storeroom.

Requisition control. Form of beverage control based on the daily requisitioned cost of items issued from the storeroom.

Reserva. Spanish for aged or matured wine.

Retsina. Generic Greek wine flavored with pine resin.

Rickey. Type of cocktail.

Riserva. Italian for aged or matured wine.

Robust. Descriptive term for a full-bodied or sturdy wine.

Rosado. Spanish and Portuguese word for rosé.

Rosato. Italian word for rosé.

Roseewein. German for rosé wine.

Rosé wine. Wine made from red- (or black-) skinned grapes whose must is fermented with the skins long enough to give it a pink or rose color.

Rosso. Italian for red.

Rotwein. German for red wine.

Rouge. French for red.

Ruby port. Type of wood port. See **Wood port**.

Rum. Spirit distilled from sugarcane molasses.

Rye. U.S. whiskey made from at least a 51 percent rye base. In Canada the name given to Canadian-produced whisky, even though it may contain no rye grain.

Saké. Japanese wine made from fermented rice.

Sales check. Document on which is recorded the description, quantity, price, and total value of each drink served to a customer or round of drinks to a group of customers.

Sales mix. Quantity, or mix, of each different type of drink consumed by customers over a period of time.

Sales register. Control machine for recording revenue earned from drinks as they are sold. See also **Precheck register** and **Preset–precheck register**.

Sangria. Mixture of wine, sugar, water, soda, and fruits.

Schaumwein. German for a sparkling wine made by the champagne method.

Schiedam. See **Dutch gin**.

Schloss. German for castle or château.

Schnapps. Type of German vodka.

Scotch. Whisky made in Scotland, usually blended. See also **Malt scotch**.

Sec. On a champagne bottle label, means dry (that is, drier than **Demi-sec**), even though the champagne may be slightly sweet.

Secco. Italian for dry.

Seco. Spanish and Portuguese for dry.

Sekt. Type of German Schaumwein. See **Schaumwein**.

Selected late harvest. Wine produced in the United States from grapes having noble rot. See **Noble rot**.

Shelf life. Length of time that a product can be stored before its quality starts to decline.

Shell out. Discarding a lemon or lime shell after its juice has been squeezed into a cocktail.

Sherry. Type of fortified aperitif or dessert wine originally made in Spain.

Shot glass. Measuring device for pouring a specific amount of liquor.

Simple syrup. One part sugar to one part water—a mixture used in certain cocktails.

Sling. Type of cocktail.

Slivovitz. Brandy with a plum base, made in some Central European countries. Also known as **Mirabelle** or **Quetsch**.

Sloe gin. Plum-flavored liqueur.

Snifter. Footed glass with a large round bowl, often used for brandy.

Soda out. Cocktail topped up with soda.

Solera. Spanish method of blending sherry.

Sommelier. In a restaurant, the person with considerable wine knowledge who orders and serves wines.

Sour. Type of cocktail.

Sour mash. In bourbon manufacture, a portion of fermented mash from an earlier fermentation added to the present mash before distillation.

Southern Comfort. Peach-flavored liqueur with a bourbon base.

Sparkling wine. Wine containing carbon dioxide, which provides effervescence when the wine is poured.

Spätlese. German term meaning late picked, or grapes picked after the normal harvest, producing a high-quality Q.m.P. wine.

Speed rail. Stainless steel compartment of the underbar, containing frequently used bottles of bar beverages.

Spillage allowance. Allowance given to bartenders, as it is not always practical to assume that every last drop, or ounce, can be drained from a bottle.

Spritzer. Type of cocktail made with a wine base.

Spritzig. German for crackling or slightly sparkling.

Spumante. Italian sparkling wine.

Standard cost. What the cost should be for an individual drink or a given level of sales. For control purposes, this standard cost can then be compared with the actual cost.

Standard cost percentage. What the cost percentage should be for a given level of sales. For control purposes, this percentage can then be compared with the actual cost percentage.

Standard drink size. Amount of alcohol and other ingredients that an establishment specifies is to be served in each kind of drink.

Standard glass. Correct type and size of glass in which a standard drink is served. See **Standard drink size.**

Standard recipe. Recipe listing ingredients of a particular drink, the quantity to be used, the mixing method, and the glass to be used.

Standard revenue control. Method of control that converts the quantity of liquor used, according to inventory records, into standard revenue, to be compared with actual revenue from sales. Also known as **Standard sales control.**

Standard sales control. See **Standard revenue control.**

Steinwein. Name sometimes given to wines of Germany produced in the Franken (Franconia) district.

Stemmed glass. Glass having a base or foot, a stem, and a bowl.

Still wine. Nonsparkling wine.

Storeroom reconciliation. Comparison of the amount of each beverage brand that should be in the storeroom according to perpetual inventory records, with the actual or physical count of that item in cases and/or on shelves.

Stout. Type of dark ale.

Straight up. Cocktail stirred in a mixing glass and then strained into a drinking glass without ice.

Straight whiskey. In the United States, an unblended whiskey containing at least 51 percent of a single grain type, such as corn or rye.

St. Raphael. Type of French aperitif wine.

Strawberry brandy. Strawberry-flavored liqueur.

Strega. Herb/spice-flavored liqueur.

Sugar syrup. Sugar and water mixture used in some cocktails.

Supérieur. French for a wine with a higher alcohol content than normal.

Superiore. Italian for a wine with a higher alcohol content than normal.

Sweet/sour mix. Mixture of sugar syrup and lime or lemon juice used in some cocktails.

Swizzle stick. Short stick used to stir a mixed drink in the glass.

Table wine. Any wine that is neither fortified nor sparkling.

Tafelwein. German for table wine.

Tannin. Astringent element in wine derived from the grapes' skins, stalks, and seeds.

Tap. Beer-dispensing faucet. See **Tapping.**

Tap beer. See **Draft beer.**

Tap box. Enclosed area in the underbar in which one or more kegs of tapped beer are housed, ready for dispensing.

Tapping. Process of opening a new keg of beer to attach it to the carbon dioxide hoses so that it can be dispensed at the tap.

Tastevin. Special wine-tasting cup that is part of the sommelier's uniform. See also **Sommelier**.

Tawny port. Type of wood port. See **Wood port**.

Tennessee whiskey. Type of bourbon filtered through maple charcoal and made in Tennessee.

Tenuta. Italian for estate or farm.

Tequila. Distilled spirit made in Mexico from the fermented juice of the agave plant (a type of cactus).

Tia Maria. Coffee-flavored liqueur with a rum base.

Tinto. Spanish and Portuguese word for red.

Toddy. Liquor base with sugar and hot water added.

Tokay. Rich sweet dessert wine made in Hungary.

Top fermentation. Method of fermenting beer in which the yeast acts at the top of the fermenting vat.

Très sec. French for very dry, and on a champagne bottle label, actually means that the wine will be slightly sweet.

Triple Sec. Orange-flavored liqueur.

Trocken. German for dry.

Trockenbeerenauslese. German term meaning selected dry berry picking, or the picking of grapes that have become almost raisinized from noble rot. Used for Q.m.P. wines.

Tulip glass. A footed stemmed glass with a tulip-shaped bowl, often used with sparkling wine, as it prevents the bubbles from escaping too quickly.

Tumbler. Flat-bottomed glass without a stem or foot.

Turnover. See **Inventory turnover**.

Underbar. Part of the front bar that comprises the ice bin, bottle wells, and speed rail for a bartender's work station.

Vandermint. Chocolate/mint-flavored liqueur.

Variable cost. Cost that increases and decreases as sales increase or decrease. An example is the beverage cost of sales.

Varietal wine. Wine named after the grapes from which it is made.

Vatting. Process in fermentation that extracts coloring and tannin from grape skins.

VDQS. Stands for *vin délimité de qualité supérieur*—one of the better French quality-wine designations.

Vecchio. Italian for old.

Vendange. French for harvesting or vintage.

Vendimia. Spanish for vintage.

Vermouth. Aperitif wine that is also used in some cocktails.

Vigneron. French for wine grower.

Vina. Spanish for vintage.

Vin de pailles. French for straw wine—a type of wine made in the Jura region.

Vin de pays. French for country or regional wine.

Vin de table. French for table wine.

Vinha. Portuguese for vineyard.

Vinho. Portuguese for wine.

Vinho de mesa. Portuguese for table wine.

Vinho verde. Type of young Portuguese wine.

Vinifera. See **Vitis vinifera**.

Vin jaune. French for yellow wine—a type of wine made in the Jura region.

Vino. Italian and Spanish for wine.

Vino da tavola. Italian for table wine.

Vino de crianza. Type of Spanish wine that is aged for only a short time.

Vintage. The year in which the grapes were harvested and crushed for wine making.

Vintage chart. Table showing for a wine region year by year the relative quality of the wines produced there.

Vintage port. Well-aged port, usually with a heavy sediment in the bottle.

Virgin. Cocktail made without alcohol.

Viticulteur. French for grower.

Vitis labrusca. Type of grapevine used to produce wine in some North American regions.

Vitis vinifera. Type of grapevine from which most of today's best wine grapes are produced.

Vodka. Colorless, odorless, and often tasteless distilled spirit.

Weighted average sales value. Method of calculating the standard sales value of a bottle of liquor when its contents are used in a variety of drinks and/or cocktails.

Wein. German for wine.

Weinbaugebiet. German for viticultural region.

Weingut. German for estate or vineyard.

Weinkellerei. German for wine cellar.

Well brand. Brand of liquor used when a customer does not specify a brand or ask for a call or premium brand. Also known as a house or nonpremium brand.

Whiskey, whisky. A spirit distilled from a grain.

Wild beer. Draft beer that froths uncontrollably when dispensed.

Wine. Fermented juice of grapes or other fruits.

Wine basket. Wicker basket for carrying certain wines from cellar to table and then for pouring them so as not to stir up their sediment.

Wineglass. Stemmed glass in which wine is served.

Wine steward. Person who handles wine orders and service. See also **Sommelier**.

Winzergenossenschaft. German for wine cooperative.

Winzerverein. German for wine cooperative.

Wood port. Type of port aged in casks and then consumed soon after bottling.

Wort. In beer and whiskey making, the liquid in which the grain starches have been converted into sugar.

Yeast. Natural element required to produce fermentation.

Zest. Outer peel of a citrus fruit.

Zester. Hand tool used to obtain zest from citrus fruit.

Bibliography

Adams, Leon D. 1985. *The Wines of America*. New York: McGraw-Hill.

Allison, Norman, and Sonia Allison. 1978. *Drinks Dictionary*. London: Collins.

Ambrosi, Hans. 1976. *Where the Great German Wines Grow*. New York: Hastings House.

Amerine, M. A., and E. B. Roessler. 1976. *Wines: Their Sensory Evaluation*. San Francisco: Freeman.

Anderson, Burton. 1980. *Vino, the Wines and Winemakers of Italy*. Boston: Atlantic–Little, Brown.

Broadbent, Michael. 1980. *The Great Vintage Wine Book*. New York: Knopf.

Broadbent, Michael. 1984. *The Complete Guide to Wine Tasting and Wine Cellars*. New York: Simon & Schuster.

Evans, Len. 1985. *Complete Book of Australian Wine*. Sydney: Hamlyn.

Fadiman, Clifton, and Sam Aaron. 1975. *The Joys of Wine*. New York: Abrams.

Gold, Alec, ed. 1972. *Wines and Spirits of the World*. Coulsdon, England: Virtue.

Grossman, Harold J. 1977. *Grossman's Guide to Wines, Beers, and Spirits*. New York: Scribner.

Hannum, Hurst, and Robert S. Blumberg. 1976. *Brandies and Liqueurs of the World*. New York: Doubleday.

Johnson, Hugh. 1984. *The World Atlas of Wine*. New York: Simon & Schuster.

Johnson, Hugh. 1988. *Hugh Johnson's Pocket Encyclopedia of Wine*. New York: Simon & Schuster.

Lichine, Alexis. 1979. *Alexis Lichine's Guide to the Wines and Vineyards of France*. New York: Knopf.

Lichine, Alexis. 1985. *New Encyclopedia of Wines and Spirits*. New York: Knopf.

Misch, Robert Jay. 1977. *Quick Guide to the Wines of All the Americas*. New York: Doubleday.

Muscatine, Doris, Maynard A. Amerine, and Bob Thompson, eds. 1984. *Book of California Wine*. Berkeley and Los Angeles: University of California Press/Sotheby.

Penning-Rowsell, E. 1976. *The Wines of Bordeaux*. London: Penguin.

Read, Jan. 1980. *The Wines of Spain and Portugal*. London: Faber.

Robards, Terry. 1976. *The New York Times Book of Wine*. New York: New York Times.

Schoonmaker, Frank. 1983. *The Wines of Germany*, revised by Peter Sichel. New York: Hastings House.

Spurrier, Steven, and Michel Dovaz. 1983. *Academie du Vin, Complete Wine Course*. New York: Putnam.

Sutcliffe, Serena. 1981. *Andre Simon's Wines of the World*. New York: McGraw-Hill.

Wildman, Frederick S., Jr. 1976. *A Wine Tour of France*. New York: Vintage.

Index